# Authentic Listening Resource Pack

**Mark Hancock and Annie McDonald**

DELTA Publishing
Quince Cottage
Hoe Lane
Peaslake
Surrey GU5 9SW
England

www.deltapublishing.co.uk

© DELTA Publishing 2014

All rights reserved. No reproduction, copy or transmission of this publication may be made without written permission from the publishers or in accordance with the provisions of the Copyright, Designs and Patents Act 1988, or under the terms of any licence permitting copying issued by the Copyright Licensing Agency, Saffron House, 6–10 Kirby Street, London EC1N 8TS.

First published 2014

Edited by Catriona Watson-Brown
Designed by Caroline Johnston
Cover design by Peter Bushell
Illustrations by Kathy Baxendale
Printed in China by RR Donnelley

ISBN 978-1-905085-88-0

### Author acknowledgements

We would like to offer thanks to Iain Wilson at **Insight Radio** for permission to use the audio material in Lessons 2, 4, 9 and 24. Thanks also to Peter Dixon at **Radio Teesdale** for the material we used in Lessons 7, 12, 14, 17, 19, 22, 27 and 34. Thanks to Sutish Sharma at **91.8 Hayes FM** for Lessons 8, 32 and 44. Thanks to Phil Gibbons at Bristol's community radio station **BCFM 93.2** for the material used in Lessons 18, 28, 37 and 38. Thanks to Paul Holloway and the young volunteers at Stockport's **PURE 107.8 FM** for the material in Lessons 29 and 42. And thanks also to Ajit Singh at west London's Punjabi community radio station **Desi Radio** for Lesson 39.

We would also like to thank the speakers who featured in the radio material mentioned above, including Simon Pauley, Mel Giedroyc, Ian Pauley, Mary-Jess Leaverland, Trevor Sharman, Maggie Rosen, Katie Wallace, Corrine Sweet, Phil Beer, Malcolm Love, Jenny Riker, Julie Summers, Małgorzata Makowska and her band Dautenis, Mike Burton, John Jackson's family, Annela Seddon, Anu Bains, Dennis Locorriere, Antonia Forster and Keith Waithe.

For the video material in Lessons 1, 6, 11, 16, 21, 26, 31, 36 and 41, we would like to thank Richard Hackett, Toby Meredith and Massimo Marzullo of the University of Portsmouth's Faculty of Creative and Cultural Industries, as well as teachers and students from LSI Portsmouth Alan Daysh, Anisa Daud, Hue Tu Thanh, Maria Shkurina, Thuy Vu Ngoc Diem, Tom Easey, Zhang Ning (Nicole) and Ezgi Bilcic.

For the video material in Lessons 3, 13, 23, 33 and 43, we would like to extend a big thanks to FameLab, and to the individual presenters Bechara Saab, Lucy Thorne, Hazem Shoira, Monika Koperska and Aneesha Acharya.

Thank you to teachers and students at **The Chester School** in Madrid, who trialled some of the material. Thanks also to our colleagues and students at **English in Chester** in the UK for working with the material.

### Photo acknowledgements

Alamy: pages 10, 61, 70
Aneesha Acharya: page 92
Antonia Forster: page 82 (bottom)
Bechara Saab: page 12
Cartoonstock: pages 19, 26
Corbis: page 84
Judy Totton: page 74
Keith Waithe LRSM/PGCEA: page 94 (bottom)
Mark Hancock: pages 8, 18, 28, 36, 37, 38, 48, 58, 67, 68, 77, 78, 79, 88, 89
Mary-Jess Leaverland: page 20
Monika Koperska: page 73
Phil Beer: page 40 (bottom)
© John Noel / Royal Geographical Society (with IBG): page 44
Shutterstock: pages 11 (B), 30, 42, 56 (both), 62, 82 (top), 94 (top group), 96
The Island Trust/MAX: page 40 (top)
Thinkstock: pages 11 (A), 22 (top)
Trevor Sharman: page 22 (bottom)

The authors and publishers have made every effort to indentify the source of copyright material used in this book or to trace copyright holders, but this has not always been possible. If any omissions are brought to our notice, we will be happy to include the appropriate acknowledgements on reprinting.

The British Council is the international partner for FameLab but has not been involved in the production or quality assurance of these educational materials.
FameLab® is a trademark of Cheltenham Festivals Ltd.

Vox-pop videos produced by The Media Production Centre, Faculty of Creative and Cultural Industries, University of Portsmouth
Production team: Richard Hackett, Lucas Holzhauer, Toby Meredith and Matt Saxey

# Introduction

Learners of English often consider listening to be their weakest skill, and this is confirmed when they listen to 'real' spoken English. They have inevitably grown up on a diet of scripted and carefully articulated recorded listening material, the main purpose of which is to provide a vehicle for vocabulary and structure. When they come across real-time spoken English – with its various accents, ums and ahs, repetitions, hesitations and false starts – they often barely understand anything at all. *Authentic Listening Resource Pack* has been written to provide teachers with resources to teach listening and to help learners develop the ability to understand scripted and unscripted everyday spoken language outside the classroom.

## Accents and varieties

In today's world, we listen to people who are both native and non-native speakers of English, from a variety of countries and regions, and so learners need exposure to different varieties and to develop flexibility when it comes to how they expect people to sound. The speakers in *Authentic Listening Resource Pack* represent a rich resource of various speakers of English, and by listening to these speakers, learners will broaden their accent repertoire.

## Topics

*Authentic Listening Resource Pack* contains 45 stand-alone lessons, based on a variety of authentic video and radio materials. The lessons are roughly graded in terms of difficulty, with the easier ones coming earlier in the book. The tasks that accompany the audio materials have been crafted so they are achievable for students around B1/B2 level on the CEFR. There are a variety of everyday informal conversational topics (e.g. culture, music, theatre, education, complaining, hobbies and pastimes, the weather, cooking, sport and competitions, places of interest, festivals), more serious conversation and discussion topics (e.g. fuel shortages, health, geography, trends, the news, communication, scientific research) and popular science and academic topics (e.g. health, space travel, neuroscience).

## Texts and tasks

The listening text in each lesson is generally between three and six minutes long. The texts have been divided into short, manageable blocks, and each one is accompanied by a range of achievable tasks. The prime objective is to provide learners with activities offering inherent support and scaffolding to offset the challenge of understanding authentic audio and video texts. In other words, the tasks have been oriented for success, so that learners gain in confidence, and their sense of achievement will maintain motivation. They will finish a lesson having employed a variety of strategies, which will be of use in the understanding of other audio texts of their choice. They will thus be better equipped to develop their listening skills autonomously.

## Lessons

The materials in *Authentic Listening Resource Pack* give learners practice in understanding different types of texts, e.g. informal radio chats, video interviews, news programmes, guided tours, instructions, discussions, explanations, adverts and videos of mini popular science lectures and informal discussions. Each lesson is divided into four or five sections, which include tasks for before, while and after listening.

- The **before listening** sections (*Thinking about the topic*, *Tuning in*) prime learners for the main audio-based activities by thinking about what they already know about the topic, e.g. by brainstorming known vocabulary or extrapolating content from given vocabulary in word clouds, reading a short introduction which provides background information on the topic or speakers, or reflecting on personal experiences and opinions. Learners tune in to speakers' voices, accents and styles of speaking and the type of text they will listen to.

- The **while listening** sections (*Listening for key words and phrases*, *Listening for the main ideas and detail*, *Listening for specific information*) contain a variety of activities which direct learners to listen for particular purposes. Learners will usually listen to parts of the text twice. For the first listening, they are generally given support, in the form of questions which have been carefully worded to provide scaffolding to guide them through the text. For the second listening, learners are asked to listen more carefully and do more challenging tasks. The activities in this section give learners practice in exploiting a range of listening strategies, e.g. to listen for key words, to follow meaning by listening out for pronouns and linkers, to remember and summarize while listening, and to use features of natural speech (hesitation, fillers and repetition) as time to think.

- In the **after listening** section (*Extension and review*), learners are encouraged to summarize and discuss the content of the recordings, or to express their personal opinions on the topic, all of which helps to make the listening experience more memorable. They are also encouraged to think about the listening experience by reflecting on some of the strategies they will have used in the lesson. This, in turn, raises learners' awareness to a range of strategies they could use in other listening they might do with different texts.

## *Pronunciation for listeners*

Every fifth lesson in *Authentic Listening Resource Pack* has a more up-close focus, getting learners to analyze small fragments extracted mainly from the texts of the preceding lessons. The objective is to help them notice features of connected speech, such as linking and assimilation, frequently reduced words in spoken English such as *actually*, as well as aspects of speech which vary across different accents. Listening to small fragments of speech taken out of context helps the listener to notice more objectively how things sound – often, when we hear the same material in context, we 'hear' what we expect to hear instead of what we actually hear though our ears.

## **Audio-visual material**

All the audio and video material for this book is contained on three disks: the audio material is on two data CDs (disks 1 and 2), and the video material is on a DVD-video (disk 3). The tracks are referred to in the lessons using reference numbers. For example, 1.62 is audio track 62 of disk 1. The video material is referred to by numbers 1–14 which appear in the video menu. The data CDs contain mp3 files and can be played on a computer or in an mp3-enabled CD player. The DVD-video can be played in a DVD player or on a computer. It also has ROM content, which can be accessed via the DVD drive on a computer. This consists of mp3 files of the audio material plus wmv versions of the videos.

## Scripts

The scripts for all of the audio and video material appear on pages 98–132 of this book. They are transcribed exactly as spoken and consequently include many features which are not standard in written text. For example, they show:

- thinking noises such as *um*
- repeated words
- false starts such as *I thi-, think*
- contracted forms such as *dunno*
- listener responses such as *uh-huh*.

## Planning a lesson

For each lesson, you will need copies of the lesson pages for all the learners in the class, or at least one set between two. You will also need a computer or DVD player for audio/video disks. The material in each lesson will take roughly an hour to cover in class. To make a complete lesson, you may want to add more activities before and after the actual listening lesson.

- **Before** the listening lesson, you could lead into the topic. For example, use the internet to prepare a few quiz questions relating to the theme for the class to answer in teams. If learners have access to the internet on their own devices, you could set a small research task related to the topic. If you have a beamer in your classroom, you could do an internet image search related to the topic, then get the class to talk about the pictures before moving on to the listening lesson.

- **After** the listening lesson, you could ask learners to work with copies of the scripts to act out sections, or to prepare their own lectures or interviews on a related topic. If they have their own devices with internet access, they could research further information on the topic. They may also listen to the podcast of selected lessons. This consists of the complete audio of the radio interviews, not broken down into sections. You and your learners can download these free from www.deltapublishing.co.uk/resources via a PIN (see below). In this way, learners can listen to the interviews again on the bus, in the car or wherever, and thus reinforce their learning outside class.

There is a useful checklist of listening techniques on page 144 that you can use with your learners.

---

Use and share this web address and PIN with your students to access and download the full versions of the radio interviews used in this course online:
**www.deltapublishing.co.uk/resources**
**PIN: 6319**

# Map of the book

|  | lesson title | lesson type | topic | genre | page |
|---|---|---|---|---|---|
| 1 | *Feeling good* | video | moods | vox pops | 8 |
| 2 | *Obsessed by the weather* | audio | weather | informal discussion | 10 |
| 3 | *Life on Mars* | video | space exploration | popular lecture | 12 |
| 4 | *Making a meal of it* | audio | cooking | cooking instructions | 14 |
| 5 | Pronunciation for listeners 1 | connected speech: weak forms of short grammar words<br>spoken English: thinking time | | | 16 |
| 6 | *Fame* | video | fame | informal discussion | 18 |
| 7 | *Talent-show winner* | audio | entertainment | anecdote | 20 |
| 8 | *Life without oil* | audio | environment | interview with an activist | 22 |
| 9 | *Living with failing eyesight* | audio | disability | personal account | 24 |
| 10 | Pronunciation for listeners 2 | connected speech: crowded syllables<br>accent variation: pronunciation of *r* and *t* | | | 26 |
| 11 | *Going places* | video | travel and tourism | vox pops | 28 |
| 12 | *Raby Castle* | audio | history | guided tour | 30 |
| 13 | *The friendly virus* | video | medicine | popular lecture | 32 |
| 14 | *Complaining* | audio | complaining | interview with an expert | 34 |
| 15 | Pronunciation for listeners 3 | connected speech: rushed adverbs<br>spoken English: vague language – *sort of*, *kind of*, *just* | | | 36 |
| 16 | *Risk* | video | adventure and risk-taking | informal discussion | 38 |
| 17 | *Baltic voyager* | audio | sea travel | personal account | 40 |
| 18 | *Under the volcano* | audio | volcanoes | interview with a geologist | 42 |
| 19 | *Mystery on Mount Everest* | audio | mountain adventure | interview with an author | 44 |
| 20 | Pronunciation for listeners 4 | connected speech: weak forms of auxiliary verbs<br>accent variation: variable vowel sounds | | | 46 |

| 21 | *First impressions* | video | first experiences of England | personal accounts | 48 |
| 22 | *Rescuing tradition* | audio | folk music | interview with performers | 50 |
| 23 | *From thought to action* | video | the human body | popular lecture | 52 |
| 24 | *Read my lips* | audio | communication | interview with a psychologist | 54 |
| 25 | Pronunciation for listeners 5 | | connected speech: weak forms of pronouns<br>spoken English: emphasis | | 56 |
| 26 | *University* | video | different university systems | interview with students | 58 |
| 27 | *Speed on ice* | audio | winter sports | chat with sportsman's mother | 60 |
| 28 | *The science of the small* | audio | physics | interview with researcher | 62 |
| 29 | *Studying abroad* | audio | university | chat about studying abroad | 64 |
| 30 | Pronunciation for listeners 6 | | connected speech: linking one word with the next<br>accent variation: the glottal stop | | 66 |
| 31 | *Technology* | video | favourite technology | vox pops | 68 |
| 32 | *Breaking news* | audio | crimes and local affairs | local news bulletins | 70 |
| 33 | *The future of paper* | video | viability of a material | popular lecture | 72 |
| 34 | *A life in the music business* | audio | a career in pop music | interview with a musician | 74 |
| 35 | Pronunciation for listeners 7 | | connected speech: titles, names, technical terms, definitions<br>spoken English: vague language – *you know*, *like* | | 76 |
| 36 | *Advertising* | video | opinions about advertising | informal conversations | 78 |
| 37 | *The language of persuasion* | audio | local businesses | radio adverts | 80 |
| 38 | *The intelligence of ants* | audio | zoology | interview with a naturalist | 82 |
| 39 | *A celebration of the sun* | audio | festivals | chat about a festival | 84 |
| 40 | Pronunciation for listeners 8 | | connected speech: cutting or changing sounds<br>spoken English: false starts | | 86 |
| 41 | *Arriving in a capital city* | video | travel experiences | personal accounts | 88 |
| 42 | *Topical chat* | audio | music; cycling safety | radio chat | 90 |
| 43 | *The silent killer* | video | oral hygiene | popular lecture | 92 |
| 44 | *The music of the rainforest* | audio | flora and fauna of a country | interview with a Guyanese man | 94 |
| 45 | Pronunciation for listeners 9 | | connected speech: intonation<br>spoken English: tag questions | | 96 |

**Scripts**   page 98

**Answer key**   page 133

**Checklist: Techniques to improve your listening**   page 144

# 1 Feeling good

Alan

Anisa

Ning

## A Thinking about the topic

1 You're going to hear Alan (English), Anisa (English) and Ning (Chinese) answering these questions. Before you listen, think about how *you* would answer them and discuss with a partner.
   1 How would you finish this sentence?
      *Happiness is …*
   2 What's your idea of fun?
   3 What puts you in a good mood?
   4 What's the best thing that's happened to you over the last week?
   5 What do people do to enjoy themselves where you're from?

2 ▶ 1 Watch the video. Alan, Anisa and Ning don't all answer all of the questions from Exercise 1. Who answers which questions? Complete this table.

|   | Alan | Anisa | Ning |
|---|------|-------|------|
| 1 | ✓    |       |      |
| 2 |      |       |      |
| 3 |      |       |      |
| 4 |      |       |      |
| 5 |      |       |      |

## B Listening for specific information

3 ▶ 1 Watch Part 1 of the video (00:00–01:32) and complete this table.

|                            | Alan                        | Anisa | Ning            |
|----------------------------|-----------------------------|-------|-----------------|
| 1 Happiness is …           | being yourself, relaxing    |       | spiritual things |
| 2 What's your idea of fun? |                             |       |                 |

4 ▶ 1 Watch Part 1 again. Who uses these phrases?
   1 Happiness is … enjoying a relaxed time.
   2 Happiness is not only the money …
   3 … have some dinner or meals …
   4 … where you've got a chance to carry out any hobby that you like …
   5 … doing something exciting …
   6 I like … going to a theme park …

5  **Watch Part 2 (01:33–03:18). Who talks about what? Write A (Anisa), N (Ning) or A+N (Anisa and Ning) next to these topics.**

| 1 friends ........ | 3 food ........ | 5 the weather ........ |
| 2 family ........ | 4 a party ........ | 6 giving gifts ........ |

6  **Watch Part 2 again and answer these questions.**
   1 Where does Anisa say she enjoys having good food? (*two places*)
   2 What puts her in an excellent mood?
   3 What type of party does Ning like best?
   4 What type of food does she like to eat? (*two things*)

7  **Watch Part 3 (03:19–04:36). Put these topics in the order you hear them.**
   a different cultures and customs ☐
   b my email account ☐
   c finishing an exam [1]
   d £30,000,000 ☐

8  **Watch Part 3 again and answer these questions.**
   1 Which day does Ning talk about?
   2 Where did she go?
   3 Why were people happy?
   4 Which day does Anisa talk about?
   5 What couldn't she remember?
   6 How much did she win?

## C  Listening for the main ideas and detail

9  **Watch Part 4 (04:37–06:32). Alan, Anisa and Ning are talking about how people enjoy themselves where they come from. Complete this table.**

|  | Alan | Anisa | Ning |
| --- | --- | --- | --- |
| place | Isle of Wight |  |  |
| main activities |  |  | going to the park |

10  **Watch Part 4 again and decide if these statements are true (T) or false (F). Compare with a partner and correct any false ones.**
   1 There's a music festival every weekend on the Isle of Wight.
   2 Alan enjoys the outdoor life.
   3 Anisa still lives in Dubai.
   4 Anisa enjoys spending time with her family.
   5 There are too many people living in Shanghai for people to go camping.
   6 It's easy to meet new people in the park.

## D  Extension and review

11 Who's most similar to you, and who's most different? Why? Discuss with a partner.

12 Which of these activities helped you understand the speakers best?
   - thinking about the topic before listening
   - thinking about who's speaking
   - listening for specific information

# 2 Obsessed by the weather

## A Thinking about the topic

1 Make a list of things which are typically associated with Britain. Make another list for your own country.

Britain: red phone box, black taxi, rain, ...

2 Read the article below. Find words or phrases with the same meaning as these.
  1 to complain
  2 lying comfortably
  3 the celebration of 60 years
  4 an image which represents something

### World's biggest deckchair placed on Bournemouth beach

**Weekend visitors to Bournemouth find the beach occupied by a deckchair taller than a double-decker bus.**

The red-and-white striped deckchair was specially constructed over a period of three weeks by artist Stuart Murdoch. It was commissioned by a well-known drinks manufacturer to celebrate the start of British Summer Time.

We British love to moan about the weather, but there was nothing to complain about this weekend, with Bournemouth basking in glorious sunshine. With the Queen's Diamond Jubilee and the London Olympics to look forward to, it promises to be a very special summer.

Mr Murdoch chose to make a deckchair because it is an iconic symbol of Britain, like red telephone boxes, black taxis or double-decker buses. He says the public response to his massive chair has been fantastic, with everybody smiling and having their photo taken with it.

3 According to the article, the 'British love to moan about the weather'. These words and phrases are connected with the weather. What do they mean, and why would you moan about them? Compare with a partner.
  1 pouring with rain   2 extreme weather   3 a tornado   4 sunstroke

4 What stereotypes do people in your country hold about themselves?

## B Tuning in

5 🎧 **1.2** Listen to Steven, a radio presenter, introducing a programme. Choose the correct answer to these questions.
  1 How many questions do you hear?
    a two   b three   c four
  2 Why does Steven ask these questions?
    a To ask the guest on the programme
    b To introduce typical British behaviour

> **Pronunciation note**
> In Steven's Scottish accent, /r/ is pronounced after a vowel, for example in these words: *weather, sport, year, sure, worth, better, start*

6 🎧 **1.2** Listen again. Number these words from the article in Exercise 2 in the order you hear them.
  a sunshine ☐   b London ☐   c moan ☐   d bask ☐   e Olympic ☐

## C Listening for specific information

**7** 🎧 **1.3** Listen to Steven and Mel talking about the weather. Who says what? Write S (Steven), M (Mel) or B (both) next to each idea.
1 The weather's getting better.
2 The clocks are going to change.
3 I've learnt something new.
4 Three months is a long time.
5 Glasgow has extreme weather.
6 The weather made me ill.

**8** 🎧 **1.3** Listen to the conversation again and answer these questions.
1 In which month was the recording made?
2 Where does Steven say people talk about the weather? (*two places*)
3 Who does Mel talk to about the weather?
4 What did Steven used to wear when he was young, even when it was cold?
5 How long did Mel stay in the Highlands of Scotland?

## D Listening for the main ideas and detail

A

B

**9** Look at photos A and B on the left. What's the occasion in each one? How could they be connected? Discuss with a partner.

**10** 🎧 **1.4** In the next part of the conversation, Mel talks about a family occasion and the massive deckchair. Listen and tick the words or phrases you hear.

**Family occasion**
a sunshine
b disaster
c football
d television
e religious

**Deckchair**
f sums up
g you know
h seven metres high
i sitting underneath it
j roll up my trousers

**11** 🎧 **1.5** Listen to these conversation extracts. Do *sort of* and *kind of* mean a) exactly or b) not exactly?
1   ... there were **sort of** 30 of my family ...
2   That for me **kind of** sums up ...
3   ... the whole of, of, the **kind of**, you know, the start ...
4   ... it's a **kind of** iconic ...
5   ... people are **sort of** crowding round it ...

## E Extension and review

**12** 🎧 **1.4** Can you remember the stories? Listen again, then write a short summary or tell a partner.

**13** Which of these activities helped you understand the radio programme best?
- thinking about the topic before listening
- listening for the main ideas

# 3  Life on Mars

## A  Thinking about the topic

1  You're going to hear a lecture containing all the words below. The bigger words occur more often, the smaller words less often. Look at them and answer these questions with a partner.

   1  What do you think the lecture might be about?
   2  Are there any words that you want to ask about or look up in a dictionary?

2  Read about the speaker. Does this information confirm your ideas from Exercise 1?

**Bechara Saab**
*Neuroscientist*
*Zürich area, Switzerland*

My research aims to show the molecules and brain structures which lie behind the drive to learn and explore. Ultimately, I hope my research will contribute to a greater understanding of life and help release the power of our imagination. I am also interested in space exploration and the possibility of living permanently on Mars.

3  ▶ 2  Watch the lecture. What did you understand? Compare with a partner.

## B  Focus on language

4  ▶ 2  Read the beginning of the lecture (1–10 below) while you watch again (00:00–00:34). Pay attention to the pronunciation. Why do you think the words are printed in different sizes?

   1  I implore you to take a look at the sky tonight.
   2  Between now and sunrise …
   3  … you'll be able to see five planets …
   4  … with your naked eye.
   5  I was staring up at the Red Planet last night, …
   6  … thinking to myself, …
   7  whenever it comes for me the opportunity …
   8  … to live on Mars, …
   9  … I will go in a heartbeat, …
   10  … and I can tell you three reasons why.

## C Listening for the main ideas and detail

5 ▶ Watch Part 1 of the lecture again (00:00–01:21) and number these points in the order you hear them

Bechara …
a asks us to imagine we live on an island. ☐
b asks if we would go to another island. ☐
c tells us that, every now and again, a giant wave destroys our island. ☐
d gives us three reasons to go somewhere new. ☐

6 Match the phrase beginnings (1–4) with the endings (a–d). Compare with a partner.

1 Mars is much colder than Earth –        a at the polar caps and elsewhere on the surface.
2 There are huge reserves of $CO_2$       b release hydrocarbons.
3 After a few thousand years,              c you can't wander around in bare feet.
4 People living on Mars                    d we'd learn how to control the climate on Earth.

7 ▶ Watch Part 2 of the lecture (01.22–03.03) and check your answers to Exercise 6.

8 ▶ Watch the whole lecture again and decide if these statements are true (T) or false (F). Correct any false ones.

1 In the imaginary world, you can see the second island all the time.
2 People might go to the second island because they're curious.
3 The greenhouse effect will produce liquid water.
4 We don't know anything about how releasing hydrocarbons will affect the planet.
5 Complex plants and animals will produce oxygen.

## D After watching

9 ▶ How many technical words and phrases can you remember from the lecture? Add them to this table. Then watch the lecture again or read the script to find more.

| chemistry | oxygen, |
| astronomy | planet, |
| climatology/geography | polar caps, |

10 In the last part of the lecture, Bechara talks about children running around Mars 'without any scuba gear'. What do you think he means? Discuss with a partner.

## E Extension and review

11 Are you convinced by Bechara's explanation of how to control the climate on Mars? Write a summary of the lecture or tell a partner. Explain why you are or aren't convinced.

12 Which of these activities helped you understand the lecture best?
- using the speaker's body language
- listening for the main ideas

# 4 Making a meal of it

## A Thinking about the topic

1  How often do you cook? What meals do you cook most frequently? What do you *never* make? Do you ever make dishes from other countries?

2  You're going to hear Ian explaining how to make a meal with these ingredients (1–9). What meal do you think he'll make? Discuss with a partner.

## B Tuning in

3  🎧 **1.6** Listen to some phrases from Ian's recipe. You'll hear each one three times. Which ingredients from Exercise 2 do you hear?

4  🎧 **1.7** Listen to more phrases from the recipe. You'll hear each one three times. Each phrase contains the word *for*. What words do you hear after *for*?

> **Pronunciation note**
> Each phrase in Exercise 3 contains the word *of*. It's pronounced very quickly, as /əv/ or /ə/. In Exercise 4, *for* is pronounced very quickly, as /fə/, or /fər/ if the next word begins with a vowel sound.

## C Listening for specific information

5  🎧 **1.8** Listen to the start of the programme. Cover the 'quantity' column of the table below and choose the correct options in the 'ingredients' column. Then listen again and choose the correct options in the 'quantity' column.

|   | ingredients | quantity |
|---|---|---|
| 1 | arborio rice or *basmati* / *carnaroli* rice | *50–60* / *60–70* grams or *1–2* / *2–3* ounces |
| 2 | mixed mushrooms | *200* / *300* grams or *6* / *8* ounces |
| 3 | *sweet* / *dry* white wine | one or two *glasses* / *tablespoons* |
| 4 | a *large* / *small* onion | one |
| 5 | garlic | as *much* / *many* as you like |
| 6 | *chicken* / *vegetable* stock | half a *litre* / *pint* |
| 7 | *olive* / *sunflower* oil | *a couple of* / *a few* tablespoons |

6 🎧 **1.8** Listen again and answer these questions.
   1 What extra information do you hear about rice and mushrooms?
   2 What should you do with the vegetable stock?
   3 Which ingredient can you leave out?
   4 Which ingredient is used to decorate the finished meal?

7 Ian often says *Um ...* or *Er ...* when he's speaking. Choose the best reason.
   a Because he can't remember what he was going to say next.
   b Because he's thinking; to show that he intends to continue.

## D Listening for the main ideas and detail

8 🎧 **1.9** Listen to the instructions. Tick these sequencing words each time you hear them. Which one does Ian use the most? Compare with a partner.

   first   ..........
   now     ..........
   then    ..........
   after   ..........
   once    ..........

9 Ian uses lots of pronouns so he doesn't have to say the same word again. Look at these phrases from the ingredients and instructions. In each one, what does the word in bold refer to?
   1 ... some dried mixed mushrooms ... **they** certainly add a real depth to the flavour.
   2 ... put the oil in a large frying pan, then let **that** warm through ...
   3 ... add in the onions, let **them** go transparent ...
   4 ... the rice is cooked through ... take **it** off the heat ...

10 🎧 **1.9** Listen again and answer these questions.
   1 Which ingredients do you chop and fry in the oil before you add the rice?
   2 When do you add the dried mushrooms?
   3 How long do you cook the rice for?
   4 What can you add at the end to make the risotto taste richer?

11 Ian uses these phrases. What do you think he means? Compare with a partner.
   1 ... and it just looks like a dog's dinner.
   2 ... you can murder a risotto.

## E Extension and review

12 Discuss these questions.
   1 Would this be a good meal to serve at a party? Why? / Why not?
   2 Would it be suitable for a vegetarian?
   3 This programme was broadcast on a radio station for blind listeners. Which stages in the cooking process would be most difficult for them?

13 Which of these activities helped you understand the radio programme best?
   • listening for specific information
   • ignoring *er* and *um* so you have more time to listen to key information
   • listening for sequencing words and pronouns to help follow ideas

# 5 Pronunciation for listeners 1

## A Connected speech: weak forms of short grammar words

1 🎧 **1.10** You're going to hear six groups of phrases. All the phrases in each group have one word in common. What is it? (Clue: It's one of these short grammar words: *an, as, a, or, and, of*.)

*Example:*
1 going about in <u>a</u> T-shirt    *a*
  We were up there for <u>a</u> week.
  Put them in <u>a</u> bowl.
  I'd booked <u>a</u> room.

> It can be difficult to hear these short grammar words because, in conversation, they are usually pronounced very weakly.
> • They all have the same weak vowel sound: /ə/.
> • Consonant sounds may be cut, e.g. *and* may be pronounced the same as *an*.
> • They may link to sounds before or after, e.g. *booked a room* sounds like *book ta room*.

2 🎧 **1.11** Listen to and read the phrases that go with these pictures. The phrases are written wrongly. Rewrite them correctly.

1 a cup a tea an a biscuit

4 a pine to milk an a loafer bread

2 one a two bags are ice

5 as coal does a block a vice

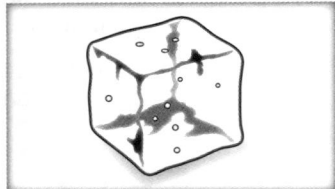

3 try a neat a bitter fruit

6 a piece a cake an a nice cream

3 How would you explain the mistakes in Exercise 2?
*Example:*
1 *A cup of tea and a biscuit* sounds like *a cup a tea an a biscuit* because:
   – the *f* is cut from the word *of* so it's pronounced like *a*
   – the *d* is cut from the word *and*.

## B Spoken English: thinking time

Writers usually have time to plan what they're going to put next. Speakers usually don't. When speakers don't know what to say next, they often:
- insert a noise such as um or er    *Fish and, um, chips!*
- stretch a word    *Fish aaand chips!*
- repeat a word    *Fish and, and chips!*

This is to give themselves thinking time.

**4** 🎧 **1.12** **Listen and show where the speaker inserts a noise using ▲.**
1 … and ▲ it's warm.
2 … but when the sun's shining, excellent mood.
3 I thought I'd do a mushroom risotto.
4 … and we were up there for a week …
5 Indeed, yes, right, this is probably enough for two people.
6 … one day, you want to send your, your daughter …
7 … and family's very important …
8 … the older I get as well, it obsesses me more and more.

**5** 🎧 **1.13** **Listen and underline the words which the speaker stretches. Notice there is often a pause after the stretched word.**
1 … and if you wanna <u>go to</u> an Italian deli, you'll find that …
2 I guess you see, you know, there's all these, sort of …
3 … then put in the rice.
4 … and I, I think it's, er, it's good for me …
5 I think, yeah, I, I would like to have the lifestyle …
6 … and then, so that's how I knew that I absolutely loved it
7 'cause he was taking part in this, er, TV show
8 particularly in terms of the impacts of climate change and
9 so when the opportunity was presented to me
10 which is not that oil's going to run out
11 in our local community to become more resilient
12 I now have to learn to like

**6** 🎧 **1.14** **Listen and circle the words or phrases which the speaker repeats.**
1 … (I think) it's looking positive.
2 … with, er, a load of Chelsea supporters.
3 … I think it's eight and a half metres …
4 … and that should be warmed then in a saucepan …
5 … to add to the risotto.
6 … and then just garnish it with, er, fresh parsley and then serve.
7 … especially maybe if you had children as well …
8 … for example, um, if you're famous person …
9 … so that was incredible.
10 It's like adding spice to food.
11 … the impact of increasing energy costs …
12 … and again how we depend on huge shopping centres …
13 … and begin to create that kind of, er, future for ourselves …
14 … and I think a lot of the ideas that are coming out of that …

**7** 🎧 **1.2–1.4, 1.8–1.9** **Listen again to the audio extracts for Lessons 2 or 4. Try to identify where the speaker inserts a noise, stretches a word or repeats a word or phrase.**

# 6 Fame

## A Thinking about the topic

1 You're going to hear Tom (English), Thuy (Vietnamese) and Ezgi (Turkish) having a conversation about fame. Before you listen, decide if the things below are good, bad or neither. You can use a dictionary. Think about the other good and bad aspects of being famous. Discuss with a partner.

2 ▶ ③ Watch Part 1 of the video (00:00–01:15). Who only mentions advantages of being famous and no disadvantages?

## B Listening for the main ideas and detail

3 ▶ ③ What can you remember? Decide if these statements are true (T) or false (F). Correct any false ones and compare with a partner. Then watch Part 1 again to check.
   1 Tom thinks the person he saw at the airport was famous.
   2 He likes the idea of having a lot of people around him.
   3 Thuy doesn't want to be admired by people.
   4 Being famous would make Thuy feel proud of what she can do.

4 Discuss these questions with a partner.
   1 How do you think Tom feels about fame? Why?
   2 Why does Thuy talk about flowers?

18 Photocopiable © Delta Publishing 2014 from *Authentic Listening Resource Pack*

## C Listening for specific information

5 ▶ 3 **Watch Part 2 (01:16–02:11). Who talks about what? Write E (Ezgi) or T (Tom) next to these topics.**
   1 the street _____   2 the paparazzi _____   3 children _____   4 the cinema _____

6 ▶ 3 **Watch Part 2 again and answer these questions.**
   1 According to Ezgi, what can't you do if you're famous?
   2 Does Tom feel that privacy is important? Why? / Why not?

7 ▶ 3 **Watch Part 3 (02:12–03:32). Number these topics in the order you hear them.**
   a school ☐
   b fashion ☐
   c children ☐ 1
   d freedom ☐
   e money ☐

8 What do you remember? What did the speakers say about school, fashion, freedom and money? Discuss with a partner.

9 ▶ 3 **Watch Part 3 again and answer these questions.**
   1 How does Thuy think being famous would help her children?
   2 What disadvantage of fame for people's children does Ezgi mention?
   3 What advantage and disadvantage of being famous does Tom give?
   4 Why does Ezgi talk about fashion?

## D Extension and review

10 Did you hear any of your ideas from Exercise 1? Whose ideas are most similar to and most different from yours? Why? Compare with a partner.

11 Which of these activities helped you understand the speakers best?
   - thinking about phrases for discussing opinions
   - remembering what people said as you listen
   - listening for specific information

'We're not intrusive – we keep a respectable distance.'

# 7 Talent-show winner

### A Thinking about the topic

1 What qualities do you think a person needs to win a TV talent show? Compare with a partner.

2 Read the newspaper article below and answer these questions.
   1 Why do you think readers of the newspaper would find the story interesting?
   2 What do you think Mary-Jess will do in the future?

## British girl wins Chinese TV talent show

**19-year-old Mary-Jess Leaverland won first place in the contest while studying Mandarin as an exchange student at Nanjing University.**

The English girl's winning performance was watched by 70 million live on television on the Chinese equivalent of *The X Factor*. During the contest, she sang songs in English and Italian, but in the final round, she sang in Chinese. **'I took Chinese Mandarin as an extra-curricular GCSE,'** she says. **'That's how I knew I absolutely loved it – I mean, it's such a fascinating language.'**

Mary-Jess found out about the show by accident during a visit to the TV studio. **'I've always wanted to be a recording artist,'** she said. **'It just looked like the most exciting opportunity that's ever been presented to me, so I definitely just went for it.'**

Mary-Jess hopes that her success in China will eventually help her to get her foot in the door of the music industry. But first, she will use her prize money to return home to Gloucestershire for a family Christmas.

3 Read the article again and find the following.
   1 the name of a British TV show
   2 a school exam course
   3 the name of a region in England

### B Tuning in

4 🎧 **1.15** You're going to hear Mary-Jess saying the quotes in bold in the article in Exercise 2. Listen and decide the best sentence ending (a, b or c). Explain your choice.

Mary-Jess is …
a reading a prepared speech aloud.
b speaking in a serious academic debate.
c speaking in a lively radio interview.

5 🎧 **1.15** Listen again a few times. Notice that Mary-Jess cuts a lot of sounds from her words – this is normal in fast speech. Look at the examples underlined below.

as a̲n extra-cu̲rricular   fasc i̲nating   wanted t̲o be a̲ recording artis̲t
jus̲t looke̲d like the most exci t̲ing   defi ni̲te ly jus̲t went

## C Listening for key words and phrases

**6** 🎧 **1.16** Listen to the first part of Mary-Jess's interview. Choose the correct options in italics to complete these sentences. Then listen again and check.
1 She started learning Chinese when she was *12 / 13 / 14*.
2 She took *Chinese / Italian / music* as her main subject at university.
3 She went to China in her *first / second / third* year at university.
4 The TV programme was *recorded / edited / live*.

**7** 🎧 **1.17** Match the two halves of these phrases. For some, there is more than one possibility. Then listen to the next part of Mary-Jess's story and check your answers.

1 a really good           a flu
2 the huge studio         b Chinese
3 the worst               c day
4 my entire               d opportunity
5 my then quite broken    e life
6 the best                f complex

**8** 🎧 **1.17** Listen again and answer these questions. Compare with a partner.
1 Who did Mary-Jess first go to the studio with?
2 Where was the singing competition happening?
3 What did Mary-Jess have to do to get on the show?
4 What problem did she have when she received a phone call to tell her that she could go on the show?

## D Listening for the main points and extra detail

**9** Number these events in a logical order.
a Mary-Jess's story was published in the local newspaper.
b Her album will be released soon.
c Mary-Jess went to the famous Abbey Road recording studios.
d A big recording company phoned Mary-Jess.
e They went to Beijing to record Chinese instruments.

**10** 🎧 **1.18** Listen to the order in which Mary-Jess talks about the events in Exercise 9. Is it the same as the logical order? Compare with a partner.

**11** 🎧 **1.18** Listen again. Make a note of one piece of extra information for each of the events in Exercise 9. Use the information to write a summary of what happened to Mary-Jess after she won the Chinese *X Factor* or tell a partner.

## E Review and extension

**12** What advice would you give to somebody who wanted to enter a talent show? Discuss with a partner.

**13** Which of these activities helped you understand the radio programme best?
- tuning in to the speaker's accent
- listening for key words and phrases
- thinking about the main ideas before detail

# 8 Life without oil

## A Thinking about the topic

1 Look at these images. What do you think *peak oil* is? How will it affect our way of life? Compare with a partner.

 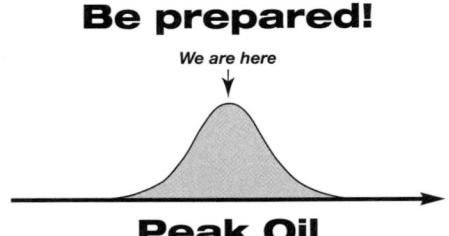

2 Read this description. How do you think 'Transition Towns' will be able to become less dependent on oil? Discuss with a partner.

### Community Podcast

Transition Towns are a network of communities working to achieve a **sustainable** way of life. The idea is a response to the impact of climate change and oil running out – a 'transition' to a more energy-efficient lifestyle. An important concept in the **transition** movement is 'peak oil' – the idea that oil **extraction** has reached its maximum level, and from now on, oil will start to become **scarce** and much more expensive. Consequently, communities will have to become less **dependent on** cars.

In this week's Community Podcast, Trevor Sharman, British local transition leader, tells Paul Goodwin how Transition Towns can help us to become more **resilient** and better able to **withstand** the challenges of a life without oil.

3 Match the words and phrases in bold in the text above with these meanings.
   1 tolerate
   2 unable to live without
   3 taking out
   4 can be continued
   5 rare
   6 strong, not vulnerable
   7 change

## B Tuning in

4 🎧 **1.19** Listen to these fragments from the podcast and notice the highlighted parts.

   ... and again, how, ¹how we depend on huge shopping centres ...
   ... fix these things for us, ²er, we can do it ourselves.
   it's about ... having, ³giving people the opportunity to, ⁴to think creatively

5 Read this explanation and find examples of a–d in the fragments in Exercise 4.
   Speakers often need time to think how to express their ideas. As a result, they:
   a pause.
   b say *er* or *um*.
   c repeat a word.
   d change a word.

## C Listening for key words and phrases

**6** 🎧 **1.20** Listen to the first part of the podcast and make notes about what Trevor says under these headings. Compare with a partner.

| peak oil | Transition Towns |
|---|---|
|  |  |

**7** 🎧 **1.21** Listen to the next part of the podcast, where they discuss a film called *The End of Suburbia*. Choose the correct word or phrase to complete each of these sentences.
1 'The End of Suburbia' is an *Australian / American / English* film.
2 It's about the importance of *society / the car / shopping*.
3 It looks at how the use of the car affects the design of *towns / shopping centres / food suppliers*.

**8** 🎧 **1.21** Read these phrases (a–f) and look up any new vocabulary in your dictionary. Match two of the phrases with each of the topics below (1–3). Then listen again and check.

a for our food supplies
b as a third leg
c about how we can be more resilient
d to get around on
e this isn't really sustainable
f in the future

Topic 1: We need a car ___b,___
Topic 2: We depend on huge shopping centres _____
Topic 3: We need to think _____

## D Listening for specific information

**9** Trevor uses pronouns to replace words and phrases. Look at these examples. What do the words in bold refer to?
1 I think the transition thing, is not about looking backwards, **it**'s about looking forwards.
2 … we've never had so much money, although **that** might be changing …
3 We've got not enough time for our children, and we're worried about our children. **These** are things that worry us now.
4 We could share more in terms of food, er, how we actually produce and, and, er, cook **it** and so on.

**10** 🎧 **1.22** Listen to the final part of the podcast and answer these questions.
According to Trevor, …
1 who works the longest hours in Europe?
2 what do we worry about paying for?
3 what can people share?
4 what will be the three advantages of planning the future?

## E Extension and review

**11** Would you be interested in living in a Transition Town? Why? / Why not? Write a summary on your opinion or tell a partner.

**12** Which of these activities helped you understand the speaker best?
- knowing when the speaker was using hesitation and repetition as time to think
- thinking about the main idea before detail
- thinking about the meaning of pronouns to help follow ideas

# 9 Living with failing eyesight

## A Thinking about the topic

1 You're going to hear someone speaking about a topic connected with these pictures. Make a list of words and phrases you might hear. Use your dictionary to help. Compare with a partner.

*Examples:* special phone, glasses ...

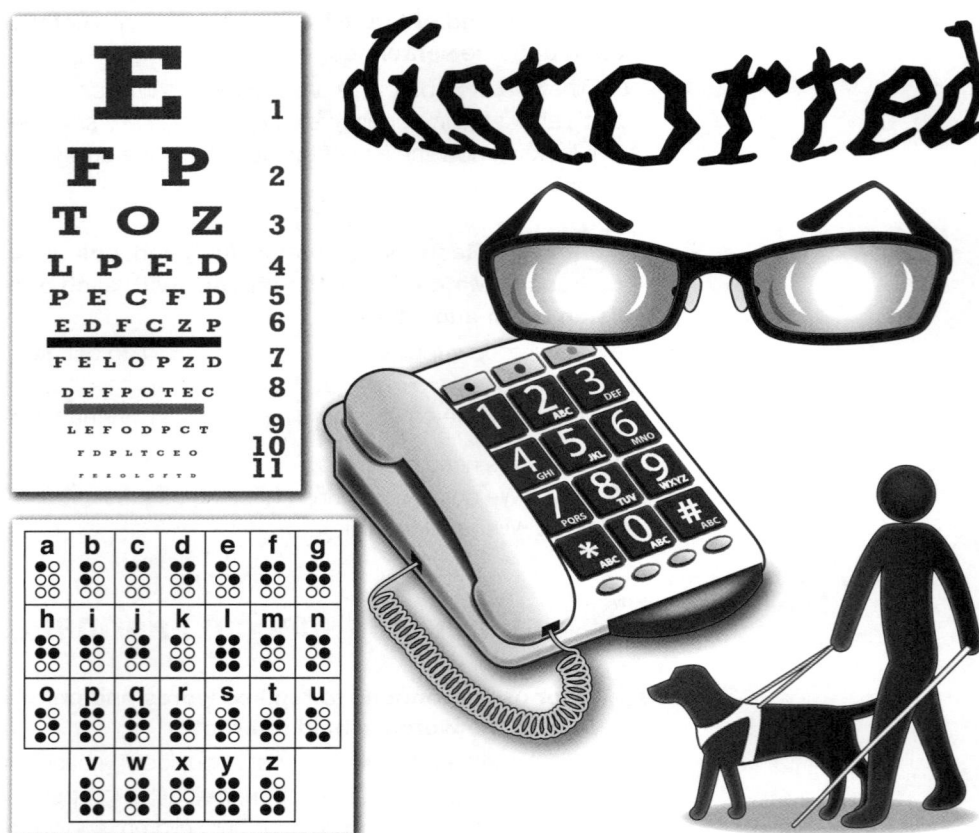

2 Check the meanings of the words in this word family.

sight    sighted    short-sighted    eyesight    sight loss

## B Tuning in

3 🎧 **1.23** Maggie is an American journalist living in London. She has failing eyesight. Listen to the first part of the interview and decide which of these questions (a, b, c or d) she's answering. Discuss with a partner.

How have your eyesight problems affected your ability to ...
a do the housework?
b use the computer?
c read the newspaper?
d travel to work?

**Pronunciation note**
In Maggie's accent, *t* often sounds like *d*. For example, *let it* sounds like *led it*.

4 🎧 **1.24** Listen to four short extracts from the first part of the interview. You'll hear each extract three times. Notice the sound of the letter *t* in these words:

let    it    sort    distorted    lot    computer

## C Listening for the main ideas and detail

**5** You're going to hear Maggie answering these questions. What do you think she might say? Discuss with a partner.
1 Have your employers been supportive? How have they reacted?
2 Do you get a lot of assistance from your friends and family? How do they help?
3 When did you first notice that you had eyesight problems?

**6** 🎧 **1.25** Listen and check your predictions from Exercise 5.

**7** Decide if these sentences are true (T) or false (F). Correct any false ones.
1 Maggie often asks her employers for support.
2 Journalism is a good profession for people who have problems with their sight.
3 Her friends and family have left her to do things on her own.
4 Maggie's friends sometimes go to the shops with her.
5 Until recently, she thought her eyesight was better than it really was.

**8** 🎧 **1.25** Listen again and make a note of some words and phrases connected with the questions in Exercise 5.

## D Listening for key words and phrases

**9** In the last part of the interview, Maggie talks about how she thinks her life will change in the future. What do you think she'll say? Before you listen, read this summary and choose the best words to complete the sentences.

Maggie thinks that people should ¹*try to / have to* make their life better in the future. People who can see ²*want to / expect to* be able to read a book, but people with eyesight problems have to find a different way. She's going to ³*have to listen / listen* to people reading to her. She thinks it's ⁴*difficult / easier* for people to do this today. She's planning on trying ⁵*to like / to find* different ways of doing things.

**10** 🎧 **1.26** Listen and check your ideas from Exercise 9. Compare and discuss with a partner.

**11** 🎧 **1.27** Listen to five slowed-down extracts from the last part of the interview. They all have the structure: 'verb + *to* + verb', e.g. *going to have to learn*. Notice that this structure has a rhythm of strong and weak syllables:

**12** 🎧 **1.26** Listen to the last part of the interview again and identify the extracts from Exercise 11.

## E Extension and review

**13** What advice would you give to Maggie? Discuss with a partner.

**14** Which of these activities helped you understand Maggie's story best?
- thinking about the topic before listening
- listening for the speaker repeating an idea
- thinking about what the speaker will say before listening

# 10 Pronunciation for listeners 2

## A Connected speech: crowded syllables

**1** Read these word groups. Why do you think some syllables are printed in bold capital letters and some are printed smaller? Read the key below to check.

| word group | 'small' syllables |
|---|---|
| it's **GON**na be a **BIG** one | (3) |
| have you **EV**er had a com**PLETE** | (4) |
| **TAKE** a look up at the **SKY** | (5) |
| you **NEV**er know what you're gonna **GET** | (6) |
| now **I** think that's very British as **WELL** | (7) |
| there's **GOT**ta be something wrong if I can't **EAT** | (8) |
| it's **NOT** gonna be something that's gonna con**TIN**ue | (9) |
| **MUS**ic in order to try and help follow my **DREAM** | (11) |
| **LOOKED** like the most exciting opportunity that's ever been pre**SENT**ed to me | (16) |

> **KEY**
> - The syllables in bold capitals are stressed.
> - The syllables in the smallest type are crowded between the stressed syllables.
> - The number in brackets shows how many 'small' (unstressed) syllables there are. Notice the number increases as you read down.

'The more there are, the more crowded it gets.'

**2** 🎧 **1.28** Listen to the word groups from Exercise 1 and read these notes.
- The unstressed syllables are spoken very weakly and very fast.
- When there are more syllables between the words in capital letters, the speech is faster and more difficult to understand.
- Reduced spellings such as *gotta* (= *got to*) or *gonna* (= *going to*) are sometimes used to represent the way these phrases sound in spoken English.
- Very long word groups, such as the last one, are common in spontaneous speech (e.g. Lesson 7) but not in prepared speeches (e.g. Lesson 4).

3 🎧 **1.29** Listen to 12 more word groups. Write the missing words and syllables in the gaps. The numbers in brackets indicate the number of unstressed syllables between the stressed syllables.

| | | |
|---|---|---|
| 1 we were **UP** ................................................ **WEEK** | (3) |
| 2 **DID**n't ................................................ **OF** it | (5) |
| 3 **I** ................................................ **RED** planet | (6) |
| 4 we **REAL**ly ................................................ **THIS** summer | (5) |
| 5 I im**PLORE** ................................................ **SKY** tonight | (7) |
| 6 **COULD** ................................................ ha**RASS**ing you | (5) |
| 7 I've **AL**ways ................................................ **ART**ist | (9) |
| 8 I've **ENT**ered ................................................ **COULD** | (9) |
| 9 I **DID**n't ................................................ **CHANCE** | (7) |
| 10 I **KNEW** ................................................ **SOUND** like | (6) |
| 11 **TELL** ................................................ **THAT** | (7) |
| 12 **TRY**ing ................................................ **NOW** | (7) |

## B Accent variation: pronunciation of *r* and *t*

4 🎧 **1.30** Listen to these phrases spoken by four different speakers. Notice the pronunciation of the letter *r* in the words in bold.

| weak *r* | strong *r* |
|---|---|
| **Mel** (southern English accent)<br>… end of **March** and, er, it's **warm** …<br>… **heard**, have you **heard** about this …<br>… they've got the **world's** biggest deck**chair** … | **Steven** (Scottish accent)<br>… **weather** disaster …<br>… not having a **care** in the **world** about the **weather** …<br>… just going about in a T-**shirt** … |
| **Ian** (southern English accent)<br>… **per person** …<br>… er, the **first** thing you do …<br>… put the oil in a **large** frying pan …<br>… fresh **parsley** and then **serve** … | **Bechara** (North American accent)<br>… to go to **Mars** …<br>… we might **learn** …<br>… how that **works** here on **Earth** …<br>… **more** and **more** complex …<br>… that liquid **water** could flow … |

5 Complete these sentences with the words *strong* and *weak*.

1 People with a southern English accent say a ................................ *r*.
2 People with Scottish and North American accents say a ................................ *r*.

6 🎧 **1.31** Listen to these phrases spoken by two different speakers. Notice the pronunciation of the letter *t* in the words in bold.

| weak *t* | strong *t* |
|---|---|
| **Maggie** (North American accent)<br>… **whatever** you need, **let** us know …<br>… you can do a **lot** of things on the phone, you can do a **lot** of things by **computer** …<br>… before I **started** using it …<br>… **better** than it was before … | **Trevor** (English accent)<br>… make much **better** sense …<br>… **waiting** for somebody else **to** fix these things …<br>… what we've **started**, we **started** by trying **to** raise …<br>… **to** think **creatively**, **to** get together … |

7 🎧 **1.32** Listen to these phrases and notice the pronunciation of *r* and *t*. Does the speaker have an American or English accent?

1 for a period of about six years in total
2 twenty-first birthday
3 they did a pretty good job of sorting it out
4 a computer program created
5 and it's a sort of search strategy
6 it was the first album ever that they wrote every song on it

# 11 Going places

## A Thinking about the topic

1 You're going to hear Tom (English), Maria (Russian) and Alan (English) answering these questions. Before you listen, think about how *you* would answer them. Compare with a partner.
   1 Where would be your ideal place to live?
   2 What's your idea of a good holiday?
   3 What's the best place you've visited recently?
   4 What advice would you give to a visitor to your country?

2 ▶ 4 Watch the video. Who do you find the easiest to understand? Why?

## B Listening for the main ideas and detail

3 ▶ 4 Watch Parts 1 and 2 of the video (00:00–02:51) and complete this table. Compare with a partner.

|   | Tom | Maria | Alan |
|---|---|---|---|
| 1 My ideal place | by the sea, no rain |  |  |
| 2 My idea of a good holiday |  |  | sitting by the pool reading a book |

4 ▶ 4 Watch Parts 1 and 2 again. Number these phrases in the order you hear them and write T (Tom), M (Maria) or A (Alan) according to who says each one.
   a ... drink an orange juice ...
   b ... I just don't really like ...
   c ... I think that an ideal place for me ...
   d ... I'm not a big city person ...
   e ... I sort of met a lot of interesting people ...
   f ... it's a bit disappointing ...
   g ... spending time at the seaside ...
   h ... which is also very lovely ...

28  Photocopiable © Delta Publishing 2014 from *Authentic Listening Resource Pack*

5 ▶ 4 **Watch Part 2 again (01:12–02:51). Who talks about what? Write T (Tom), M (Maria) or A (Alan) next to these topics. Which topic do they all mention?**
   1 friends _____
   2 family _____
   3 culture _____
   4 winter holidays _____
   5 travelling alone _____
   6 the beach / swimming _____

6 ▶ 4 **Watch Part 2 again and answer these questions.**
   1 Why does Tom like going on holiday with friends?
   2 What advantage does he mention about travelling alone?
   3 What does Maria say she'll find boring after two or three days?
   4 How can she solve this problem?
   5 What characteristic does Alan use to describe himself with holidays?

## C Listening for specific information

7 ▶ 4 **Watch Part 3 (02:52–04:36). Who's recently visited these places (1–3), and how did they describe them (a–c)?**
   1 Antibes and Normandy
   2 Cambodia
   3 Mexico and the Caribbean Sea
   a interesting
   b impressive
   c expensive

8 ▶ 4 **Watch Part 3 again and answer these questions.**
   1 Why did Tom find Cambodia interesting?
   2 What was good and bad about his holiday?
   3 What does Maria say about the beaches in the Caribbean?
   4 How does she describe the people in Mexico? Why do you think it was important?
   5 What did Alan enjoy in Antibes?
   6 What didn't he like?

9 ▶ 4 **Watch Part 4 (04:37–06:43). Tom, Maria and Alan talk about giving advice to people visiting their own country. Who mentions these things? Compare with a partner.**
   1 Cultural differences
   2 Stereotypical ideas
   3 The weather

10 ▶ 4 **Watch Part 4 again and decide if these statements are true (T) or false (F). Correct any false ones.**
   1 Tom advises visitors to Britain to go only to London.
   2 He advises people to ignore common opinions on British food.
   3 Maria lives in Moscow.
   4 She mentions several things you can do.
   5 Alan thinks that, for many visitors, driving in England is difficult at first.
   6 He says that visitors should do what other people do.

## D Extension and review

11 **Who would be the best person for you to travel with? Why? Compare with a partner.**

12 **Which of these activities helped you understand the speakers best?**
   - thinking about the topic before listening
   - ignoring background noise
   - listening for the general ideas

# 12 Raby Castle

### A Thinking about the topic

1 Read this extract from a brochure. Would you like to visit Raby Castle? Why? / Why not?

**Visiting Raby Castle**

Raby, home to Lord Barnard's family since the seventeenth century, is one of the finest medieval castles in England. Set in stunning grounds with hundreds of deer, the castle opens to the public over Easter weekend and from May until the end of September. Visitors are offered a full guided tour of the most impressive rooms in the castle, including the magnificent entrance hall, the sumptuous Octagon Drawing Room and the vast Baron's Hall.

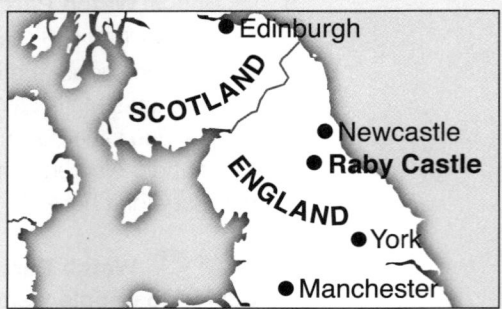

2 Work with a partner. Find three words in the extract which are synonyms of *amazing*. Check your answers in a dictionary.

### B Tuning in

3 🎧 **1.33** Listen to three people describing Raby Castle. How do they all sound? Choose the best adjective (a, b or c).
   a bored   b worried   c approving

4 🎧 **1.34** Vowels vary a lot across different accents, so listeners need to be flexible. Listen to the phrases in this table. You'll hear each phrase three times. Notice the accent difference in the vowels shown in bold.

|   | Katie Blundell (north-east England) | Claire Owen (southern England) |
|---|---|---|
| 1 | up at the c**a**stle | to the c**a**stle |
| 2 | absolutely st**u**nning | it is the most st**u**nning |
| 3 | **o**pen room | when we're **o**pen |
| 4 | I've never seen so many p**ai**ntings in my life | all the p**ai**ntings are members |

30 Photocopiable © Delta Publishing 2014 from *Authentic Listening Resource Pack*

## C Listening for specific information

**5** 🎧 **1.35** Listen to part of a radio programme in which Katie Wallace talks to Katie Blundell, a member of staff at Raby Castle, and complete these notes.

- Raby Castle: home to Lord Barnard's family since [1]............
- Katie Blundell: Marketing and [2]............ Manager
- Park: nearly [3]............ deer
- Visitor numbers last year: over [4]............
- Open: [5]............ days over Easter weekend; from May to September
- Number of rooms open to public: about [6]............

**6** 🎧 **1.35** Listen again and answer these questions.
1 Has Katie Wallace visited the castle before?
2 Who has invited her to visit the castle?
3 Where is Katie Blundell?
4 How does she feel about her job?
5 What is Claire, the Curator, going to tell Katie Wallace about?

## D Listening for the main ideas and detail

**7** 🎧 **1.36** Listen to Claire and Katie Wallace on a tour of the rooms listed in the table below. Match these people (1–6) with the correct room.
1 Henry Vane the Elder
2 the second Duke of Cleveland
3 John Carr of York
4 the Scottish architect, William Burn
5 Mary, Queen of Scots
6 the second Earl of Darlington

|  | Octagon Drawing Room | Entrance Hall | Baron's Hall |
|---|---|---|---|
| people |  |  |  |
| extra information |  |  |  |

**8** 🎧 **1.36** Listen again and note down two more pieces of information for each of the rooms in Exercise 7. Compare with a partner.

**9** 🎧 **1.37** In the last part of the programme, Claire talks about her job as a curator. What do you think she does? Listen and check your ideas.

**10** 🎧 **1.37** Listen again and decide if these statements are true (T) or false (F). Correct any false ones. Compare with a partner.
1 Claire works full time.
2 She chooses the tour guides.
3 Katie Wallace thinks Claire has an easy job.
4 Claire thinks she's got a fantastic job.

## E Extension and review

**11** Which job would you prefer, the Marketing and Event Manager's or the Curator's? Why? Write a summary or tell a partner.

**12** Which of these activities helped you understand the radio programme best?
- thinking about vocabulary before listening
- listening for different accents
- listening for key names, words and phrases

# 13 The friendly virus

## A Thinking about the topic

1 You're going to listen to Lucy Thorne giving a lecture containing all the words below. The bigger words occur more often, the smaller words less often. Look at the words and answer these questions with a partner.
   1 What do you think the lecture will be about?
   2 Are there any words that you want to ask about or look up in a dictionary? Choose five.

2 ▶ 5 Watch the video. What did you understand? Compare with a partner.

## B Focus on language

3 When people give a lecture, they usually divide what they say into short sections with pauses for breath between. Most of the pauses are in the same place as written punctuation, or where the phrase breaks naturally. How could a speaker divide this text? Use a short vertical line as shown to indicate possible pauses. There are no 'correct' answers!

Is there such thing | as a good virus? Now, this might seem like a strange thing to ask. When we think of viruses, we tend to think of the big baddies, like flu and HIV, that are exceptionally good at spreading disease. Even Hollywood's cottoned on to our fear of viruses, and has brought them to the red carpet as evil, fast-spreading, quite deadly villains. But what if we could use viruses to treat diseases, like cancer?

4 ▶ 5 Watch Lucy's introduction to the lecture (00:00–00:37). Does she divide the text in the same places as you did in Exercise 3?

5 ▶ 5 Watch Part 1 again. Why does Lucy ask questions at the beginning and end of her introduction? Compare with a partner.
   a She doesn't know the answers.
   b She wants to know if the audience can answer the questions.
   c She's introducing the main themes in her lecture.

## C Listening for the main ideas and detail

**6** ▶ 5 **Watch Part 2 (00:38–01:47) and number these points in the order you hear them.**

a The idea that viruses can treat diseases has been around for a long time. ☐1
b We now have the technology to use viruses. ☐
c The measles virus prefers to grow in tumour cells. ☐
d The tumour cell is killed. ☐

**7** ▶ 5 **Match these phrase beginnings (1–4) and endings (a–d). Use the words in bold to help you. Watch Part 2 again to check your answers. What do the words in bold refer to?**

1 This idea has been around for a century
2 Some children with measles
3 When the virus is big enough,
4 We know the virus kills the tumour cell

a and now we have the technology to use **this** information.
b and **it's** based on a natural phenomenon.
c had a reduction in **their** tumours.
d **it** starts small explosions in the cells.

**8** ▶ 5 **Watch Part 3 (01:48–03:25) and decide if these statements are true (T) or false (F).**

1 The measles virus uses a key to open a doorway into a cell.
2 Cancer cells change their locks.
3 The virus carries a harmless drug.
4 A lethal substance poisons the cancer cells from the inside.
5 The measles virus is the only virus which can do this.

**9** ▶ 5 **Watch Part 3 again and check your answers to Exercise 8. Correct any false statements.**

**10** ▶ 5 **Watch the whole lecture again and answer these questions.**

1 How long have we known that viruses can treat diseases?
2 Where does the measles virus prefer to grow?
3 What three things do we have today to help us fight diseases?
4 What is the patient given at the beginning of the treatment?
5 What type of results are scientists getting from their research?

## D After watching

**11 Try to remember the process which Lucy describes. Explain or write about it using this diagram to help you.**

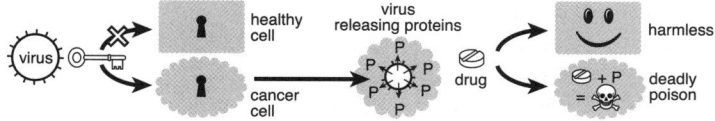

**12** ▶ 5 **Watch the lecture again to check.**

## E Extension and review

**13 Do you think Lucy's use of the Hollywood metaphor makes her lecture more interesting? Why? / Why not? Discuss with a partner.**

**14 Which of these activities helped you understand the lecture best?**
- thinking about pronouns to follow ideas
- listening for the main ideas before detail
- noticing how the speaker divided the text into short chunks

# 14 Complaining

## A Thinking about the topic

1 Look at the photo. What do you think happened here? Tell the story. Would you do this?

2 What would you say or do in each of these situations? What would you never do? Why? Discuss with a partner.
   1 You buy something online and there's something wrong.
   2 You've sent an email to a company and no one's replied.
   3 You go on holiday and the hotel food is awful.
   4 A shop assistant is rude to you.

## B Tuning in

3 🎧 1.38 Listen to Peter, a radio presenter, interviewing a guest expert, Corrine Sweet, over the phone. How have people's complaining habits changed over the last five years? Compare with a partner.

4 Who do you find easier to understand, Peter or Corrine? Why is that? Write P (Peter) or C (Corrine) in the boxes.
   He/She …
   - speaks quickly. ☐
   - has an accent I haven't heard before. ☐
   - speaks clearly. ☐
   - uses words and phrases that are new for me. ☐
   - is distorted because they are speaking on the telephone. ☐
   - pauses a lot, which gives me time to think. ☐

## C Listening for specific information

5 🎧 1.39 Listen to the next part of the interview. Who makes these points, Peter (P), Corrine (C) or both (B)?
   1 It's easy to send an email. ☐
   2 We have more to complain about today. ☐
   3 People don't want to wait for an answer to a letter. ☐
   4 It's difficult to make a general statement. ☐
   5 British people have changed their behaviour. ☐

**6** 🎧 **1.39** Corrine uses the words and expressions in bold below. What do you think they mean? Listen again and compare with a partner.

1 I think we are more **picky**, we've got higher standards …
2 We want not to **stick** a letter in the post …
3 … it **takes ages** and it sits in an in-tray …
4 I think in the British **psyche** …
5 … we don't like **whiners**, we don't like moaners …

**7** 🎧 **1.39** Listen again and answer these questions. Compare with a partner.

1 Why don't people send letters of complaint any more?
2 How has British people's behaviour changed?
3 What does Corrine think about this?

## D  Listening for the main ideas and detail

**8** 🎧 **1.40** Listen to the next part of the interview. Choose the best summary of the conversation (a, b or c).

a It's better to complain online.
b Online feedback allows people to share information about companies.
c A company is good if it lets you complain online.

**9** 🎧 **1.40** What can you remember? Match the beginnings and ends of the sentences. Then listen again and check.

1 Shy people …            a ask for positive feedback.
2 Angry people …          b just want your money.
3 Companies like eBay and Amazon …   c want to fight.
4 Some family companies …  d prefer email.
5 Companies that don't care …  e think about customer service.

**10** 🎧 **1.41** Listen to the final part of the interview. What's the best way to complain? Number these points in the order you hear them.

a Be polite. ☐
b Think about who you are complaining to. ☐
c Say what you want them to do. ☐
d Give details about the problem. ☐

**11** 🎧 **1.41** Listen again. What do you think of Corrine's advice? Choose one or two of these adjectives. Tell a partner or make some notes.

1 sensible   2 unrealistic   3 practical   4 silly

**12** Look at these phrases. Can you guess what they mean? Compare with a partner.

1 fire off            4 got that off my chest
2 huge shift          5 feel psychologically stroked
3 it's dead easy      6 sound advice

**13** 🎧 **1.38–1.41** Listen to the whole interview again and check your ideas.

## E  Extension and review

**14** How do you feel about complaining to somebody? Discuss with a partner.

**15** Which of these activities helped you understand the radio interview best?

- tuning in to the speaker's voice
- listening for the main ideas
- guessing the general meaning of new words and phrases

# 15 Pronunciation for listeners 3

## A Connected speech: rushed adverbs

**1** 🎧 **1.42** Listen to and read Alan's words. You'll hear them six times, getting progressively slower. What do you think he's really saying?

Alan: an it sachli lichri true!

**Note**
Some adverbs such as *actually* and *literally* are especially common in speech, and they're often pronounced very weakly and are consequently difficult to hear. According to the dictionary, both of these words have four syllables:
*actually* /ˈæktʃʊəli/
*literally* /ˈlɪtərəli/
However, in speech, they often have only two.

**2** 🎧 **1.43** You're going to hear 20 short fragments containing *actually*. Listen, then look at five of the fragments below, written as they sound. Write them correctly.

1. tie matchly
2. a nacksli we have
3. ayak she love it
4. we'd own tatsli say
5. hour zaxi watchin it on TV

**3** 🎧 **1.44** Some other adverbs are commonly rushed in speech. Listen and complete the gaps in the fragments below with the words/phrases in the box.

| basically | definitely | obviously | of course | particularly |

1. yeah, _____ computers, you know
2. you know, _____ celebrate something
3. I was _____ struck
4. they've _____ said, well
5. I'm _____ pleased because
6. It was _____ the best year of my life.
7. earlier and _____ he, one of the things he
8. um, you know, _____ the focus of Lohri is
9. panning out, _____ in terms of
10. so what do we need for this? _____ mushrooms
11. and _____ , people who go to visit
12. er, _____ there's, there was the sort of
13. because _____ after George
14. well, _____ , it's terribly important

## B Spoken English: vague language – *sort of, kind of, just*

**4** 🎧 **1.45** Listen to and read Anisa and Tom's words. What do you think the highlighted words are really?

*Anisa:* and I **sudduv** slept on and off

*Tom:* it **scanna** like radio that you can choose

**Notes**
- Speakers use *sort of* and *kind of* to mean 'not exactly'. For example, *kind of like a radio* means 'similar to, but not necessarily exactly the same as, a radio'.
- These expressions are so common in speech that speakers often say them almost automatically, and very fast and reduced. Consequently, they are difficult for listeners to hear. However, if you don't hear them, it makes very little difference to your understanding!

**5** 🎧 **1.46** Listen and show where the speaker inserts *sort of* or *kind of* using ▲s or ▲k.

1. for ▲s the presentation
2. lots of nice pockets of
3. there were 30 of my family
4. but I stumbled into a karaoke place
5. I mean, we went to several places
6. and you just put your case forward and
7. people are crowding round it and
8. er, you've got some lovely beach front
9. people are right to complain
10. know with the big, you know, plastic discs
11. and we tend to queue up
12. maybe a car that runs on water, you know
13. for me sums up the whole of, of the, you know, the start
14. um, until he stood up
15. and I think you're missing out a little bit

**6** 🎧 **1.47** Listen and correct the words in bold. What word do all the fragments have in common?

1. **anaw sojuss** the lifestyle
2. a **nenjuss** walking around and
3. um, **justa** try and get my foot in the door
4. and, um, **I'd yuss** wanted to get out of the heat really, so
5. you **nojuss** cars that use alternative fuel
6. it was, it was **juss** wonderful
7. **deff nijuss** went for it

**Note**
Like *sort of* and *kind of*, *just* is so common in speech that speakers often say it almost automatically, and very fast and reduced. Usually, you won't hear the final /t/ sound. Again, it makes very little difference to the meaning, so it's not important if you miss it.

# 16 Risk

## A Thinking about the topic

Maria   Alan   Ning

1 You're going to hear Maria (Russian), Alan (English) and Ning (Chinese) having a conversation about taking risks. Before you listen, number these activities in order of danger. What other risky activities can you think of? Compare and discuss with a partner.

gambling ☐
scuba diving ☐
parachute jumping ☐
hang-gliding ☐
mountain climbing ☐

2 ▶ 6 Watch the interviews. Who sounds the most adventurous? Compare with a partner.

## B Listening for the main ideas and detail

3 ▶ 6 Watch Part 1 (00:00–01:37) and choose the correct options.
 1 *Maria / Alan / Ning* would like to go parachute jumping.
 2 *Maria / Alan / Ning* would like to go scuba diving.

4 ▶ 6 What can you remember? Decide if these statements are true (T) or false (F). Compare with a partner and correct any false ones. Then watch Part 1 again to check.
 1 Ning thinks Maria is crazy.
 2 Maria's afraid of heights.
 3 Alan doesn't like heights.
 4 He thinks scuba diving is safe.
 5 Ning would like to learn how to swim.

5 Discuss these questions with a partner. Then check your ideas in the script.
 1 Why did Maria say 'I'm not going to die when I jump.'?
 2 What did Ning mean when she says 'It's just a dream.'?

38  Photocopiable © Delta Publishing 2014 from *Authentic Listening Resource Pack*

## C Listening for specific information

**6** ▶ 6 **Watch Part 2 (01:38–02:44). Who says each of these words? Write A (Alan), M (Maria) or N (Ning) next to each one.**
1 risky ☐
2 amazing ☐
3 dangerous ☐
4 fit ☐
5 height ☐

**7** What are the speakers describing when they use the words in Exercise 6? Discuss with a partner.

**8** ▶ 6 **Watch Part 2 again, then answer these questions. Compare with a partner.**
1 What did Maria's friend do?
2 Why does she say it was difficult?
3 Why wouldn't Ning like this activity? (*two reasons*)

**9** ▶ 6 **Watch Part 3 (02:45–04:29) and number these topics in the order you hear them.**
a casino ☐
b the royal baby ☐
c investment ☒
d the lottery ☐
e snow ☐

**10** ▶ 6 **Watch Part 3 again and answer these questions.**
1 Why doesn't Alan gamble?
2 Why wouldn't Maria go to a casino?
3 How much did Alan once win on the lottery?
4 Why does he get upset about people buying lottery tickets?
5 What does Ning feel about English gambling habits?

## D Extension and review

**11** What can you remember? Who used these expressions, and what did they mean? Compare with a partner.
1 Before you die? OK, come on!
2 I would chicken out.
3 … and see all the fish and stuff …
4 … would you fancy that?
5 … some crazy scheme or something like that.
6 … they gamble on all kinds of stuff.

**12** Who do you think would take the most and least risks? Discuss with a partner.

**13** Which of these activities helped you understand the speakers best?
- listening for key words
- listening for general ideas
- guessing the general meaning of expressions

# 17 Baltic voyager

## A Thinking about the topic

**1 Look at the map and read the text. Then find the names of the things below (1–8).**

**The Pegasus** is a boat belonging to The Island Trust, a charity which aims to provide sail-training experiences for young people in need. Sailing provides trainees with a challenging adventure, encouraging independence, teamwork, communication and life skills. The Pegasus, skippered by Diggory Rose, won prizes in the 2009 Tall Ships race.

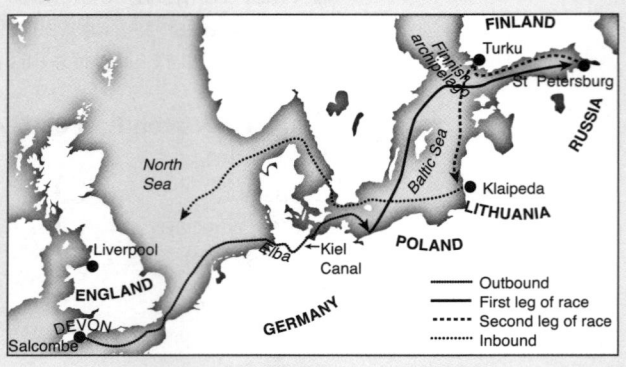

1 a boat — the Pegasus
2 a charity
3 a competition
4 a group of islands in the Baltic
5 a port in Russia
6 a boat captain
7 a river in Germany
8 a county in England

**2 Would you enjoy the voyage shown on the map? Why? / Why not? Compare with a partner.**

## B Tuning in

**3  1.48 Musician Phil Beer took part in the voyage shown on the map. Listen to him explaining how it happened. Tick the names in Exercise 1 that you hear.**

## C Listening for specific information

**4  1.49 Listen to the next part of the interview with Phil and choose the correct summary (a, b or c).**

a They came last in the first stage, and came second in the next stage to St Petersburg.
b They won the first stage of the race, but the boat broke after they left St Petersburg.
c The boat broke in the first stage and had to be fixed in St Petersburg. They won the stage from Finland.

5 🎧 **1.49** Listen again and complete this table.

| BOAT AND CREW | | |
|---|---|---|
| length<br>number of standing crew<br>trainees sent by | 1 _____ – _____ feet in the water<br>2 _____<br>3 _____ Fire Service | |
| **BALTIC VOYAGE** | | |
| 1st leg of race | problem<br>city where repair work done | mast worked loose<br>4 _____ |
| Finnish archipelago cruise | number of days<br>number of islands | 5 _____<br>6 _____ |
| 2nd leg of race | starting city<br>finishing city<br>position of Pegasus in race | 7 _____<br>Klaipeda<br>8 _____ in class<br>9 _____ overall |

## D Listening for key words and phrases

6 🎧 **1.50** Listen to the last part of the interview and answer these questions.
  1 What was the weather like around Finland?
  2 What was the weather like crossing the North Sea?
  3 Was anyone sea-sick?
  4 What did Phil do when he visited other ships?

7 🎧 **1.50** Match the phrase beginnings and endings. Then listen again to check.
  1 a few **heavy-duty** …           a  fleets
  2 and oil …                        b  **gale**
  3 Did you sing any sea … ?         c  occasions
  4 sea-sick on **odd** …            d  **rigs**
  5 through a near …                 e  **shanties**
  6 trying to avoid fishing …        f  storms

8 Guess the meaning of the words in bold in Exercise 7. Use the context of the whole phrase to help you.

9 Look at the phrases in bold in this extract from the script. Can you guess what they mean? Compare with a partner.
  … we were **bashing our way through** a, a near gale and, of course, when you, when you're just **nose on to it**, you know, and you're trying to avoid fishing fleets and oil rigs and all the rest of it, it's, er, quite unpleasant.

## E Extension and review

10 Do you think Phil would enter the Tall Ships race again? Why? / Why not? Make a note of three reasons or tell a partner.

11 Which of these activities helped you understand the radio programme best?
  • tuning in to the speaker's voice
  • using context to guess meaning of key words and phrases
  • listening for specific information

# 18 Under the volcano

## A Thinking about the topic

1 Look at this infographic. Where and when did the event happen? Do you know any other volcanoes and stories about them? Discuss with a partner.

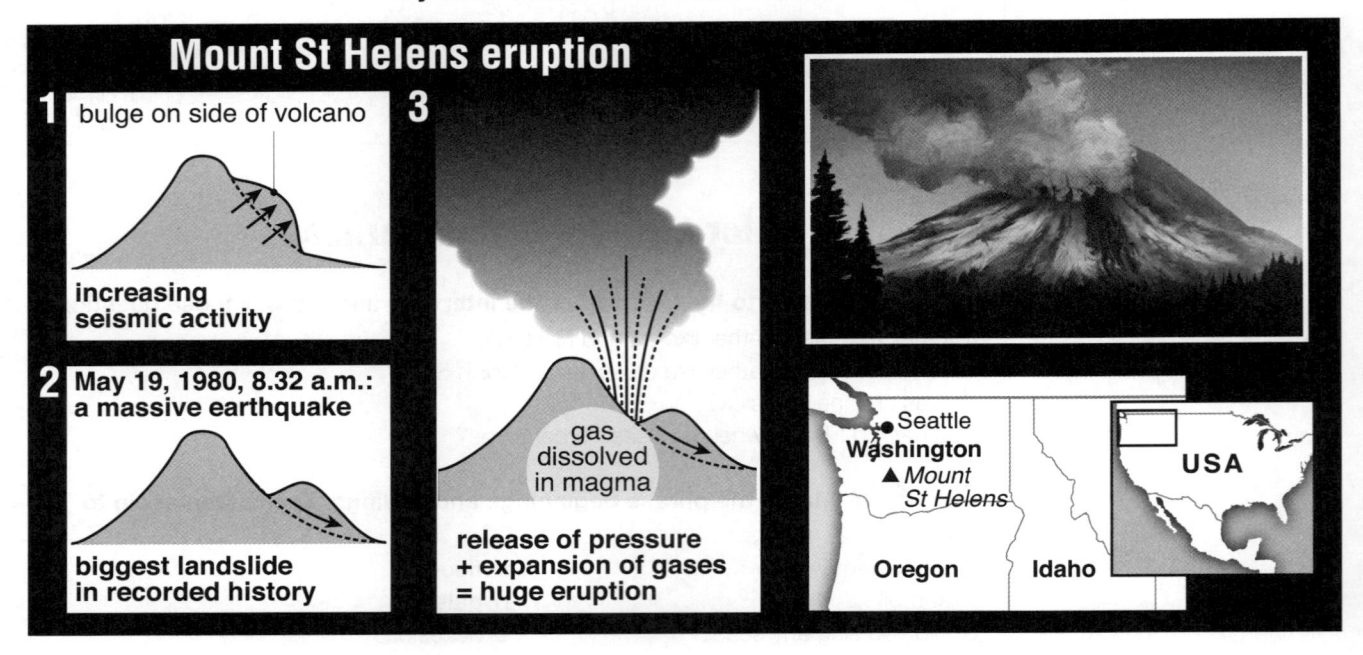

**Mount St Helens eruption**

1. bulge on side of volcano — increasing seismic activity
2. May 19, 1980, 8.32 a.m.: a massive earthquake — biggest landslide in recorded history
3. gas dissolved in magma — release of pressure + expansion of gases = huge eruption

Seattle • Washington ▲ Mount St Helens — Oregon — Idaho — USA

2 Find words in the infographic with these meanings. Compare with a partner.
1 explosion
2 very big (*two words*)
3 ground moving (*two words*)
4 area which sticks out
5 liquid inside a volcano

## B Tuning in

3 🎧 **1.51** Malcolm, a radio presenter, is talking to Jenny Riker, a volcanologist, about Mount St Helens. Listen and read. You'll hear it first at normal speed and then slowed down.

**Malcolm:** It must have been absolutely terrifying [I think] for people 'cause it, because [good question, yeah, because] it's not, it's not a highly **populated** area, is it?

**Jenny:** Um, no, it's not very **populated**, but, er, you can see that volcano from Portland, Oregon, which is a city probably about the size of Bristol.

**Malcolm:** So, the bulge **started**, [Yeah] and then, and then what happened, er, after? [Well, the bulge **started**] So, I mean, er, did, did, people like yourself, volcanologists, sort of run …

4 🎧 **1.51** When speakers are very involved in a conversation, they often a) interrupt the other speaker, and b) repeat themselves. Listen again and find examples of a and b in the highlighted text in Exercise 3.

5 🎧 **1.52** The sound /t/ is often pronounced differently in British and American accents. Listen and compare the way *populated* and *started* are pronounced.

## C  Listening for the main ideas and detail

**6** 🎧 **1.53** Listen to the first part of the interview and choose the correct statement (a, b or c). Compare with a partner.
  a  Mount St Helens had always been very active, with many earthquakes in the region.
  b  People could see the changes happening to Mount St Helens before it erupted.
  c  Mount St Helens is in a heavily populated area, and many people were affected by the eruption.

**7** 🎧 **1.53** Listen again. Tick the information you hear.
  1  Washington State is on the north-west coast. ☐
  2  Washington, DC, the capital, is on the east coast. ☐
  3  People ran away from the volcano. ☐
  4  Most people remember the 1980 eruption. ☐
  5  You can see the volcano from Portland. ☐
  6  The side of the volcano exploded. ☐

**8** 🎧 **1.54** Listen to the next part of the interview. Number these topics in the order you hear them. Compare with a partner.
  a  Mount St Helens today ☐
  b  Scientists went to Mount St Helens. ☐
  c  A story from history ☐
  d  The eruption ☐

**9** 🎧 **1.54** Match the sentence beginnings and endings. Then listen again and check your answers.
  1  The scientists                a  started the eruption.
  2  The first volcanologist       b  is quieter than that in 1980.
  3  A landslide                   c  came from all parts of the country.
  4  Recent activity               d  died at Vesuvius.

## D  Listening for specific information

**10** 🎧 **1.55** Listen and decide if these statements are true (T) or false (F). Correct any false ones.
  1  Volcanologists don't go to places where volcanoes are exploding.
  2  Volcanic areas with lava flows are easier to work in.
  3  Jenny knows a lot about the preservation processes like those at Pompeii.
  4  The eruption at Pompeii happened very slowly.

**11** 🎧 **1.55** Listen again and complete these sentences.
  1  Jenny and her colleagues work at volcanoes all over the _____ .
  2  Some volcanic areas, like Hawaii, produce lava flows which move quite _____ .
  3  People living in Pompeii didn't have time to _____ what they were doing.
  4  The _____ preserves living things.

## E  Extension and review

**12**  Would you like to work as a volcanologist? Why? / Why not? Make notes of your reasons or tell a partner.

**13**  Which of these activities helped you understand the speakers best?
  • thinking about vocabulary connected to the topic
  • knowing when the speakers were using hesitation and repetition as time to think
  • listening for the main points

# 19 Mystery on Mount Everest

## A Thinking about the topic

1 **What do you know about Mount Everest? Can you answer any of these questions? Compare with a partner.**
   1 Where is it?
   2 How high is it?
   3 Who first climbed it?
   4 When?

2 **Read this flyer advertising a talk about an early Everest expedition. Who are the people in the photo?**

---

### Everest needs you, Mr Irvine

In 1924, George Mallory and Sandy (real name Andrew) Irvine set out to become the first people to climb Mount Everest. They were never seen alive again. What happened to them? Did they reach the summit or not? Their story has become one of the greatest legends of mountaineering, and Irvine's great-niece, writer and historian Julie Summers, brings it alive in this fascinating, beautifully illustrated performance.

---

3 **Mark these sentences N (Nobody knows) or D (The text doesn't say).**
   1 Mallory and Irvine reached the summit of Everest. ☐
   2 Mallory and Irvine's bodies were never found. ☐
   3 Irvine's older sister was Julie's grandmother. ☐

## B Tuning in

4 🎧 **1.56** **Listen to the beginning of a telephone interview with Julie. Does she answer any of the questions in Exercise 3? Compare with a partner.**

5 🎧 **1.56** **Listen again. Who do you find easier to understand, the interviewer or Julie? Why? Tick the reasons.**
   He/She ...
   ... speaks quickly. ☐
   ... has an accent I've heard before. ☐
   ... speaks clearly. ☐
   ... says some words with emphatic stress. ☐
   ... isn't speaking on the telephone. ☐
   ... says *er* and *um* a lot. ☐

## C Listening for key words and phrases

**6** 🎧 **1.57** Listen to Julie talking about her family history. Number the names of these people, places and events in the order that you hear them.

a Dick Summers ☐
b Spitzbergen ☐
c Evelyn ☐
d Everest ☐
e the Oxford and Cambridge boat race ☐
f Sandy's sister and brothers ☐
g Uncle Sandy ☐

**7** 🎧 **1.57** Julie uses different types of pronouns and adjectives to refer to different people. Look at these extracts. Who do you think the words in bold refer to? Listen again and check.

1 … his older sister Evelyn was **my** grandmother …
2 … I knew very little about him, except **he** was Uncle Sandy …
3 … my grandmother refused ever to speak about him … even when **her** own children questioned **her**.
4 He did have a love affair with **his** best friend's stepmother …

## D Listening for the main ideas and detail

**8** 🎧 **1.58** Listen to the next part of the interview. Number these points in the order you hear them.

a Julie hopes no photographs will be published. ☐
b Both families hope that no more bodies will be found. ☐
c Mallory's granddaughter lives near Julie. ☐
d In 1960, a Chinese climber saw the body of Sandy Irvine. ☐
e George Mallory's body was found. ☐

**9** 🎧 **1.58** Listen again and add one extra piece of information to each point in Exercise 8. Compare with a partner.

**10** 🎧 **1.59** Listen to the final part of the interview. Choose the correct word or phrase to complete each of these sentences.

1 Sandy's story is *terrible / romantic / incredible*.
2 *Everybody believes / Nobody believes / Some people believe* they got to the top of Everest.
3 Mallory planned to leave a picture of his wife *in his pocket / at the top of Everest / on a snowy peak*.
4 Hillary got to the summit of Everest in *1929 / 1935 / 1953*.

**11** 🎧 **1.59** Listen again and answer these questions. Compare with a partner.

1 Why did the story capture people's imagination?
2 What does Julie think of the stories about whether or not Irvine and Mallory got to the summit?
3 Why did people think they had got to the top?
4 What did Hillary do when he got to the top of Everest?
5 What two questions did finding Mallory's body raise?

## E Extension and review

**12** Would you go to the talk *Everest Needs You, Mr Irvine*? Why? / Why not? Make some notes or tell a partner.

**13** Which of these activities helped you understand the radio programme best?
- thinking about the speaker's style
- thinking about the meaning of pronouns to follow ideas
- listening for the main points before detail

# 20 Pronunciation for listeners 4

## A Connected speech: weak forms of auxiliary verbs

**1** 🎧 **1.60** In each of the sentences below, the part in bold has been misunderstood. Listen and decide what the speaker actually wanted to say, using words and phrases from the box.

| is | are | was | were | have | has | ~~I was~~ | have been | there was |

1 **hours** two years old     *I was two years old*
2 my watch**es** broken
3 the man, who **as** a doctor
4 **though as** only one left
5 it must **of bin** terrible
6 the place **as** changed a lot
7 the birds **a** singing
8 they must **of** gone
9 I thought you **a** French

> **Note**
> The verbs in the box in Exercise 1 are usually pronounced very weakly, and it may be impossible to hear the difference between these and other weakly pronounced words such as *of*, *a* or *as* (see Lesson 5).

**2** 🎧 **1.61** Listen and complete these fragments of speech with a form of *be*: *is, are, was, were*.

1 which _____ in Washington state
2 because they _____ interested in what _____ going on
3 and this _____ exactly
4 Evelyn _____ my grandmother
5 I _____ two years old
6 for your colleagues who _____ in the field
7 things that _____ there at the time of the eruption
8 what's exciting _____ that we now
9 and we realized that it _____ actually working loose

**3** 🎧 **1.62** All of these verb phrases contain forms of *be* and *have*. Listen to 12 fragments and number the phrases in the order you hear them.

was going to leave ☐    were carrying ☐    was found ☐

were never seen ☐    has grown ☐    has never been ☐

has replaced ☐    might have been ☐    must have been ☐

must have got ☐    would have written ☐    would've been solved ☐

## B Accent variation: variable vowel sounds

**4** 🎧 **1.63** Listen to seven pairs of phrases. For each pair, identify a word (or part of a word) that they have in common. You'll hear each pair three times.

**5** 🎧 **1.63** Vowel sounds are like handwriting: just as a letter can be written in many different ways, a vowel sound may be pronounced in a variety of different ways. Listen again. Notice the speakers have different accents. The vowel sound is pronounced differently in each pair.

**6** All the vowel sounds of English may vary in different accents. The vowel sounds which are often spelt with the letters 'a' and 'o' are particularly variable. Look at this table.

| main letter | sound | dictionary pronunciation (British English) | pronunciation in a different accent |
|---|---|---|---|
| a | /eɪ/ | stay /steɪ/ | /steə/ (sounds like *stair*) |
|   | /ɑː/ | example /ɪgˈzɑːmpl/ | /egˈzæmpl/ (sounds like *eggs ample*) |
|   | /ɔː/ | caught /kɔːt/ | /kɒt/ or /kɑːt/ (sounds like *cot* or *cart*) |
| o | /ɒ/ | hot /hɒt/ | /hɑːt/ (sounds like *heart*) |
|   | /əʊ/ | cold /kəʊld/ | /kɔːld/ (sounds like *called*) |

**7** 🎧 **1.64** Listen to 41 fragments of speech containing the words in this table. Tick them as you hear them. Notice how the sound varies in different accents.

| sound | examples on the audio | | | | | | | |
|---|---|---|---|---|---|---|---|---|
| /eɪ/ | way ❏ change ❏ today ❏ | | say ❏ today ❏ say ❏ | | days ❏ came ❏ | | stranger ❏ way ❏ | |
| /ɑː/ | can't ❏ photograph ❏ example ❏ | | castle ❏ castle ❏ | | example ❏ examples ❏ | | castle ❏ example ❏ | |
| /ɔː/ | abroad ❏ talks ❏ | | causes ❏ thought ❏ | | all ❏ | | water ❏ | |
| /ɒ/ | lottery ❏ dogs ❏ | | job ❏ stop ❏ | | from ❏ shop ❏ | | from ❏ | |
| /əʊ/ | phone ❏ process ❏ don't ❏ | | coast ❏ know ❏ know ❏ | | boat ❏ over ❏ know ❏ | | know ❏ know ❏ | |

# 21 First impressions

## A Thinking about the topic

1 You're going to hear Maria (Russian), Ezgi (Turkish) and Thuy (Vietnamese) describing their impressions of England when they arrived for the first time. Which of these topics do you think they'll talk about? What do you think they'll say about them? Which of these topics *won't* they talk about? Discuss with a partner.

music food people culture weather beaches accommodation sports wildlife transport cities

## B Listening for specific information

2 ▶ 7 Watch Part 1 (00:00–03:45). Which topics from Exercise 1 does Maria mention?

3 ▶ 7 Watch again and answer these questions.
  1 What did Maria expect to find when she first arrived?
  2 What did she find that was different?
  3 What did she find strange?
  4 What does she say about English food?
  5 What does she say about cycling in London?

4 ▶ 7 What can you remember? How do think Maria feels about the English way of life? Why? Compare with a partner, then watch again.

## C Listening for the main ideas and detail

**5** ▶ 7 **Watch Part 2 (03:46–05:03). Number the topics Ezgi mentions in the order you hear them.**
   a taxis ☐
   b national characteristics ☐
   c bathrooms ☐

**6** ▶ 7 **Watch Part 2 again and answer these questions.**
   1 What was Ezgi's first impression of England? Why?
   2 What does Ezgi say is different in Turkey?

**7** ▶ 7 **Watch Part 3 (05:04–07:34). Which topic from Exercise 1 does Thuy mention?**

**8** ▶ 7 **Watch Part 3 again. What does Thuy say about these situations? Make some notes in the table, then compare with a partner.**

| situation | notes |
|---|---|
| Where she lives |  |
| Problem 1: the broken cooking pot |  |
| Problem 2: going places |  |
| General impressions |  |

## D Extension and review

**9** Who do you think enjoys living in England the most? And the least? Why? Discuss with a partner.

**10** What do you know about the countries the speakers come from? What would you expect to be the same or different in your country? Compare with a partner.

**11** Which of these activities helped you understand the speakers best?
   - thinking about the topic before listening
   - listening for the main ideas
   - watching and listening for feelings

# 22 Rescuing tradition

## A Thinking about the topic

1 Read the advert below. If you went to this concert, which of these would you expect to see? Compare with a partner.

colourful folk costumes    a vocalist    Polish pop hits    electric instruments

---

**Cotherstone Arts Centre**

Sat. 4th April, 7.30

**Dautenis**

*Folk music from the north-east of Poland*

For the members of Dautenis, folk culture is not a colourful spectacle for tourists to see, but a living reality. Come along and see how these four talented young musicians bring back to life the old songs and melodies of their region, using a combination of traditional and modern instruments.

---

2 Read the advert again and find words with these meanings.
1 skilled  2 tunes  3 mix  4 performance  5 old-fashioned

## B Tuning in

3 🎧 **1.65** Małgorzata is a musician in Dautenis. Listen to her explain the meaning of the band's name to Peter, a radio interviewer. What phrase does she mention from the advert in Exercise 1? Compare with a partner.

4 For most English speakers in the world today, English is *not* their mother tongue. Małgorzata's mother tongue is Polish.
1 Is her accent easier or more difficult for you to follow than Peter's?
2 What do you think makes it easier / more difficult?

## C Listening for key words and phrases

**Note**
Some words show the relationship between the ideas a speaker is talking about. If you listen for these words, they can help you understand some general information in a text.

5 Match the words and phrases (1–7) with their functions (a–f). One of the functions can be matched with two words/phrases. Then check in a dictionary.

1 instead of        a to add information
2 but              b to introduce a difference
3 and              c to introduce a reason
4 because          d to introduce an action after a reason
5 and then         e to introduce one action after another
6 so               f to introduce an alternative
7 also

6 🎧 **1.66** Listen to the next part of the interview. Tick the words and phrases in Exercise 5 as you hear them.

7  🎧 **1.66** Listen again. Choose the best word or phrase to complete each sentence. Compare with a partner.
   1 Peter says the members of the group are *young / old / very young*.
   2 People *want to / don't want to / already* know about their culture.
   3 To find out about their culture, the group speaks to *older people / other groups / children*.
   4 According to Małgorzata, *the government / folk groups / children* adapted folk music.
   5 The group *are trying / are going to try / tried* to get to their roots.

## D Listening for specific information

8  🎧 **1.67** Listen to the next part of the interview. Number these topics in the order you hear them.
   a Comparing two places: the north-east of Poland and England ☐
   b What we've been doing in Teesdale ☐
   c Pop music in Poland ☐

9  🎧 **1.67** Listen again. Make notes for these points. Compare with a partner.
   1 Name two English pop groups which are known in Poland.
   2 Name two other countries whose music is known in Poland.
   3 Give one similarity between the north-east of Poland and England.
   4 Give one difference between the north-east of Poland and England.
   5 Name one thing the members of the group have enjoyed about their visit.
   6 Name one thing they haven't really enjoyed about their visit.

10 🎧 **1.68** In the last part of the interview, Małgorzata talks about how the group combines old and new music. Listen and make notes in this table. Then listen again and check.

| old music | new music |
|---|---|
|  |  |

11 At the end of the interview, Małgorzata uses the Polish word *zapraszamy*. What do you think it means? Discuss with a partner.

## E Extension and review

12 🎧 **1.65–1.68** Listen to the interview again. Would you like to go to the show? Why? / Why not? Write some notes or tell a partner.

13 Which of these activities helped you understand the radio programme best?
   • tuning in to the accent of the speakers
   • listening for joining words
   • listen for the main points before detail

# 23 From thought to action

## A Thinking about the topic

**International FameLab TALKINGSCIENCE**

1 You're going to hear a lecture containing all the words below. The bigger words occur more often, the smaller words less often. Look at the words and answer these questions with a partner.
   1 What do you think the lecture might be about?
   2 Are there any words that you want to ask about or look up in a dictionary? Choose five.

2 Read about the topic. Does this information confirm your ideas from Exercise 1?

### Introduction

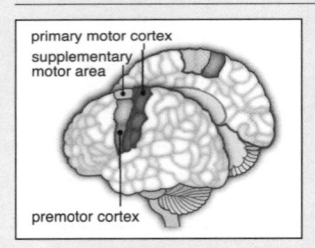

It's easy to forget how amazing the human brain is. In our daily lives, we perform many thousands of actions without even noticing. For example, before you read on, raise your right arm for a moment. Have you done that? Now think about this: how did you do it? Perhaps the thought, 'Raise my arm' came into your mind first. But what *is* a thought, and how can it transform into action? These are exactly the kinds of question which neuroscientists ask.

In this chapter, we will look at areas of the brain called the *primary motor cortex* and the *supplementary motor area*, how they connect so that intentions can lead to motion, and what happens when this connection fails.

3 Watch the video of Egyptian neuroscientist Hazem Shoira giving the lecture. What did he say? Compare with a partner.

## B Focus on language

4 Watch Part 1 of the lecture again (00:00–01:09) and read the first few sentences below. Pay attention to the pronunciation. Why do you think the text is printed like this?

so we're **often asked**
to think **outside of** the box
but for a **brain** scientist
the brain **is** the box
and so sometimes it **really helps**
when you're **trying to study humans**
to **think** like an alien

## C  Listening for the main ideas and detail

**5** ▶ 8 **Watch Part 1 again. Choose the best reason why Hazem asks the audience to do these two things.**
1 Think like an alien to *add some facts / understand aliens / suggest a way of seeing things differently*.
2 Put their left arm up to *answer some questions / introduce the main idea / explain an experiment*.

**6** ▶ 8 **Watch Part 2 of the lecture (01:10–02:00) and number these phrases in the order you hear them.**
a  a little crack in the brain ☐
b  your intention centre and your motion centre ☐
c  supplementary motor area ☐
d  the primary motor cortex ☐

> **Note**
> Lecturers often use phrases to introduce or signpost extra detail.

**7** ▶ 8 **Watch Part 2 again and number these signposts as you hear them.**
a  … this is basically … ☐      c  … which is, basically, … ☐
b  … what we call … or … ☐     d  And when there's … ☐

**8** ▶ 8 **Watch Part 2 again and match the items (1–4) with the details (a–d).**
1 a little crack in the brain.            a  an intention centre
2 the primary motor cortex              b  responsible for movement
3 supplementary motor area              c  thought turns to action
4 your intention centre and your motion centre   d  motor area

**9** ▶ 8 **Watch Part 3 of the lecture (02:01–03:23) and decide if these statements are true (T) or false (F).**
When there's a disconnection between a person's intention and motion, …
1 people's arms and hands don't move.
2 it could be embarrassing.
3 neuroscience doesn't help us understand.
4 it causes problems which healthy people rarely consider.

**10** ▶ 8 **Watch Part 3 again. Correct any false statements in Exercise 9.**

## D  After watching

**11** ▶ 8 **What can you remember from the lecture? Complete this summary. Watch the complete lecture again and check your answers.**

When studying human behaviour and the brain, it helps to think like an [1]_____ . The brain changes thought to [2]_____ , but sometimes there is a disconnection between your intention and your [3]_____ centre. When this happens, hands and arms behave on their own, especially the [4]_____ arm. Some people have problems with this every day, and [5]_____ science can help us understand what's happening. Healthy people should remember how amazing their [6]_____ are.

## E  Extension and review

**12 Did you find Hazem's lecture enjoyable? Why? / Why not? Make notes to explain your answer or tell a partner.**

**13 Which of these activities helped you understand the lecture best?**
- thinking about the topic before listening
- tuning in to the 'parcels of information' in the lecture
- listening for signposts

# 24 Read my lips

## A Thinking about the topic

1 2 3 4 5 6 7 8

**1 Work with a partner. Look at the pictures and answer these questions.**

1 What emotions or moods do the faces represent? Match them with these adjectives:
   a alert ☐         e happy ☐
   b angry ☐         f naughty ☐
   c bored ☐         g sad ☐
   d confused ☐      h shocked ☐

2 How can they be communicated if you can't see the face?

3 How can they be communicated if you can't hear the voice?

**2 Work with a partner. Try to say the phrase *Oh, really?* with some of the moods in the pictures.**

## B Tuning in

**3 🎧 1.69 Listen to and read this piece of unplanned speech. What differences do you notice between this and written English? Discuss with a partner.**

The same is true for *m*, *m* for *Michael* and *n* for *Nicholas*. They actually sound rather similar, but they look rather different, and so what you find is – this is just sort of gross examples, there are also … it goes more subtly than that – but what you find is if you can see a person – and this is true for people with perfect vision – if you can see a person, you get much more of the content of their speech than if you can't.

## C Listening for the main ideas and detail

**4 🎧 1.70 Listen to Mike Burton talking on a radio show for blind people about what you can learn from seeing a face. How many things does he mention: one, two or three?**

**5 🎧 1.70 Listen again and decide if these statements are true (T) or false (F). Correct any false ones. Compare with a partner.**

1 Mike Burton is a professor of psychology.
2 You can tell who somebody is from their face.
3 You need to know the person to tell what they're feeling.
4 Lip-reading doesn't help.
5 Seeing a person's face helps us understand communication more than we realize.

**6 🎧 1.71 Listen to the next part of the interview. What's Mike's main point (a, b or c)? Discuss with a partner.**

a We are born with no ability to understand facial expressions.
b We only learn to understand facial expressions as we grow older.
c We are born with a basic ability to understand facial expressions, and learn about the subtleties as we get older.

**7** 🎧 **1.71** **Listen again and number these points in the order you hear them.**
  a People often say a baby looks like his father.
  b Some emotions, like happiness, are universal.
  c The skill we are born with is basic.
  d Some behaviour comes from our genes – we are born with it.
  e We learn to understand facial expressions according to our cultures and upbringing.
  f We would be more sensitive to Japanese faces if we were born in Japan.

## D Listening for specific information

**8** 🎧 **1.72** **In the next part of the interview, Mike talks about the differences between understanding in face-to-face situations and when you can't see the speaker's face. Make a note of two things he might say, then listen to check. Did you hear either of your ideas?**
  1 ........................................................................................................................................
  2 ........................................................................................................................................

**9** 🎧 **1.72** **Decide if these statements are true (T) or false (F). Then listen and check your answers.**
  1 People use lip-reading all the time.
  2 Some consonant sounds are more difficult to understand on the telephone.
  3 It's easier to understand somebody speaking on the telephone than in a noisy place.
  4 Sighted people are aware of how much they use a person's lip movements.

**10** 🎧 **1.72** **Listen again and correct any false statements. Add some more information to each statement. Compare with a partner.**

**11** 🎧 **1.73** **In the final part of the interview, Mike explains how we can help people with poor sight to understand us. Make a note of two things he might say, then listen to check. Did you hear either of your ideas?**
  1 ........................................................................................................................................
  2 ........................................................................................................................................

**12** 🎧 **1.73** **Listen again and answer these questions.**
  1 Why might people lose the ability to recognize somebody?
  2 Does this mean that they won't be able to recognize emotional expressions?
  3 Which emotion does Mike use as an example of an easy thing to see on people's faces?
  4 What does he advise people to do in noisy environments?

## E Extension and review

**13** 🎧 **1.69–1.73** **Listen to the whole interview again. What advice would you give to somebody who wants to help a partially sighted person understand them better? Write some notes or tell a partner.**

**14 Which of these activities helped you understand Mike Burton best?**
  • tuning in to his voice
  • listening for the main points
  • thinking about what he might say before listening

# 25 Pronunciation for listeners 5

## A Connected speech: weak forms of pronouns

1 🎧 **1.74** You're going to hear five groups of phrases. Each group of phrases has one word in common. Listen and identify it. Clue: In each case, the word in common begins with the letters *th*.

2 🎧 **1.75** In these sentences, the part in bold has been misunderstood. Listen and decide what the speaker actually wanted to say. Note that in each bold phrase, there's at least one pronoun which is joined to the word before or after it.

1 **abetya** very proud
2 **Ana** started to cry
3 **telya hawa** feel about **'im**
4 'cause **anew iwez** excited
5 **Ana** did, **agot** very, very emotional
6 but **akump** bear to watch it
7 **aget** very nervous **forrim**
8 **Ana** hadn't realized
9 **ani** had the scars **wenee** came back
10 **aldoo** it
11 **will** never know **kuzwi** broke the boat
12 **athing** one or two people were slightly seasick
13 because **yether** great-niece
14 **yenoe wada** mean
15 **shiad** very young friends
16 **budakan** still read my
17 **yukandoo** a lot of things on the phone
18 **anell** come and **meepmi** at the bus stop

*I bet you're very proud and I started to cry*

3 Read this phrase: *Watch or a dress?* It may be pronounced exactly the same as the question *What's your address?*

Now find questions which may be pronounced like these phrases. Each question contains a personal pronoun and/or a possessive adjective.

1 What do the eat?
2 What's a name?
3 Where did she lose a ram bag?
4 When Diddy loses money?
5 Watch an aim?
6 What Daisy arriving?
7 Where am a shoes?

## B Spoken English: emphasis

> **Note**
> To give emphasis to a word, speakers say the stressed syllable higher, louder and longer. They do this because they think the word is important to the meaning of what they're saying.

**4** 🎧 **1.76** Listen to and read these two fragments. In the first one, notice how the speaker gives emphasis to the underlined words. In the second one, underline the words which you hear emphasized.

1 That's, that's <u>such</u> an interesting observation, and it is <u>completely</u> borne out by, er, research, um, over <u>many</u>, many years, you know, people with <u>perfect</u> vision use lip-reading <u>all</u> the time.
2 … in your situation, where you are, er, you just cannot resolve, er, the person's lip movements because you can't see them, you are inevitably going to suffer some loss in, er, in what sounds like hearing, but actually it's the full comprehension of the sentence.

**5** 🎧 **1.77** In fragment 1 in Exercise 4, the adverb *completely* is said with emphasis. There are a number of adverbs and adjectives which are typically said with emphasis, because they have a strong meaning. Listen and complete these phrases.

1 it looks _____ incredible
2 look _____ differently
3 you've got _____ the right reaction there
4 it is the most _____ and sumptuous room
5 _____ impressive entrance hall
6 this is absolutely an _____ room

> **Note**
> Compare the strongly pronounced adverbs here to the rushed adverbs featured in Lesson 15, such as *actually*, which are often pronounced so weakly that they're difficult to hear.

> **Note**
> Compare Speakers A and B in item 3 of Exercise 6. Speaker A reduces the auxiliary *is* to *'s*, but in Speaker B's reply, he gives the full form of *is* for emphasis.

**6** 🎧 **1.78** Lesson 20 showed how auxiliary verbs (*is, are, do, have, will, can,* etc.) are usually reduced. However, if speakers want to give a positive emphasis to the sentence, they may choose to put emphasis on the auxiliary. Listen to these examples.

1 Wow! What **is** this room where you've brought us to, Claire?
2 A: Three months! That's a long time, isn't it?
  B: That **is** a long time, actually.
3 A: Now that's bold!
  B: That **is** bold!

**7** 🎧 **1.79** Listen to 12 more fragments of speech. Tick each of these auxiliary verbs each time you hear it emphasized in a fragment.

1 is _____
2 do _____
3 does _____
4 have _____
5 will _____
6 can _____

> **Note**
> In the case of emphasized *do* and *does*, these may appear where they don't exist in the same sentence without emphasis:
>
> | without emphasis | with emphasis |
> |---|---|
> | People ask me … | People **do** ask me … |
> | It obsesses us … | It **does** obsess us … |

# 26 University

## A Thinking about the topic

Alan

Maria

Ning

1 You're going to hear Alan (English) interviewing Maria (Russian) and Ning (Chinese) about universities in their countries. Before you listen, make a note of three or four topics you think Alan will ask about. Compare and discuss with a partner.

2 ▶ 9 Watch the video. How many of your topics did you hear? Can you remember any other topics?

## B Listening for the main ideas and detail

3 ▶ 9 Watch Part 1 (00:00–01:45). Choose the correct options in these sentences. Compare with a partner.
   1 Maria and Ning *are / aren't* currently studying for a degree at university in the UK.
   2 You *have to / don't have to* pay to study at a university in England.

4 ▶ 9 What can you remember? Decide if these statements are true (T) or false (F). Correct any false ones. Then watch Part 1 again to check. Discuss with a partner.
   1 Maria has a degree from a Russian university.
   2 All Chinese universities are expensive.
   3 Some people who study at English universities take gap years to help them pay.
   4 Student numbers are increasing in England.

5 What can you remember? Make some notes on what the speakers said about the following. Compare with a partner.
   1 a private school
   2 state university
   3 a student loan

58  Photocopiable © Delta Publishing 2014 from *Authentic Listening Resource Pack*

## C Listening for specific information

6 ▶ 9 **Watch Part 2 (01:46–03:52). Check any new vocabulary in your dictionary. Number these words and phrases in the order you hear them.**
   a research ☐
   b scholarship ☐
   c Bachelor's degree ☐
   d grants ☐
   e postgraduate school ☐
   f homework ☐

7 ▶ 9 **Watch Part 2 again and answer these questions.**
   1 What don't you pay for in China?
   2 Why doesn't Maria pay for her university studies?
   3 What does she say about judges?
   4 What do Maria and Ning say about the last two weeks of term?

8 ▶ 9 **Watch Part 3 (03:53–05:44). How many times do you hear these words or phrases? Tick each one as you hear it.**
   1 accommodation
   2 (share/rent) a flat/apartment
   3 hall(s) of residence
   4 student house

9 ▶ 9 **Watch Part 3 again and complete this table about university accommodation in Russia, China and England.**

|  | Russia | China | England |
| --- | --- | --- | --- |
| free accommodation? | Yes, but only if you don't pay for your education. | 1 | Doesn't say |
| type of accommodation | 2 | Apartment or 3 | 4 |

10 **What can you remember? Answer these questions, then compare with a partner.**
   1 Why do Russian students prefer to rent a flat?
   2 What's the disadvantage of renting a flat?
   3 Why do most Chinese students choose to stay in university accommodation?
   4 Why are many students in England offered accommodation for the first year only?

## D Extension and review

11 What impression do you think Alan has of Russian and Chinese universities? How do you know? Discuss with a partner.

12 In which of the three countries would you prefer to study? Why? Compare with a partner.

13 Which of these activities helped you understand the speakers best?
   - thinking about the topic before listening
   - listening for repetition of key words and phrases
   - listening for tone of voice to identify attitude

# 27 Speed on ice

## A Thinking about the topic

1 Read the infographic below and complete the gaps (1–7) with the words in the box.

> burns   driver   lucky   runners   slope   speed   team

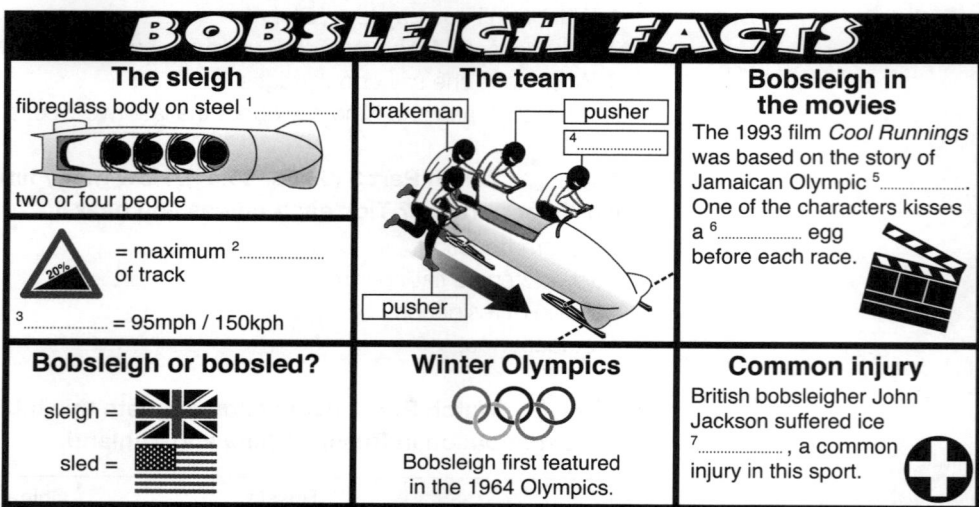

### BOBSLEIGH FACTS

**The sleigh**
fibreglass body on steel ¹..............
two or four people

20% = maximum ² .............. of track

³ .............. = 95mph / 150kph

**The team**
brakeman, pusher ⁴.............., pusher

**Bobsleigh in the movies**
The 1993 film *Cool Runnings* was based on the story of Jamaican Olympic ⁵.............. One of the characters kisses a ⁶.............. egg before each race.

**Bobsleigh or bobsled?**
sleigh = 🇬🇧
sled = 🇺🇸

**Winter Olympics**
Bobsleigh first featured in the 1964 Olympics.

**Common injury**
British bobsleigher John Jackson suffered ice ⁷.............., a common injury in this sport.

2 Answer these questions about the infographic. Compare with a partner.
  1 Why do you think the members of the team wear helmets?
  2 In what order do you think the members of the team jump into the sleigh?
  3 Why is a Jamaican bobsleigh team an interesting subject for a film?
  4 How do you think John Jackson got the injury described?

## B Tuning in

3 🎧 **2.1** Listen to and read the beginning of a radio interview with Julie Jackson about her son's bobsleigh career. What differences do you notice between this and written English? Discuss with a partner.

**Katie:** Julie has arrived. Hello, Julie. [Hi] Hello, how are you doing today?
**Julie:** Fine, thank you.
**Katie:** Julie is, of course, er, John, who is currently over in, er, Vancouver at the Olympic Games, John Jackson, in the bobsleigh. This is his mum. I bet you're very proud.
**Julie:** I am – very, very proud of what he's achieved. I can't explain, I can't tell, start to tell you how I feel about him, [um] just bursting with pride.

> **Pronunciation note**
> Julie's accent is from north-east England. Note the pronunciation of these words:
> - *can't, start*: The final /t/ is replaced by a very short silence (a 'glottal stop'), so they sound like *can'*, *star'*.
> - *bursting*: The final sound is /n/, not /ŋ/, so it sounds like *burstin*.

## C Listening for key words and phrases

**4** 🎧 **2.2** Underline the key words in these sentences. Then listen to the first part of the interview and number the information in the order you hear it.
a John is in Vancouver at the moment. ☐ 1
b Julie couldn't watch the race, so she sat on the stairs. ☐
c Julie cried. ☐
d John texted his mum before the opening ceremony. ☐
e Julie thought John was going to have an accident. ☐
f John had an accident. ☐

**5** 🎧 **2.2** Listen again. Add one more piece of information to each of the sentences in Exercise 4. Compare with a partner.

**6** 🎧 **2.3** Listen to the next part of the interview and decide if these statements are true (T) or false (F). Correct any false ones.
1 John watched a film called *Cool Runnings* on the plane to Vancouver.
2 John likes to puts his hand on his knee before he starts a race.
3 John checks a lot of things before he drives his car.

**7** 🎧 **2.3** Listen again and choose the correct answer (a, b or c) for each of these questions.
1 What does Julie think about John watching *Cool Runnings* on the plane?
 a It's strange.   b It's funny.   c It's sad.
2 Does Julie think John is superstitious?
 a No, she doesn't.   b She's not sure.   c Yes, she does.
3 What does Julie mean when she says, 'He'll tell me off for this'?
 a John will be very angry with her.
 b She thinks she shouldn't be telling people about this.
 c John will be happy she's telling people about him.
4 How does the interviewer react when Julie tells her about the things John does before he drives his car?
 a She's surprised.   b She's worried.   c She's pleased.

## D Listening for specific information

**8** 🎧 **2.4** Listen to the final part of the interview. Which sentence is correct?
a John expects to get a gold medal.
b John doesn't believe he'll get any medals.
c John hopes to do well.

**9** 🎧 **2.4** Listen again and complete these sentences.
1 John hopes to finish in the top ten or ............... .
2 Julie thinks that the top ............... skiers have a lot of pressure to perform well.
3 John likes to be ............... .
4 Julie says that John will give ............... %.

## E Extension and review

**10** How would you feel about a friend or relative doing a dangerous sport? Make some notes or tell a partner.

**11** Which of these activities helped you understand Julie best?
• thinking about the characteristics of natural conversation
• tuning in to her accent
• listening for key words and the main points

# 28 The science of the small

## A Thinking about the topic

1 Put these things in order from smallest to biggest. Two of them are roughly the same size. Compare with a partner.

   a bacterium   b atom   c human hair   d molecule   e red blood cell

2 Read this text. What do you think *nano* means?

### What is nanoscience?

Nanoscience is the study of objects in the size range of 1–100 nanometres, where a nanometre is one billionth of a metre. For comparison, something which is 100 nanometres wide is 10,000 times smaller than the width of a human hair. Nanoscientists manipulate objects which are bigger than an atom but much smaller than bacteria or red blood cells. This is an exciting new area of science, because materials at the nanoscale have very different properties from the same materials in the metre-scale world. New methods in nanotechnology have allowed us to measure and harness these properties.

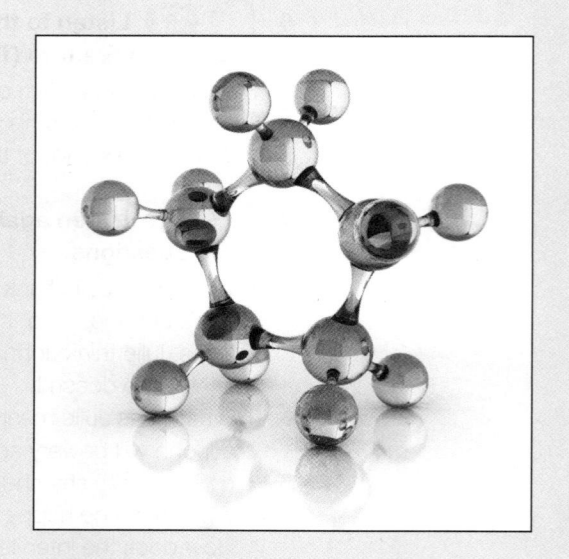

3 Find words in the text with these meanings.

   1 control and use   2 change   3 characteristics   4 distance from side to side

## B Tuning in

**Note**
Words/syllables like *as, than, an, for, -er*, etc. are pronounced very weakly, joined to the words before and after.

4 🎧 **2.5** You're going to hear Annela Seddon, a nanotechnologist, saying four comparative phrases. Listen and write the phrases. You'll hear each phrase three times.

## C Listening for the main ideas and detail

5 🎧 **2.6** Listen to the first part of the interview. Who says the following? Write I (Interviewer), A (Annela) or B (both).

1 nanotechnologist ☐
2 nanotechnology ☐
3 nanoscience ☐
4 physicists ☐
5 bacterium ☐
6 experiments ☐

**6** 🎧 **2.7** Listen to the next part of the interview and decide if these statements are true (T) or false (F). Correct any false ones.
1 Nowadays, it's usual to hear people talking about nanoscience.
2 *The Pleasure of Finding Things Out* is a history of scientific experiments.
3 Richard Feynman was a famous chemist.
4 Richard Feynman thought quantum mechanics was hard to understand.

**7** 🎧 **2.7** What do you learn about Richard Feynman and his famous book/lecture? Listen again and add some key words/phrases to this table (not whole sentences).

| the man | the book/lecture |
|---|---|
| frequently quoted | 1959 |
| | |

**8** 🎧 **2.6–2.7** Read these sentences from audio 2.6 and 2.7. Can you guess what the words/phrases in bold mean? Listen again to check that your ideas make sense in context.
1 … the word 'nanotechnology' is **bandied around** […] all over the place …
2 … not quite as small as what they do with their **quarks** and subatomic particles …
3 … we've been **digging** deeper and deeper and deeper and understanding more and more …
4 … quite a famous lecture, and […] it's **written up faithfully** in a fantastic book …
5 … he's frequently quoted **chap** …

## D Listening for key words and phrases

**9** 🎧 **2.8** Listen to the last part of the interview. Choose the best description (a, b or c) of what Annela says. Compare with a partner.
a She talks about cooking to explain nanoscience.
b She uses the example of aluminium foil to explain how it changes when it is made smaller.
c She gives examples of all the changes that happen to materials when they are made smaller.

**10** 🎧 **2.8** Listen again and complete this summary. The first two letters of each missing word are given.

When some materials are reduced to the nanoscale, they become ¹ex_____ . The surface of the particles ²ch_____ , and the materials stop behaving how scientists ³ex_____ them to. Not knowing what ⁴ma_____ will do at a very small scale makes nanoscience very exciting. When scientists identify the new ⁵pr_____ of material on a nanoscale, they can use these to do ⁶in_____ science.

## E Extension and review

**11** Use your notes from Exercise 7 to write a summary of or tell a partner about Richard Feynman and *The Pleasure of Finding Things Out*.

**12** Which of these activities helped you understand Annela best?
- thinking about the topic before listening
- guessing the meaning of words and phrases
- listening for key words and phrases

# 29 Studying abroad

## A  Thinking about the topic

1  Read this text and do the mini-quiz. Compare with a partner.

### Dutch University Challenge

With tuition fees rocketing at British universities, many school-leavers are considering the option of studying abroad. One popular destination is the Netherlands, where you can take your Bachelor's degree in English, and for a fraction of the price of a similar course in the UK. But there are some things you should know before you go. Try this Netherlands mini-quiz!

1  What's the capital of the Netherlands?
   a  Amsterdam      c  The Hague
   b  Eindhoven      d  Utrecht

2  What's used as an alternative name for the Netherlands?
   a  Holland         c  The Low Countries
   b  Benelux         d  Dutch

## B  Tuning in

2  You're going to hear two short segments from the beginning of a radio programme about studying in the Netherlands. Look at this information about the segments (A and B) and decide which segment is described in each of the sentences below (1–4).

Segment A: News reading, presenting from a prepared script
Segment B: Interviewing, speaking without a prepared script

1  The speaker uses long, complete sentences.
2  The speaker often repeats phrases.
3  The speaker starts, changes his mind and begins again.
4  The speaker uses longer words.

3  🎧 2.9  Listen and check your answers to Exercise 2. Compare with a partner and give examples of each of the features if you can.

## C  Listening for the main ideas and detail

4  🎧 2.10  Listen and number these topics in the order you hear them.
   a  Courses at Utrecht University of Applied Science
   b  There hasn't been a big increase in students going to Utrecht from Britain yet.
   c  It's going to get more expensive to study in England.
   d  Many people in the Netherlands speak English.

5 🎧 **2.10** Listen again. What do these numbers/phrases refer to?
   a 9,000   b 36   c 1,500   d 40,000   e quite a few

6 In the next part of the interview, Paul talks about his experiences in Utrecht. What topics do you think he might talk about? Compare with a partner.

7 🎧 **2.11** Listen. Did you hear any of your ideas from Exercise 6?

8 🎧 **2.11** Listen again and answer these questions.
   1 How long ago did Paul study at the University of Utrecht?
   2 What did he learn about while he was away from home? Give two examples.
   3 Who did he meet while he was there?
   4 Which two other countries does he mention visiting?

## D Listening for specific information

9 🎧 **2.12** Listen to and read the beginning of the next part of the interview. Does Sandra agree with Paul that Utrecht is a big student town? Underline the words and phrases which help you answer the question.

   **Paul:** Oh, Utrecht is absolutely, what do you think, Sandra? It's, it's a brilliant student town, isn't it, there's a big student population.

   **Sandra:** It is, yeah. It's very popular with Dutch students as well, I mean, um, it's very close to Amsterdam, but it's, you know, it's the biggest student city, I think, er, one out of every five residents is a student, so no, it's, it's, it's a lot of fun.

10 🎧 **2.13** In the final part of the interview, Sandra and Paul compare studying in Utrecht and Manchester. Listen and add information to this table about both places. Compare with a partner, then listen again to check.

| UTRECHT | |
|---|---|
| characteristics | café culture, ... |
| transport | cheap to get there, ... |
| cost of course | |
| website | www. |
| MANCHESTER | |
| advantages | near to Stockport (7 miles) |
| disadvantages | |

## E Extension and review

11 Imagine you lived in Stockport and were planning to go to university. Use your notes from Exercise 10 to write a summary of your choice and explain your reason(s) for it, or tell a partner.

12 Which of these activities helped you understand the speakers best?
   • understanding the features of unprepared speech
   • ignoring background noise
   • ignoring fillers and repetitions
   • listening for the main ideas

# 30 Pronunciation for listeners 6

## A Connected speech: linking one word with the next

**1** These sentences have been written as they sound, but they're incorrect. Read them aloud to yourself, then write the correct version.

1 I bought sick seggs and a napple.   I bought six eggs and an apple.
2 Please way tin the corridor.
3 Do you want an eye scream?
4 It snow good, I can't do it!
5 Most student steak the school bus.
6 The Atlantic's a notion.
7 We walk tover the bridge.
8 I phone dim on his mobile.
9 You can see cat size in the dark.
10 I went to were, curly.

> **Note**
> Sometimes the consonant sound at the end of one word sounds as if it's at the beginning of the next word. Find examples in the sentences in Exercise 1.

**2** 🎧 **2.14** You're going to hear ten speech fragments. They include these wrongly written fragments, which you'll then hear repeated four times. Write them correctly.

1 the na natom   than an atom
2 it srit nup
3 thin kabout
4 eva non
5 ka ti tup
6 suddenly take so na
7 thing a thing kabout
8 determin di yiz
9 stop tat the scene
10 mau than nose

**3** These sentences have been written as they sound, but they're incorrect. Read them aloud to yourself, then write the correct version.

1 It doesn't get dark till after rate.   It doesn't get dark till after eight.
2 I studied law rut university.
3 I saw rim coming out of his house.
4 Under-rage drinking's against the law.
5 If your rears are cold, put your hat on.
6 Margaret's got blue wise.
7 It's a quarter to wait.
8 My poor back's starting to wake.
9 He looks pale – is he your right?
10 I can't hear – I've got my fingers in my years!

> **Note**
> Sometimes if one word ends with a vowel sound and the next begins with a vowel sound, you may seem to hear one of these three consonant sounds between them: /r/, /w/ or /j/. Find examples in the sentences in Exercise 3.

4 🎧 **2.15** You're going to hear ten speech fragments. They include these wrongly written fragments, which you'll then hear repeated four times. Write them correctly.

1 small a run small a run smaller     *smaller and smaller and smaller*
2 they're reible to like vote fa ra nest
3 lay more reggs rather than laying their rown
4 be yable to wakshaly use
5 funny side to wit
6 lucky yegg
7 at around two way yem

## B Accent variation: the glottal stop

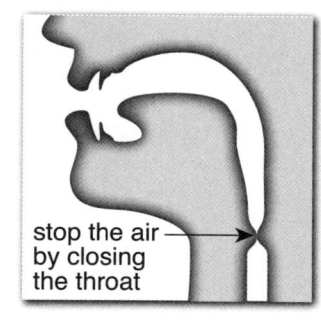

5 🎧 **2.16** Many speakers replace the sound /t/ with a very short silence, made by closing the throat. This is known as a 'glottal stop'. Listen to the pronunciation of *(little) bit* in these fragments.

1            tell us a **little bit** about, about their intelligence
2            tell me a **bit** about universities in your country
3            develop a **little bit** of a
4            tell me a **little bit** more about
5            could you tell me a **little bit** about that
6            to tell us a **little bit** more
7            stick out a **little bit**
8 in England at the moment, this is a **bit** of a, a big issue
9            can you tell us a **little bit** about that?
10           you can tell me a **little bit** more about it in a minute
11           tell me a **little bit** about
12           in a **little bit** of a cart thing

6 🎧 **2.17** Listen to these fragments. You'll hear each one three times. Circle the letter 't's which are pronounced as a glottal stop.

1 they have something called *nomihodai*
2 but, sort of, interesting, and
3 something occurs to me
4 but exactly how we wanted them
5 what is it like from a mother's point of view
6 the way he likes to set off with
7 ten per cent drop in premature birth rates
8 quiet mountain
9 what it involves, etcetera
10 I don't know nothing about it

7 🎧 **2.18** The first part of this lesson looked at how speakers link words together, so, for example, *turn on* sounds like *tur non*. Some non-native speakers of English don't do this, but separate words with a glottal stop instead. Listen to these fragments spoken by Thuy, a Vietnamese speaker, and show the glottal stops with / .

1 he turn / on his computer
2 when I go out
3 and I usually ask, er, the people
4 you live in, er, Portsmouth in the UK
5 I will, er, tell this story to my friends and my family
6 because I live in a hostel

# 31 Technology

## A Thinking about the topic

1 Look at these words. Do you know of and use all or some of these?

Facebook  email  smartphone  Twitter  YouTube  apps  Grooveshark  Skype  iPhone  Google  washing machine  website  mobile phone  internet

2 You're going to hear Tom (English), Ezgi (Turkish) and Thuy (Vietnamese) answering these questions. Before you listen, think about how *you'd* answer them. Compare with a partner.
   1 What do you use your computer for?
   2 What gadget could you not live without?
   3 What website is your favourite for work purposes?
   4 What was the biggest technological breakthrough in your lifetime?
   5 What do you think will be the next big technological breakthrough?

3 ▶ 10 Watch the video. Who do you think enjoys new technology the most? Why? Discuss with a partner.

## B Listening for specific information

4 ▶ 10 Watch Part 1 of the video (00:00–03:16) and complete this table.

|  | Ezgi | Tom | Thuy |
|---|---|---|---|
| 1 Computer use at home | 1.................... Facebook | 2.................... Grooveshark, YouTube |  |
| 2 Most important gadget | iPhone | 3.................... | 4.................... |

Photocopiable © Delta Publishing 2014 from *Authentic Listening Resource Pack*

5 ▶ 10 **Watch Part 1 again. Tick these phrases as you hear them.**
1 **it**'s so important for me ☐
2 so **it**'s kind of like ☐
3 I guess I could live without **it** ☐
4 I wouldn't like to part with **that**. ☐
5 and **it**'s useful ☐
6 **it**'s really important ☐

6 ▶ 10 **What can you remember? Who says each of the phrases in Exercise 5, and what do the words in bold refer to? Watch Part 1 again and compare with a partner.**

## C Listening for the main ideas and detail

7 ▶ 10 **Watch Part 2 (03:17–06:28). Who talks about what? Write To (Tom), E (Ezgi) or Th (Thuy) next to these topics. Each topic is mentioned by two people.**
1 favourite websites ............
2 technological breakthroughs ............
3 mobile phones ............

8 ▶ 10 **Watch Part 2 again and decide if these statements are true (T) or false (F). Correct any false ones and compare with a partner.**
1 Thuy usually checks the internet for world news once a week.
2 Ezgi's favourite website is Science Daily.
3 Tom remembers what computers were like when he was seven.
4 Ezgi was nine years old when her brother had his first cellphone.
5 Thuy thinks people will be able to do more things on their smartphone in the future.
6 Tom thinks that cars may run on water in the future.

9 ▶ 10 **What can you remember? Answer these questions. Then watch Part 2 again and compare with a partner.**
1 Thuy described two things as being *useful*. What were they?
2 Who described something as a *benefit*? What was it?
3 Who talked about something which is important because they are *specialized* in a particular area? Which area are they specialized in?
4 Who talked about being able to fit something into *the palm of my hand*? What was it?
5 Who talked about something being *convenient* and *comfortable*? What was it?
6 Who mentioned the word *alternative*? Alternative what?

## D Extension and review

10 **Whose ideas are most similar to yours? And the least? Why? Compare and discuss with a partner.**

11 **Which of these activities helped you understand the speakers best?**
- thinking about the topic before listening
- following ideas across sentences
- listening for key words

# 32 Breaking news

## A Thinking about the topic

1 What kinds of story would you expect to read or hear in a local newspaper or on a local radio station? Add to this table. Compare with a partner.

| incidents | accidents | car crash, ... |
| --- | --- | --- |
| | crimes | mugging, ... |
| other events | marriage, ... | |

2 Read this news article and decide which section of the table in Exercise 1 it belongs in. There's more than one possibility!

### Body found by canal

A man's body was discovered at Hanwell Flight in the early hours of Thursday morning. The police have not yet named the man, who was found at around 3 a.m. by the Grand Union Canal.

The 31-year-old man was taken to Ealing Hospital, where he was pronounced dead. Relatives have been informed. Police are investigating the circumstances of the incident.

## B Tuning in

3 🎧 **2.19** Listen to four short phrases from a news bulletin. Try to write down what you hear. You'll hear each phrase three times.

4 🎧 **2.20** Listen to the complete news bulletin and check your answers to Exercise 3. Notice that auxiliary verbs in the passive (*was, were, has been,* etc.) are usually pronounced weakly.

5 🎧 **2.20** Listen again. Find three differences between the radio bulletin and the information in the article in Exercise 2. Compare with a partner.

## C Listening for specific information

6 🎧 **2.21** You're going to hear two news items about transport-related incidents. Check that you understand the meaning of these words and phrases. Use your dictionary to help. Then listen and put the words/phrases in the correct column of the table below.

arrested   collision   head injury   information   killed   platform
pronounced dead   stable condition   suspicious   tracks

| train-station incident | road incident |
| --- | --- |
| | |

7 🎧 **2.21** Listen again and answer these questions.

Train-station incident
1 How old was the Tube passenger?
2 What happened?
3 When did the incident happen?
4 What do the police think?

Road incident
5 How old was the boy?
6 What happened?
7 When did the incident happen?
8 What do the police want people to do?

8 🎧 **2.22** Listen to another three news items. Write 1, 2 or 3 next to each of these names and numbers, according to the story each one occurs in.

West Drayton ☐   Broadway ☐   3 p.m. ☐   John Gordon ☐
West Avenue ☐   Stockley Park ☐   University of West London ☐
Nico Alijoki ☐   800 homes ☐   under-25s ☐   23-year-old ☐
0208 721 7253 ☐

9 🎧 **2.22** Listen again. Make notes in this table about the three stories. Then choose one story and tell it to a partner.

| story 1: watch theft | story 2: unexploded bomb | story 3: art prize |
|---|---|---|
|  |  |  |

## D Listening for the main ideas and detail

10 🎧 **2.23** At the end of the programme, four people exchange opinions on a topical news item. Listen to the final news item. Which topic are they going to discuss (a, b or c)?
a Children and illness
b Smoking in confined spaces
c Laws against smoking in public places

11 🎧 **2.24** Listen and number these opinion summaries in the order you hear them.
a Laws to stop people smoking in their own homes and cars wouldn't work. ☐
b People will smoke at home with or without laws, and it's difficult to check what people do at home. ☐
c Freedom of choice is important – people should be allowed to do whatever they want to. ☐
d Parents know the dangers of smoking and should be responsible for their children. ☐

12 🎧 **2.24** Listen again. Do you agree with any of the speakers' opinions, or do you have another opinion on the subject? Compare with a partner.

## E Extension and review

13 Do you ever listen to local news? Why? / Why not? Make some notes about your reasons or tell a partner.

14 Which of these activities helped you understand the news programme best?
- thinking about the type of programme before listening
- listening for key words and specific information
- summarizing what the speaker says as you listen

# 33 The future of paper

## A Thinking about the topic

1 You're going to hear a lecture by Polish chemist Monika Koperska containing all the words below. The bigger words occur more often, the smaller words less often. Look at the words and answer these questions with a partner.

1 What do you think the lecture might be about?
2 Are there any words that you want to ask about or look up in a dictionary? Choose five.

2 ▶ 11 Watch the video. What did you understand? Compare with a partner.

## B Focus on language

3 ▶ 11 Read the beginning of the lecture below while you watch Part 1 again (00:00–01:03). Pay attention to the pronunciation and insert a full stop each time you think the speaker begins a new idea.

Time is passing by all the time and although everything that surrounds us seems to be stable and durable it is in fact constantly drawn by a mechanism that slowly but consequently leads to its total decomposition and if we wanted to preserve an idea for hundreds of years, what do we save it on?

> **Notes**
> - In writing, it's considered wrong to start a sentence with words like *and*. However, in speech, speakers often begin a new idea with such words.
> - Even fluent speakers sometimes make mistakes with words. In the lecture, Monika actually says *discomposition* instead of *decomposition*, but you can still work out what she means.

## C Listening for the main ideas and detail

**4** ▶ 11 Watch Part 1 again and tick these items as you hear them.
1 stone ☐   2 parchment ☐   3 magnetic tape ☐   4 CD-ROM ☐
5 USB ☐   6 clouds ☐

**5** ▶ 11 Monika says that each of the items in Exercise 4 has problems. Match these problems (a–f) with the items (1–6). Compare with a partner, then watch Part 1 again and check your answers.

a will start to decay in 30–50 years
b information in too many places
c storage capacity too small
d will lose information after two to five years
e too expensive
f won't last very long

**6** ▶ 11 Watch Part 2 of the lecture (01:04–01:51). What is Monika's main point?
a Data is disappearing.
b We need more archaeologists.
c Paper is what we're looking for.

**7** ▶ 11 Watch Part 2 again and answer these questions. Compare with a partner.
1 Why does Monika talk about tape memory banks?
2 How much stored data has already disappeared?
3 Why is paper a good solution?

**8** ▶ 11 Watch Part 3 of the lecture (01:52–03:11) and underline the key words in these sentences. Then listen for the key words and number the points in the order you hear them.
a We can de-acify paper and make it stronger. ☐
b Books can last hundreds of years. ☐
c We need to improve the paper-making process. ☐
d In the 19th century, the manufacture of paper left a chemical that weakened it. ☐

## D After watching

**9** What can you remember from the lecture? Work with a partner and explain what Monika says about these things.

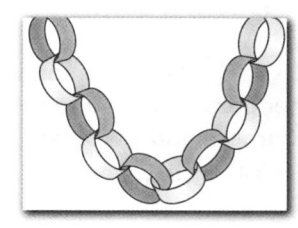

1   2   3

## E Extension and review

**10** Do you agree with Monika that civilization isn't ready for the book to disappear? Discuss with a partner or in small groups.

**11** Which of these activities helped you understand the lecture best?
- thinking about the topic before listening
- listening for the main ideas before detail
- noticing where the speaker begins a new idea

# 34 A life in the music business

## A Thinking about the topic

1 Look at the photo of musician Dennis Locorriere. What do you think these words mean in this context? Compare with a partner.

album
charts
covers
fan
hit
tour
track

2 Complete these phrases using the words from Exercise 1.
1 a mixture of original songs and ................
2 a song from my last ................
3 I'm a huge ................ of The Beatles
4 I'm often away from home on ................
5 number one in the ................
6 the first ................ on my new album
7 this song was a massive ................ in America

## B Tuning in

> **Accent note**
> Katie speaks with an accent from the north-east of England. Dennis speaks with a New York accent.

3 🎧 **2.25** In conversation, speakers often use short questions to involve the other person. Listen to seven extracts from a telephone interview with Dennis Locorriere and say which of these questions is in all of them.
a isn't it?   b you know?   c you see?   d know what I mean?   e no?

4 🎧 **2.26** Listen to the beginning of the interview. Why does Dennis think Katie's introduction is funny? Compare and discuss with a partner.

## C Listening for the general ideas and detail

5 🎧 **2.27** Listen to the next part of the interview. Which summary (a, b or c) reflects Dennis's main point? Compare with a partner.
a Everything happened too quickly for him to know he was famous.
b He only realizes how big he was when he looks back at the past.
c He knew he was famous because he was making lots of records.

6 🎧 **2.27** **Listen again and choose the best answer (a, b or c) to each of these questions.**
   1 In how many countries did Dr Hook have a number one in the charts?
     a 62   b 52   c 42
   2 When somebody introduces Dennis, he …
     a realizes how famous he was.
     b thinks it's all over.
     c feels everything was crazy.
   3 How does Katie sound when she's talking to Dennis?
     a excited   b philosophical   c bored
   4 How does Dennis sound when he's talking about his past?
     a excited   b serious   c bored

7 🎧 **2.28** **Listen to the next part of the interview and number these points in the order your hear them.**
   a He still has lots of Beatles memorabilia. ☐
   b His mum listened to lots of music. ☐
   c It was unusual for groups to write all their own songs for an album. ☐
   d He decided to sing when The Beatles went to America. ☐
   e His favourite Beatles album is *Rubber Soul*. ☐

8 🎧 **2.28** **Listen again and add one piece of information to each of the points in Exercise 7. Compare with a partner.**

## D Listening for key words

9 🎧 **2.29** **Listen to the next part of the interview. Decide if these statements are true (T) or false (F). Then listen again and correct any false ones.**
   1 Dennis has changed the way he writes his songs.
   2 His songs are usually autobiographical.
   3 He prefers to write the words and music together.
   4 It's always easy to put the music to the words.
   5 He likes his words to sound good even if they weren't put to music.

10 🎧 **2.30** **Listen to the final part of the interview. Tick these words and phrases as you hear Dennis saying them. Use your dictionary to help with meaning as necessary.**
   a a big fan ☐   b guitar ☐   c album tracks ☐
   d career ☐   e hits ☐   f solo stuff ☐

11 🎧 **2.30** **What can you remember? Look again at the words and phrases in Exercise 10. What does Dennis say about them? Then listen again and check.**

## E Review and extension

12 **Would you like to go and see Dennis's show? Why? / Why not? Use the words and phrases from Exercise 10 and make some notes or tell a partner.**

13 **Which of these activities helped you understand the interview best?**
   • tuning in to the speaker's conversational style
   • summarizing the general idea as you listen
   • listening for key words

# 35 Pronunciation for listeners 7

## A Connected speech: titles, names, technical terms, definitions

**Note**
It's important to recognize when a speaker is giving a title, name, term or definition. These are often introduced by a word or phrase such as the ones in the gaps in Exercise 1.

1 🎧 **2.31** Listen and complete this extract. You'll hear the extract three times.
… it's written up faithfully in [1]_____ Richard Feynman, [2]_____ *The Pleasure of Finding Things Out*, and the lecture is [3]_____ *There's Plenty of Room at the Bottom*.

2 🎧 **2.32** Listen to ten extracts. After the word *called* in each extract, you'll hear one of the words or phrases below. For each phrase, choose a description (a–e) and note any other information you hear about it.
a the name of a person
b the name of a group
c the name of an album
d a technical term
e a non-English word

**Note**
The word *called* is often very reduced so that you can hardly hear it.

Dautenis   mitochondrial DNA
Post Cool   Diggory Rose
Emily Grigsby   morgh
William Byrne   Frank Potter
temnothorax albipennis   ant algorithm

3 🎧 **2.33** Listen and complete these extracts.
1 according to _____ *Scientific American* story
2 in front, um, of a little crack that you have in your brain there's _____ the *motor area*
3 _____ Eleanor Jones of Uppsala University
4 and _____ Beechwood
5 we're _____, um, Annela Seddon
6 and a _____ Penguin Books
7 and _____ *nanotechnology* is
8 *nano* actually comes from _____ 'dwarf'
9 from my _____, Nigel Franks
10 but the most significant person in the Punjab was, er, _____ Dhulla Bhati
11 the word *Guyana* _____ 'land of many waters'
12 a computer program _____ Professor David Cope of Santa Cruz University
13 there's _____ the *supplementary motor area*
14 it was _____ previously to the Second World War called Mollinson
15 and there's another _____ *The Ants*
16 it was, er, built about 1709 by a _____ George Cowdry
17 it is a name that refer to two lakes in our region, they are _____ Dowcien
18 one _____ of the Mallory family, Virginia Arnott
19 um, there's a _____ about bees, um, by Thomas Seeley called the *Honeybee Democracy*
20 they have _____ *nomihodai*

## B Spoken English: vague language – *you know, like*

**Note**
You know is so common in speech that speakers often say it almost automatically, and very fast and reduced. Consequently, it's difficult for listeners to hear. However, if you don't hear it, it makes very little difference to your understanding!

4 🎧 **2.34** Listen to and read Tom's words. Notice how the phrase *you know* is spoken very quickly and low, so that you can hardly hear it.

> ... er, also for the internet access, you know, if ever something occurs to me, you know, 'Oh, I wonder what, you know, this is or that is,' you know, I can quickly Google it and find out about it.

5 🎧 **2.35** Listen and show where the speaker inserts *you know* using ▲.
1 well, yeah, no, it's one of those things like anything else
2 it just kind of happens, what I mean, it's not until it's all over
3 now we have to have another one, what I mean
4 and so you don't really stop
5 they wouldn't do that
6 but I, so, it, I just got involved
7 it was the thing that opened my eyes. It was really
8 and artists didn't do that back then. You did covers
9 I write the song in 30 minutes. And then sometimes I deliberate over it
10 I could tell you why I wrote every single song
11 something solid like that
12 um, it's better when it comes at the same time
13 me, a, a guitar and 40 years of songs that I can draw from
14 you want everything to be included. You just do
15 can't really imagine having to remember all my friends
16 well, I guess, I mean, there seems to be some progress being made on, um, sort of electric cars or just cars that use alternative fuel
17 definitely computers, um

**Note**
Conversational *like* is spoken very quickly and low, and it may be inserted in almost any position in a phrase. It's also a common way of introducing a piece of direct speech or thought, as in items 6 and 14 in Exercise 6.

6 🎧 **2.36** Another common conversational word is *like*. Listen and show where the speaker inserts *like* using ▲.
1 it was the best opportunity that I've ever had
2 but it seems, sort of, you know, once every five years
3 that all happened in sequence
4 was it just sort of the eye of the storm
5 but it wasn't until, you know, The Beatles
6 it was, 'Wow, that's really wonderful'
7 um, really good robust decision-making
8 a seemingly, you know, simple creature
9 um, their nest choice behaviours are very democratic
10 so collectively, they're able to, er, vote for a nest
11 the sun represents on the one hand the rays of light
12 and it's, it's a pagan, pagan ritual
13 and they've got, you know, say lorries and buses
14 if I see a cyclist now, I'm, 'Oh no'

# 36 Advertising

## A Thinking about the topic

1 **You're going to listen to three conversations about advertising. Before you watch the video, answer these questions and compare with a partner.**
   1 Which adverts do you enjoy the most: adverts on TV or on web pages? Why?
   2 Which of these sentences best summarizes your feeling about pop-up ads?
      a They can be useful.
      b They're usually annoying.
      c They're not necessary.
   3 What's your favourite website or webpage? Why?
   4 Do you ever shop online? Why? / Why not?
   5 Do you ever get junk mail / spam? Where does it come from? How do you feel about it?

## B Listening for specific information

2 **Watch Part 1 (00:00–02:10) and choose the best ending (a, b or c) to complete this sentence about the opinions of Tom, Ezgi and Thuy.**
   They all think email advertising …
   a can be useful.
   b is always annoying.
   c is not necessary.

3 **Watch Part 1 again. Who mentions these things, Tom (To), Thuy (Th) or Ezgi (E)? Some are mentioned by more than one person.**
   1 junk mail
   2 university
   3 a watch
   4 a film

4 **What do you remember? What was said about the things in Exercise 3? Make some notes, then compare with a partner.**

## C Listening for main ideas and detail

5 ▶ 12 **Watch Part 2 (02:11–04:31). Who talks about each of these topics, Massimo (M), Hue (H) or Anisa (A)?**
   1 Changing passwords ☐
   2 Companies following personal interests ☐
   3 Having more than one email account ☐

6 ▶ 12 **Watch Part 2 again and answer these questions. Compare and discuss with a partner.**
   1 Why does Massimo say people get spam emails?
   2 Does he think people can do anything to stop them?
   3 Why does Anisa talk about her private email account?
   4 What does Hue feel about shopping online?

7 ▶ 12 **Watch Part 3 (04:32–06:13) and number these topics in the order you hear them.**
   a a new camera ☐
   b a favourite movie ☐
   c pop-up ads ☐
   d the latest kitchen gadget ☐
   e a football match ☐

8 ▶ 12 **Watch Part 3 again and decide if these statements are true (T) or false (F). Correct any false ones.**
   1 Anisa thinks it's good that people's interests can be tracked or followed.
   2 Anisa seems to be easily influenced by adverts.
   3 Hue is never influenced by adverts.
   4 Hue finds adverts during a film or football match annoying.

9 **Anisa said these things. What point was she making in each case?**
   1 I'm gonna have about 400 spam emails in a week.
   2 Nobody wants to talk to me.
   3 How have I lived my life without one?
   4 It sits there, you know, for years …

## D Extension and review

10 **Whose opinion is closest to yours? Why? Compare with a partner.**

11 **Which of these activities helped you understand the speakers best?**
   - thinking about the topic before listening
   - listening for general opinions
   - understanding the main points

# 37 The language of persuasion

## A Thinking about the topic

**1 Read the advert below and answer these questions.**
1. a) What is being advertised, b) where is it, and c) what's it called?
2. What goods and/or services does it offer?
3. What are the benefits?

### Kate's Kitchen

★ The perfect place to relax and enjoy great food and drinks.
★ Open all day long.
★ Pop in for a refreshing cup of tea or coffee, and try one of our delicious home-made cakes.
★ Or why not try our lunch menu?
★ Fresh food at affordable prices!

26 Station Road, Baker's Green   Open 9 a.m.–9 p.m.

**2 What benefits could companies offering these goods/services mention in their adverts? Compare with a partner.**
1. an internet café   2. a gift shop   3. a language school
4. a mobile-phone service provider   5. a bank / building society

## B Tuning in

**3 🎧 2.37 Listen to a short advert and try to answer the questions in Exercise 1. Which question isn't answered explicitly?**

**4 🎧 2.37 Radio adverts often include these features. Listen again and tick the features which make the advert *easier* to understand.**

background music ☐   repetition of key information ☐
fast delivery ☐   professionally recorded ☐

## C Listening for key words and phrases

**5 🎧 2.38 The next two adverts are for similar places. Listen and make notes to answer question 1 in this table.**

|  | Advert 1 | Advert 2 |
|---|---|---|
| 1 What is being advertised, where is it, and what's it called? | | |
| 2 What goods and/or services does it offer? | | |
| 3 What are the benefits? | | |

6 🎧 **2.38** Listen again and make notes to answer questions 2 and 3 in the table on page 80. Compare with a partner.

7 🎧 **2.39** Listen to the next two adverts. Number these words and phrases in the order you hear them.
a £800 ☐
b Jamaica National Building Society ☐
c 0207 708 2442 ☐
d 25% off ☐
e energy bills ☐
f Purchase or build your own home ☐
g Mick Siddle ☐
h 0800 954 5255 ☐
i mortgage product ☐

8 🎧 **2.39** Listen again and answer these questions.
1 What's happening on 14th November?
2 Who's it for?
3 What can you find out?
4 What service is Mick Siddle offering?
5 What do most people say to his idea?
6 What should you do if you want to know more?

## D Listening for the main ideas and detail

9 🎧 **2.40** Listen to the next three adverts. What goods are they offering?

10 🎧 **2.40** Listen again and answer these questions. Compare with a partner.
**Advert 1**
1 Why does the advert mention women? How does this help advertise Amulet?
2 What did the man buy at Amulet? Who helped him?
3 What do these facts suggest about Amulet?

**Advert 2**
4 What backgroung noise can you hear near the beginning of the advert? What does it suggest?
5 Where does The Fish Shop get its fish from? Why is this information important?

**Advert 3**
6 Where are the people in the advert? What does this suggest about the Bristol Wood Recycling Project?
7 Why does the man ask about bird boxes and picture frames? What does the answer tell us about the Bristol Wood Recycling Project?

11 🎧 **2.40** Listen again. Write one example of a type of background noise for each of the adverts. How do they help you understand the advert? Compare with a partner.

## E Review and extension

12 Do you like adverts? Why? / Why not? Make some notes or tell a partner.

13 Which of these activities helped you understand the adverts best?
- thinking about typical information in an advert
- listening for key words and phrases
- thinking about context and background noise

# 38 The intelligence of ants

## A Thinking about the topic

1 Read these ant facts with the help of a dictionary. Guess which fact is false. Compare with a partner.

### ANT FACT CHALLENGE

*One of these facts is false. Can you guess which?*
- Ants outnumber humans a million to one.
- There are over 12,000 species of ant.
- There were ants in the age of the dinosaurs.
- Ants leave a trail of scent to lead the others to food.
- Ants can carry 50 times their own body weight.
- Ants choose a new nest democratically.
- The ants in a colony can think together, like one collective brain.
- One species of Australian ant has eight legs.
- Only one female in the colony breeds; all the others care for her brood.
- The ant biomass in the rainforest is four times the rest of the creatures put together.

## B Tuning in

2 **2.41** You're going to hear Malcolm, a radio interviewer, asking Antonia Forster, a researcher, about her work. Listen to and read her reply. Notice how you can tell from her intonation in phrases 1–8 that she'll continue. In phrase 9, her voice goes down so you know she's finished.

1 Um, well, we work with one species of ant primarily
2 called, er, *temnothorax albipennis*.
3 It's a really small ant,
4 so in the lab, we keep it in between glass slides
5 and mostly we study its behaviour,
6 er, we give it nest choice experiments,
7 um, one person in our lab, Jamie, studies their fighting strategy,
8 um, so there's all sorts of various things we look at,
9 mostly their collective behaviours.

3 **2.42** Listen to six more extracts from the interview and, for each one, say whether Antonia is going to continue (C) or has finished her point (F).
1 ☐  2 ☐  3 ☐  4 ☐  5 ☐  6 ☐

## C Listening for the main ideas and detail

4 **2.43** Decide if these statements are true (T) or false (F). Then listen and check your answers. Correct any false statements.

1 Colonies of ants behave differently to the way they do as individuals.
2 People have become fascinated by ants in the last few years.
3 Ants are approximately the same size.
4 Ants may seem simple creatures, but they're not.

**5** 🎧 **2.43** Match these pieces of information (a–d) with the points in Exercise 4 (1–4). Then listen again and check your answers.

a Some ants are several centimetres long, some are very small. ☐
b Ant behaviour is complicated. ☐
c We can learn a lot from studying ants. ☐
d Individual ants aren't capable of complicated thoughts or processes. ☐

**6** 🎧 **2.44** Listen to the next part of the interview. What's Antonia's main point?

a Studying ant group behaviour has shown us many different ways of doing things.
b Ant intelligence is best seen when they are studied as a group.
c Ants have many problems, and when they work together, they are able to find solutions.

**7** 🎧 **2.44** Listen again and answer these questions. Compare and discuss with a partner.

1 According to Antonia, what is 'colony-level cognition'?
2 What is an 'ant algorithm'?
3 Why does Antonia compare a colony of ants to the human brain?

## D Listening for specific information

**8** 🎧 **2.45** In the next part of the interview, Antonia talks about *eusociality* – the ways in which certain creatures organize themselves. Underline the key words in these statements. Then listen for the key words and number the statements in the order you hear them.

a The queen lays all the eggs. ☐1
b Female eggs are fertilized, male eggs aren't. ☐
c The others don't lay their own eggs. ☐
d Female ants have sisters rather than daughters. ☐
e The others in the colony are the queen's daughters. ☐

**9** 🎧 **2.46** How can you find out more about ants? Listen to the final part of the interview and tick the information you hear.

1 visiting the Bristol Ant Lab website ☐
2 going to the cinema ☐
3 reading academic papers ☐
4 reading magazines ☐
5 reading different books ☐

**10** 🎧 **2.46** Listen again. Antonia mentions three different books. Note down one piece of information about each book.

1 *The Superorganism*
2 *The Ants*
3 *Honeybee Democracy*

## E Extension and review

**11** Would you like to visit the Bristol Ant Lab? Why? / Why not? Write a brief explanation or tell a partner.

**12** Which of these activities helped you understand Antonia best?
- thinking about the topic before listening
- listening to intonation to decide if a speaker's going to continue their point
- listening for keys words and phrases

# 39 A celebration of the sun

## A Thinking about the topic

**1 Look at the photo of a festival and answer these questions. Compare and discuss with a partner.**
1 Where in the world do you think this festival takes place?
2 What do you think happens at the festival?
3 Do you know any festivals which are similar?

## B Tuning in

**2** 🎧 **2.47** You're going to hear a conversation about the Lohri festival on Desi Radio, a Punjabi radio station in London. Listen to the first part of the interview, in which the interviewer, Dea, asks her guest, Taranjit, to explain Lohri. Who do you find easier to understand, Dea or Taranjit? Compare and discuss with a partner.

**3** 🎧 **2.47** Listen again and read Taranjit's reply. Why are some of the words in *italics*? Notice how these words *sound* in the flow of speech.

Lohri, um, before I start, Dea, thank you very much to Desi Radio for inviting me and letting me speak about, er, Lohri. Now, Lohri's a fantastic, colourful Punjabi celebration. Um, you know, basically the focus of Lohri is, er, a big bonfire in the evening, and, er, it's a singing, dancing, buying of gifts, *saag*, and *makki di roti*, eating *rewri* and *gur* and throwing peanuts, roasted peanuts, onto the fire.

**4** 🎧 **2.48** Listen to these sentences. You'll hear each one three times. Notice the examples of *t* in bold. In the interviewer's London accent, the sound /t/ is often replaced with a very short silence (called a *glottal stop* – see Lesson 30).

wha**t** i**t** involves, e**t**cetera
I don'**t** know nothing about i**t**
Could you tell me a li**tt**le bi**t** about tha**t**?

## C  Listening for main ideas and detail

**5** 🎧 **2.49** Listen to the next part of the interview. Notice the three words below. They are key words in this section of the interview, and Taranjit repeats them several times. As you listen, tick each word each time you hear it.

beginning ............................  sun ............................  spring ............................

**6** 🎧 **2.50** Listen to the next part of Taranjit's description of the Lohri festival and decide if these statements are true (T) or false (F). Correct any false ones.
1 The Indus Valley civilization existed before any religion.
2 Lohri is a pagan festival.
3 Lohri is dedicated to the moon.
4 The sun represents light and gold.
5 No food is thrown onto the fire.
6 People from different communities meet to celebrate Lohri.
7 Some people get married at the Lohri festival.
8 It's a good occasion for girls and boys to meet each other.

**7** 🎧 **2.50** Write some words and phrases you remember. Then listen again and put them in order. Compare with a partner.

## D  Listening for specific information

**8** 🎧 **2.51** Listen to the next part of the interview and choose the best answer (a, b or c) for each of these questions.
1 How old is the Lohri festival?
   a  4,000 years old    b  5,000 years old    c  6,000 years old
2 Who was Dulla Bhatti?
   a  a bank robber    b  a freedom fighter    c  a slave
3 What did Dulla Bhatti do?
   a  helped the rich    b  worked in a market    c  saved girls from poor families

**9** Match the words and phrases in bold (1–4) with their meanings (a–d). Compare and discuss with a partner.
1 it's a pagan **ritual**                                   a  stories
2 there's lots of **legends** about Lohri                   b  money or property
3 he'd actually arrange for their marriages                 c  part of a ceremony
  and provide their **dowry**                               d  made to
4 so they won't be **forced to** be sold

**10** 🎧 **2.51** Listen again. Check to see if your answers in Exercise 9 make sense. What's the connection between Lohri and Dulla Bhatti?

## E  Extension and review

**11** Which celebrations or festivals are most important where you are from? Write a short description or tell a partner.

**12** Which of these activities helped you understand the interview best?
• thinking about the accent of the speakers
• guessing the general meaning of foreign-sounding words
• using repetition to identify key ideas

# 40 Pronunciation for listeners 8

## A Connected speech: cutting or changing sounds

**1** 🎧 **2.52** Listen to four different speakers. In each extract, the speaker says something which sounds like *fuss fall*. What are they really saying? You'll hear the four extracts three times.

**2** 🎧 **2.53** Listen to and read these fragments. The words in bold are written as they sound. Correct them.
1 and this is **exackly**
2 **infeck** cancer cells
3 any bad side **effecks**
4 up on the north-**wess** coast
5 **perfeck** vision
6 the **easiess** thing to see
7 exchange of **giffs**
8 **rainforess**
9 the **satistics** of this
10 the thing is, **is** not about looking backwards, **is** about looking forwards

> **Note**
> In Exercise 2, the speakers do not pronounce the sound /t/ in some places. In fast speech, speakers often cut sounds in this way.

**3** If a speaker doesn't pronounce a /t/ or /d/ at the end of the word, it sometimes sounds as if they're saying something else. What do you think these speakers were really saying?
1 Better luck necks time!   *Better luck next time!*
2 Would you like a coal drink?
3 Who bill the pyramids?
4 I fell very tired last night.
5 I one to hole your hand.
6 I when to the doctor's yesterday.

**4** 🎧 **2.54** You're going to hear each of these words in isolation three times. Then you'll hear them in a short fragment. They've been written as they sound. Correct them.
1 kuz    *because*       8 responsbu
2 bout                   9 excepshny
3 praps                  10 absoo'i
4 praps                  11 clecting
5 p'tickly               12 tradishny
6 p'tickly               13 unde
7 probly                 14 jeck'n (three words!)

> **Note**
> In fast speech, speakers may cut more than one sound, and sometimes entire syllables. Find examples in Exercise 4.

**5** 🎧 **2.55** Listen to and read these fragments. The words in bold are written as they sound. Correct them.
1 the **goog** guys
2 and it **coob** be like almost harassing you or
3 the virus **kung** carry in a protein
4 **coob** be good at this
5 we **womp** more
6 you **shub** be polite
7 cruising **ing** company
8 I **cump** bear to watch it
9 **cum** be more than the sum of their parts

> **Note**
> Items 1–3 in Exercise 5 show how speakers may cut sounds in fast speech. They may also change sounds. For example, *good guys* sounds like *goog guys*, because the speaker changes the /d/ to /g/ in preparation for the next word.

## B Spoken English: false starts

> So how do they ... te-, tell us a little bit abou-, about their intelligen-, do ... now, here's an important question: Do ants have an individual intelligence, or is it entirely a, a group thing?

> In a, in a wa-, I would argue that no, individually, they don't really have cognition, but as a colony, they do.

**6** 🎧 **2.56** Listen to and read the interviewer's question and Antonia's answer above. This is spoken English; how is it different from written English?

> **Note**
> The speakers are deciding what to say at the same time as they're speaking. As a result, they ...
> - repeat sections to give themselves time to think
> - correct themselves if they make an error
> - change their minds about what they're going to say next.
>
> As a listener, you mustn't be distracted by these repetitions and changes.

**7** 🎧 **2.57** Listen to these fragments. Underline the syllable, word or phrase which is repeated in each one.
1 I think it's looking positive
2 all over the place
3 um, if I was doing, um, jazz

**8** 🎧 **2.58** Listen and read. For each fragment, decide if the speakers are correcting the grammar (G), a single word (W) or both (G/W).
1 so that it hasn't, it will only
2 hadn't fought in the Se-, in the First World War
3 in your situation where you are, er, you just cannot, er, resolve the person's lip movements
4 to 95 deg-, er, miles per hour
5 again, like I said, it's, it marks the beginning
6 leading a sen-, sedentary lifestyle

**9** 🎧 **2.59** Listen and indicate with a slash (/) the places where the speakers change their mind about what they're going to say. In some cases, they change their minds several times in the same extract!
1 journalism may be one profession where it almost doesn't ma-, it depends what you do, obviously, but
2 suddenly people were talking, er, when I was a kid, people weren't talking about nanoscience
3 wha-, what, why do you think – and we're going to get on to some of the specific things – but wha-, wha-, why do you think they have fascinated us
4 yeah, no, you know, it's one of those things, like anything else, it sometimes, it seems like it was yesterday
5 I mean, the, if you actually, it's, I think sometimes you probably have to pinch yourself
6 with vinyl and stuff, they get, it gets, as it, it gets better, as, as it gets warmer, doesn't it?

# 41 Arriving in a capital city

## A Thinking about the topic

1 What do you tend to notice or look for when you arrive in a new city for the first time? Compare with a partner.

|  | you | your partner | Alan | Anisa |
|---|---|---|---|---|
| • public transport | ☐ | ☐ | ☐ | ☐ |
| • food/drink | ☐ | ☐ | ☐ | ☐ |
| • entertainment | ☐ | ☐ | ☐ | ☐ |
| • people | ☐ | ☐ | ☐ | ☐ |
| • geographical features | ☐ | ☐ | ☐ | ☐ |
| • danger | ☐ | ☐ | ☐ | ☐ |
| • historical monuments | ☐ | ☐ | ☐ | ☐ |
| • fashion | ☐ | ☐ | ☐ | ☐ |
| • something else | ☐ | ☐ | ☐ | ☐ |

## B Listening for specific information

Alan

2 ▶ 13 Alan is talking about Tokyo. Watch Part 1 (00:00–02:39) and tick the topics from Exercise 1 that he mentions.

3 ▶ 13 Watch Part 1 again and answer these questions.
   1 What did Alan say about travelling by train? What surprised him about it?
   2 How did he feel about the *kayten sushi* restaurant?
   3 Why did he go to the karaoke place? What happened there?
   4 What's *nomihodai*?

4 ▶ 13 Alan uses the phrases shown below. Can you remember which topic he was talking about for each one? What did he mean? Make some notes in the table, then watch Part 1 again and compare with a partner.

| phrase | topic | general meaning |
|---|---|---|
| no hassle or anything like that | the train | no problems |
| like a conveyor belt | | |
| weird and wonderful stuff | | |
| I kind of stumbled into | | |
| in very broken Japanese | | |

### C  Listening for main ideas and detail

Anisa

5  ▶ 13  Anisa is talking about Mexico City. Watch Part 2 (02:40–05:48) and tick the topics from Exercise 1 she mentions.

6  ▶ 13  Watch Part 2 again and answer these questions. Compare and discuss with a partner.
1 What does she say about the bus journey?
2 Had she planned what she was going to do in Mexico City before she arrived? Why? / Why not?
3 Do you think she felt frightened when she first arrived? Why? / Why not?
4 How did she feel about Mexican food?
5 Do you think she liked living in Mexico City? Why? / Why not?

7  ▶ 13  Anisa talks about two people she met. Why does she talk about them, and what do we learn about them? Make some notes in the table, then watch Part 2 again to check.

| the woman | the man |
|---|---|
|  |  |

8  ▶ 13  Anisa uses the phrases below. Can you remember which topic she was talking about for each one? What did she mean? Make some notes in the table, then watch Part 2 again and compare with a partner.

| phrase | topic | general meaning |
|---|---|---|
| very cramped | the bus | extremely full |
| bundles of food |  |  |
| this huge sprawling area |  |  |
| it was love at first sight |  |  |
| all my worldly possessions |  |  |
| they really went out of their way |  |  |
| I couldn't get over the fact that |  |  |

### D  Extension and review

9  Do you think Alan and Anisa would like to visit the same cities? Would they be interested in the same things? Why? / Why not? Compare with a partner.

10 Which of these activities helped you understand the speakers best?
 • thinking about the topic before listening
 • listening for general ideas before detail
 • using context to guess the meaning of words and phrases

# 42 Topical chat

## A Thinking about the topic

1 Read this article and look at the pictures below. Is newer technology always better? Compare with a partner.

### Is this the end of the CD?

CD sales have seen a significant year-on-year drop in the first three months of 2012, according to figures from BPI and the official charts company. Sales fell 25% from 20.5 million in the first three months of last year to 15.3 million this year. Digital sales continue to rise, with almost a third of all albums now being bought digitally.

a   b   c   d

2 Which of these words relate to the pictures in Exercise 1? One word can be used more than once. Use your dictionary to help.

1 CD
2 album
3 vinyl
4 iTunes
5 download
6 tape
7 record
8 cassette

## B Tuning in

3 Compare these two sentences. Which one do you think would be more typical in a casual conversation? Why? Compare with a partner.
Specific: 'We used to get vinyl, cassettes or CDs.'
Vague: 'We used to get things like vinyl and stuff.'

**Note**
The underlined section in item 3 of Exercise 4 looks wrong in writing, but it's completely normal in casual conversation.

4 🎧 2.60 Listen to these extracts from an informal discussion. Check any new vocabulary in your dictionary. Notice the vague words and phrases that are highlighted. These phrases are often spoken very quickly and unclearly, but here they're slowed down. You'll hear each extract twice.

1 Well, that's it with iTunes and things like that, though, **isn't it**? But you get things like vinyl and stuff.
2 some of the original, like Pink Floyd albums do sound better on record than sort of the digitally remastered, which is a bit bland
3 Yeah, I know they are, sort of getting better, **aren't they**? But with vinyls and stuff, they get, it gets, as it, it gets better as it, as it gets warmer, **doesn't it**?
4 I think it's really good, **isn't it**? But like you say, you've got to have the space, **haven't you**? for them to go

**Note**
Speech which is very fast and unclear is often not essential for understanding. Instead, listen for key words which are pronounced more loudly and clearly.

5 🎧 2.60 Listen again and notice the phrases in bold. These are used to involve the listener, not to ask a real question. They're often spoken very quickly and unclearly, e.g. *isn't it* sounds like *intit*.

90 Photocopiable © Delta Publishing 2014 from *Authentic Listening Resource Pack*

## C Listening for key words and phrases

**6** 🎧 **2.61** Listen to three people discussing ways of storing music today. Tick the words and phrases in Exercise 2 as you hear them.

**7** 🎧 **2.61** Listen again and follow the conversation on the chart below. Then complete the gaps (1–5) using these words. Compare with a partner.

cassettes    record    sleeves    sound    space

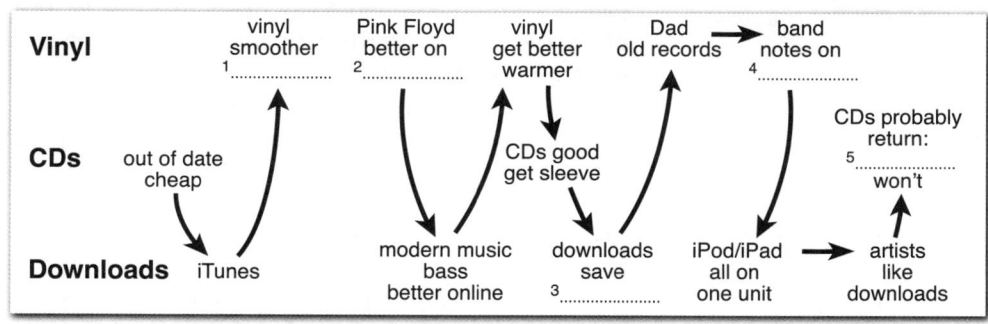

| | | | | | |
|---|---|---|---|---|---|
| **Vinyl** | vinyl smoother 1....... | Pink Floyd better on 2....... | vinyl get better warmer | Dad old records → | band notes on 4....... |
| **CDs** | out of date cheap | | CDs good get sleeve | | CDs probably return: 5....... won't |
| **Downloads** | iTunes | modern music bass better online | | downloads save 3....... | iPod/iPad all on one unit → artists like downloads |

**8** What do you think about the future of CDs? Why? Make some notes and compare with a partner.

## D Listening for the main ideas and detail

**9** 🎧 **2.62** The topic of the discussion changes to cycling safety on British roads. Listen to the conversation and number these points in the order you hear them. Discuss with a partner.

a Cyclists don't follow safety rules. ☐
b Don't go on the road. ☐
c Don't get a bike. ☐
d Cyclists need to take tests. ☐

**10** 🎧 **2.62** Match these pieces of information (1–4) with the points in Exercise 9 (a–d). Then listen again and check your answers.

1 They can have licence registration. ☐    3 Cyclists don't wear helmets. ☐
2 Cycling is too dangerous. ☐    4 It's too frightening. ☐

## E Extension and review

**11** 🎧 **2.61–2.62** People often provide statistics when they talk about change. Complete these statements, then listen again and check your answers.

1 CD sales have seen a significant y............-y............ drop in the first three months of 2012 …
2 Sales f............ 25% from 20.5 million in the first three months of last year to …
3 Digital sales c............ to rise, with almost a third of …
4 … the number of cyclists killed or seriously injured r............ by 36% this year …
5 … other casualties on British roads is on the d............ .

**12** Choose a topic you know about and check some facts and figures about how it's changing. Tell a partner.

**13** Which of these activities helped you understand the discussions best?
- thinking about key words and phrases before listening
- listening for synonyms
- listening for the main points before detail

# 43 The silent killer

## A Thinking about the topic

**International FameLab — TALKING SCIENCE**

1 You're going to listen to Aneesha Acharya, a dental researcher from India, giving a lecture containing all the words below. The bigger words occur more often, the smaller words less often. Look at the words and answer these questions with a partner.
   1 What do you think the lecture might be about?
   2 Are there any words that you want to ask about or look up in a dictionary? Choose five.

2 ▶ 14 Watch the video. What did Aneesha say? Compare with a partner.

## B Focus on language

3 ▶ 14 Watch the first part of Part 1 of the lecture (00:00–00:21) and complete this transcript. The gapped words are all function words (prepositions, pronouns, connectors, articles, auxiliary verbs, etc.).

Now, most [1]_____ know that [2]_____ least someone [3]_____ _____ family [4]_____ friends [5]_____ suffered [6]_____ heart disease, [7]_____ heart disease [8]_____ know today [9]_____ number-one killer, especially [10]_____ _____ developing world.

### Accent note
In many English accents, function words are pronounced very weakly. In Aneesha's Indian accent, they're very clearly pronounced, so there's less contrast between function and content words.

92 Photocopiable © Delta Publishing 2014 from *Authentic Listening Resource Pack*

## C Listening for the main ideas and detail

4 ▶ 14 Watch the whole of Part 1 (00:00–00:56) and tick these phrases as you hear them.
1 heart disease ☐   2 developing world ☐   3 Asian continent ☐
4 risk factors ☐

5 When you're watching a lecture, you sometimes need to make notes. However, you can't write everything the presenter says, so it's helpful to use abbreviations or symbols for some words. Match these suggested abbreviations or symbols (a–d) with the phrases in Exercise 4 (1–4).
a dev. w. ☐   b rf ☐   c ♥ ☐   d As. con. ☐

6 ▶ 14 Look at these notes. Can you guess what they might represent? Compare with a partner. Watch Part 2 (00:57–01:52) and number the notes in the order you hear the points.
a bact → bst → art ☐
b most common infect = gd ☐
c ↑ risk – hd ☐
d gd devel – bact on teeth ☐
e gd = silent ☐

7 ▶ 14 Watch Part 2 again and make notes using the abbreviations and symbols in Exercises 5 and 6. Invent your own if you prefer.

8 ▶ 14 Decide if these statements are true (T) or false (F). Then watch Part 3 (01:53–02:33) and check your answers.
1 People with gum infections are three times as likely to develop heart disease.
2 Gum disease can be easily controlled.
3 Solving gum disease doesn't affect general health.

9 ▶ 14 Watch Part 3 again and correct any false statements in Exercise 8.

## D After watching

10 ▶ 14 What do you remember from the lecture? Add more information about the main topics in the table using abbreviations and symbols. Watch the lecture again or read the script to find more information.

| hd (heart disease) | no. 1 killer; nos ↑ |
|---|---|
| rf (risk factors) | |
| gd (gum disease) | |
| res (research) | |

## E Extension and review

11 Are you convinced by Aneesha's message? Why? / Why not? Use the information in Exercise 10 to write a summary of the lecture or tell a partner.

12 Which of these activities helped you understand the lecture best?
- thinking about the topic before listening
- thinking about the speaker's accent
- using abbreviations and symbols to write key points

# 44 The music of the rainforest

## A Thinking about the topic

1 You're going to hear an interview with Keith Waithe, a musician, talking about his native country, Guyana. Write ten words or phrases you expect to hear in the interview. Compare with a partner.

cock of the rock

harpy eagle

howler monkey

caiman

Kaieteur Falls

## B Tuning in

2 🎧 **2.63** Listen to Keith explaining what *Macusi* is. Choose the correct meaning (a, b or c).
  a  an Amerindian tribe
  b  a bamboo flute
  c  the Guyanese rainforest

3 🎧 **2.64** Listen to these phrases from Keith's explanation. You'll hear each phrase three times, getting progressively slower. Notice that the function words in bold are very reduced.

Macusi **is the** largest
**and their** main instrument
**for the** first time
nine weeks ago **I was** trekking
how **I was able to** meet

**Accent note**
Keith lives in the UK, but he has a Guyanese accent.

94   Photocopiable © Delta Publishing 2014 from *Authentic Listening Resource Pack*

## C Listening for specific information

**4** 🎧 **2.65** Listen to the first part of the interview and tick these names of places and geographical features as you hear them.
Macusi ☐   Guyana ☐   Guyanese ☐   Oronoque River ☐
Kaieteur Falls ☐

**5** 🎧 **2.65** Listen again and answer these questions. Compare and discuss with a partner.
1. Who did Keith buy his flute from?
2. What does the word *Guyana* mean?
3. What can you see when you fly over Guyana?
4. What is the height of the Kaieteur Falls?

**6** 🎧 **2.66** Listen to the next part of the interview. How does Keith feel about Guyana? Choose the sentence (a, b or c) which best summarizes his feelings.
a. He prefers to live in Guyana rather than England.
b. He thinks he's got the best of both worlds.
c. He wouldn't like to live in Guyana.

**7** 🎧 **2.66** Listen again and answer these questions. Compare with a partner.
1. How long has Keith lived in England?
2. What does he take back to Guyana when he goes?
3. What's he got in his back garden?
4. Who bought them?
5. What happens to them in winter?
6. What else has he got in the garden?

## D Listening for key words and phrases

**8** 🎧 **2.67** Underline the key words and phrases in these statements. Then listen out for the key words/phrases in the last part of the interview and number the statements in the order you hear them. Compare with a partner.
a. There's a lot of conservation work going on in the Guyanese rainforest. ☐
b. Keith was helped by older Guyanese musicians. ☐
c. Flutes and the sounds of the rainforest have things in common. ☐
d. The cock-of-the-rock is difficult to see. ☐
e. Many people write about the birds and animals in the rainforest. ☐
f. The sound of the birds in the morning is amazing. ☐

**9** 🎧 **2.67** What can you remember? Add some key words and phrases to the statements in Exercise 8. Then listen again and check.

**10** How does Keith sound when he's describing the rainforest?
a. sad   b. worried   c. happy

## E Extension and review

**11** Would you like to visit the Guyanese rainforest? Why? / Why not? Make some notes or tell a partner.

**12** Which of these activities helped you understand the interview best?
- tuning in to the accent of the speaker
- listening for function words
- listening for key words and phrases

# 45 Pronunciation for listeners 9

## A Connected speech: intonation

1 🎧 **2.68** Listen to and read this text. It shows a fragment of speech, with the intonation.

1 a**ppar**ently
2 eh, **mice**
3 **Vik**ing mice
4 sailed as far as **Green**land

**Notes**
- Each line of text is a 'speech unit'.
- Each speech unit contains one main syllable, shown in larger print.
- The words from the main syllable to the end of each unit either go down then up, or simply down.
- The down–up pattern shows the information is incomplete.
- The down pattern shows the information is complete.

2 🎧 **2.69** Listen. You'll hear the text again and then three more times with one or more of these speech units added each time. Number them in the order they're added.

a er, let me just get this **ab**solutely right, ☐
b it's from a, a Scientific **Amer**ican story, ☐
c er, **mice**, ☐
d er, according to a re**port**, ☐

**Note**
The added speech units have a down–up pattern, showing that they add information to the story but don't complete it.

3 🎧 **2.70** Listen to these speech units. You'll hear each one three times. Which one has a down pattern, showing that it completes the information?

1 **DNA**
2 on Iceland and **Green**land,
3 in **Swe**den
4 dating right back to the **Vik**ing heyday
5 according to Eleanor **Jones**
6 from **mice** skeletons,

4 🎧 **2.71** Guess where the speech units from Exercise 3 go in this text, then listen and check.

a _____
of Uppsala Uni**ver**sity
b _____
and her **coll**eagues,
they looked at the, er, what's called the mito**chon**drial
c _____
d _____
or **mouse** skeletons,
e _____
f _____

96 Photocopiable © Delta Publishing 2014 from *Authentic Listening Resource Pack*

5 🎧 **2.72** Listen to the entire report about Viking mice. Pay attention to the intonation. Notice that the speaker uses short, clear speech units for the key information, and longer and accelerated speech units for additional information.

## B  Spoken English: tag questions

6 In conversational English, tag questions such as *isn't it?* are very common. Look at these different ways you may hear *isn't it?* pronounced.

intip?   isni'?   innit?   iz'ntit?   iznip?

> **Note**
> Conversational tag questions are usually not true questions, so the intonation goes down. They are really an invitation for the other person to agree with the speaker.

7 🎧 **2.73** Listen to six fragments of conversation. Notice the way that *isn't it?* is pronounced.

8 🎧 **2.74** Complete these fragments with tag questions, then listen and check. You'll hear each fragment three times.

1 and you've got a specialism, _____ ?
2 you've got some fairly extreme weather up there, _____ ?
3 um, ants are incredibly intelligent creatures, _____ ?
4 they're not questioned immediately, _____ ?
5 it's not a highly populated area, _____ ?
6 first, another bulge appeared, _____ ?
7 ants have a very particular way, _____ ?
8 it's an iconic symbol, _____ , the deckchair?
9 'cause you've got a big job, _____ , there really?

9 One of the tag questions in Exercise 8 is a real question, and the intonation goes up. Which one is it?

> **Note**
> Tag questions are not always at the end of a sentence, as you can see in fragments 8 and 9 in Exercise 8.

10 🎧 **2.75** Listen to and read these fragments of conversation. You'll hear each fragment at normal speed and then slowed down.

1 … well, that's it, with iTunes and things like that, though, isn't it, but you get things like vinyl and stuff …
2 … yeah, I know they are sort of getting better, aren't they? But with vinyl and stuff, they get, it gets, as it, it gets better as it, as it gets warmer, doesn't it …
3 … I think it's really good, isn't it, but like you say, you've got to have the space, haven't you, for them to go …

> **Note**
> Tag questions may appear almost anywhere within the flow of casual conversation, often very unclearly pronounced. However, if you don't catch them, it won't affect your understanding!

# Scripts

## Lesson 1  Feeling good

### Video 1, Part 1
**Alan**: Happiness is being yourself and relaxing.
**Anisa**: Happiness is being surrounded by friends and family, and enjoying a relaxed time, without any stress.
**Ning**: Happiness is not only the money, um, it's, but also the spiritual things, er, happiness is not, er, it's not just about, er, have some dinner or meals, you, er, you can also, er, gain happiness from the, er, spiritual things like, er, music or love, yes.

\*\*\*

**Alan**: Fun? Er, anything I think where you've got a, a chance to, to carry out any hobby that you like, er, do anything which you actually get a lot out of yourself, not, not doing things for other people, and then sharing that with, with people you actually want to be with, so yeah, going out for a, a beer is great as well.
**Anisa**: Um, fun, I'd say, doing something exciting, so not necessarily just sitting down and curling up and reading a book, but actually travelling somewhere or going somewhere and doing something, so I'm really an active person, and I like going out and, um, say going to a theme park, an amusement park, something like that, that would be fun.

### Video 1, Part 2
**Anisa**: I'm actually pretty easy to be in a good mood, because, as long as I'm relaxed, around friends or family, sort of good food, sitting in a restaurant, or at someone's house having a nice big meal with everybody, then that's pretty nice, um, it doesn't hurt if the weather's good, and I have to say, this summer has been very nice. Normally in England it's not very nice, but when the sun's shining, um, excellent mood.
**Ning**: Well, there's a lot of way to push me good, feel good, er, like, er, but my best way is to have party, especially family party, I don't like a teenager party because it's, er, it's too messy, I like to, er, take part in the family parties, especially there's a lot of, er, er, peer, of my age, um, but, er, I prefer to go with my family, not, er, not just me, because, er, you know, I don't know how to prepare my gifts, so they can give me some advice, and, er, in the family party, um, I, I don't, I don't want to drink, er, er, any alcohol, I prefer the dessert, and, er, the food, I like taste all kinds of food of different countries, um, but er, um, er, every time, when I feel sad, I will call my friends up and advise them, actually it's not, um, advice, just ask them to, er, maybe prepare, er, family party and they invite their relatives and their friends, and we can meet together so I can, er, forget the sadness and, and enjoy them, so I will, I will become better, better after that.

### Video 1, Part 3
**Ning**: OK, the bestest thing I want to talk about is the last Sunday, I went to a family party – yes, I love family party – and, er, because the day before, before the party, I just finish my IELTS exam, so I need to relax, so I really happy to enjoy the, and, er um, I've never been to the UK, so I, er, went to, er, British people's house and meeted them and bring them, er, gifts from China, and they're really happy, and we talked a lot about our different cultures and the customs like, er, the weddings or something, yes.
**Anisa**: Definitely, I got very excited on Tuesday, when I opened my email account and I had won the lottery. Um, I was thrilled, it took me a long time to actually remember my password and get into my account to find out just how much I had won. Um, while I was doing this, in my mind, er, the figure went up from ten thousand to a million to well, of course, I'd won about 30 million pounds. In reality, it was two pounds seventy, but it was exciting, it put me in a good mood for the rest of the day.

### Video 1, Part 4
**Alan**: On the Isle of Wight, well, the thing is we get lots and lots of festivals every year, er, it seems that every weekend there's another festival going on, so we've got lots of chances to go to music festivals, er, classic-car festivals or whatever, er, and there's a lot of, there's a big arts scene on the Isle of Wight, so if you're into, um, I don't know, anything where you can take a picnic out and listen to some music, you've got a lot of chance for this, er, and the island is also brilliant for scenery, just walking, lots of cycle tracks, er, footpaths, that kind of thing, so, um, it's a bit different from a city environment, it's not so much theatre, that kind of thing, it's more, it's more outdoor life, I think.
**Anisa**: Um, well, when I lived in Dubai, it was very different to the city it is right now, so at that time, it was trying to keep cool, which meant living in a swimming pool or going to the sea and swimming in the sea, um, but, I think that's where I got my idea of sitting around and eating and having a good time with friends and family, 'cause it's a very family-oriented environment, and, er, family's very important to a lot of people, so that would be one of the main activities.
**Ning**: Well, there's a lot of activities, um, but, er, in my family and in my city, because, er, Shanghai is crowded city, we usually go to park, because, er, there is no place for us to camping, I really love camping, and, er, most of the, er, office ladies, they all like to relax about … but, er, we usually go to the park and, er, maybe we do not know each other, but we met in the park, so we can be together and talk about family of each other and, er, well, and kids can be friends, and something like that, yeah.

## Lesson 2  Obsessed by the weather

### Audio 1.2
**Steven**: If talking about the weather was an Olympic sport, then you could guarantee that Britain would top the medal tables this year at London 2012. Is there anything more British than having a right good moan about the weather? Even when you go abroad, what do you do? You check the weather back home, just to make sure you're getting your money's worth as you bask in the sunshine. But, far from being a weird British quirk, talking about the rain or shine can be pretty positive. Is there any better way to start a conversation with a stranger? I'm now joined by comedienne Mel Giedroyc. Hi, Mel!
**Mel**: Hello, Steven. How are you?

**Steven**: I'm great. How are you?
**Mel**: I'm good. I'm good. I'm particularly pleased because the weather's looking up.

## Audio 1.3
**Mel**: Hello, Steven. How are you?
**Steven**: I'm great. How are you?
**Mel**: I'm good. I'm good. I'm particularly pleased because the weather's looking up.
**Steven**: Ahhh! It is at the moment. At the moment.
**Mel**: It's looking up. What are we? End of March and, er, it's warm, the blossom's out, and, er, well, of course, British Summer Time starts officially, the old clocks going forwards so I think, I think it's looking positive.
**Steven**: Now, do you think being British and talking about the weather are just inseparable?
**Mel**: I have to say I think because our weather is so mad [Mmm] and so changeable, I think it does obsess us as a nation, actually. Did you know, for example, Steven, that we Brits spend an average of three months over the course of our lifetimes, talking about the weather.
**Steven**: I did not know that, but I can believe that.
**Mel**: Three months! That's a long time, isn't it?
**Steven**: That is a long time, actually. But it is a great way to talk to people, though, isn't it? Er, in a taxi, in a shop. It's the first thing that you talk about.
**Mel**: Yes. I find the older I get, as well, um, it obsesses me more and more. I have a daily chat with my mum about the weather, but that I really enjoy – it's not something that I regard, you know, as, as a chore, I actually love it because it's always changing. You never know what you're going to get.
**Steven**: Yeah, that's something I can definitely relate to. I remember being younger, not having a care in the world about the weather, just going about in a T-shirt and th-this is in Glasgow.
**Mel**: Now that's bold.
**Steven**: That is bold.
**Mel**: You've got some fairly extreme weather up there, haven't you?
**Steven**: We do, actually. I mean, in the last few years, we've had extreme weather all over the UK, really. We've had, um, some incredible winters, many tornados, and even recently, we've had, um, some of the driest winters on record as well.
**Mel**: Yeah. I have to say Scotland is the only place I've ever had sunstroke.
**Steven**: Really?
**Mel**: Yes. It was in the Highlands of Scotland, up near Ardgye, and, er, we were up there for a week, and the sun came out, didn't think anything of it. Two days later, terrible sunstroke, in bed, couldn't even eat, Steven, and for me, I'm telling you, there's got to be something wrong if I can't eat.
**Steven**: Me too, I'm exactly the same.
**Mel**: Yeah.

## Audio 1.4
**Steven**: Have you ever had, apart from your sunstroke, have you ever had a complete weather disaster where you just think, 'Oh, why today?'?
**Mel**: I've got to say a few family occasions have been marred somewhat with, er, in fact, disastrously two years ago, one of my daughters had her first holy communion. I'd booked a room in a pub. It was pouring with rain. We went into the pub, and they were showing a Chelsea match. And, er, there were sort of 30 of my family, little daughter in white dress, trying to, you know, obviously celebrate something quite special, a little bit holy, with, er, with a load of Chelsea supporters. It wasn't good, Steven, we needed that weather outside.
**Steven**: Yeah, I'm sure it was a bit of a religious experience for the Chelsea fans, mind you.
**Mel**: It might have, it might have been. But I don-, I don't know if you've heard, have you heard about this story in Bournemouth on the beach, they've got the world's biggest deckchair.
**Steven**: Yes, I did, actually.
**Mel**: Have, have you heard about it?
**Steven**: I have, yeah.
**Mel**: That, it, that for me kind of sums up the whole of, of, the kind of, you know, the start of British Summer Time, it's a kind of iconic, it's an iconic symbol, isn't it, the deckchair, and they've got this huge red-and-white stripy deckchair, which is, I think it's eight, eight and a half metres high or something? It looks absolutely incredible, and people are sort of crowding round it, and hiding underneath it, and trying sit on top of it.
**Steven**: Now, I think that's very British as well. It's like we're saying, 'Look, it's summer, OK, it is.'
**Mel**: Yes.
**Steven**: 'We've go a massive deckchair, that means it's summer.'
**Mel**: Yes. Whatever else is happening, I will get my deckchair out, and I will roll up my jeans.

## Audio 1.5
1 … there were sort of 30 of my family …
2 That for me kind of sums up …
3 … the whole of, of, the kind of, you know, the start …
4 … it's a kind of iconic …
5 … people are sort of crowding round it …

## Lesson 3  Life on Mars
### Video 2, Part 1
**Bechara**: I implore you to take a look at the sky tonight. Between now and sunrise, you'll be able to see five planets with your naked eye. I was staring up at the Red Planet last night, thinking to myself, whenever it comes for me the opportunity to live on Mars, I will go in a heartbeat, and I can tell you three reasons why.
Imagine that you live on an island, in the middle of the ocean, and that on your island there's a myth, a legend, that every so many generations, a giant wave arrives, tall as the moon, and wipes out your civilization. Also imagine that on the distant horizon, and perhaps only on the clearest of days, you can see a second island, but you have no way to get there, and then someone invents a boat. Would you take that boat and go to the second island? You might go out of pure curiosity. You might go as a means to safeguard your civilization from the next cataclysmic wave. These are good motivations, but perhaps the most compelling reason for you to go to that second island, or for me to go to Mars, is what we might learn.

### Video 2, Part 2
**Bechara**: Despite its fiery appearance, Mars is much much colder than Earth, you can't wander around in bare feet – no. To live on Mars, we would have to terraform it. We'd have to change the climate to make it a little more like Switzerland, and this is not, this is not science fiction. It's possible on Mars because there are huge reserves of carbon dioxide, frozen at the polar caps and elsewhere on the surface. And if we could add just a little heat, we could release so much $CO_2$ through a runaway greenhouse

effect that the pressure and the temperature on Mars would be thick enough and hot enough, that liquid water would flow.

Scientists suggest that we could do this by smashing asteroids into the planet or by exploding hydrogen bombs, or even with super space mirrors that would redirect sunlight onto the polar caps. But probably, the most practical method would be for people living on Mars to release hydrocarbons. We already know a little bit about how that works here on Earth.

And then after a few thousand years of introducing more and more complex plants and animals, there'd be enough oxygen on Mars that my great-great-great-grandchildren could run around barefoot and without any scuba gear. So, in addition to satisfying our curiosity and helping protecting the community of life from events that, for example, killed the dinosaurs, going to Mars could teach us things that we cannot yet imagine. We may even learn how to control the climate back here on Earth. So, tonight, please when you leave here, take a look up at the sky and find your second island.

## Lesson 4 Making a meal of it

### Audio 1.6
there's a wide variety of mushrooms (x3)
glass of dry white wine (x3)
half a pint of vegetable stock (x3)
a couple of tablespoons of olive oil (x3)
one or two grains of the rice (x3)
scrape some parmesan on top of that (x3)

### Audio 1.7
probably enough for two people (x3)
one for you, one for the risotto (x3)
need to leave them for about ten to 15 minutes (x3)
let them go transparent for about three or four minutes (x3)
let that go for a minute (x3)
fry them in the oil for about two or three minutes (x3)
for about 20 minutes or so (x3)
possibly for about another minute or two after that point (x3)
you can go for about 25 minutes (x3)

### Audio 1.8
**Presenter**: All right. Well, what have we got today, then?
**Ian**: Er, today, I thought, um, I'd do a mushroom risotto.
**Presenter**: All right, so we've got mushroom risotto. Wh-, what do we need for this – obviously mushrooms?
**Ian**: Er, indeed, yes, um, right, this is probably enough for two people. Er, the important thing to choose is the right rice. Um, the rice is, is a wild grass seed, and there's thousands of varieties. But the two most commonly used for risotto are, are arborio or carnaroli. Um, both are widely available in, um, most supermarkets, and if you wanna go to an Italian deli, you'll find that, er, you'll be able to get hold of some, certainly carnaroli will be available. Um, you'll need about 50 to 60 grams or two to three ounces per person. Um, I'd also invest in some dried mixed mushrooms, again available in any supermarket. Um, and they add, er, an added di-, they certainly add a real depth to the flavour. Then, I'd get about 300 grams or six ounces of your mushrooms of your choice. There's, now, thankfully, er, there's a wide variety of mushrooms now available in most supermarkets. Jus-, get about as much as you can, different types, throw them all together. You need a glass of dry white wine [Mm!] or two, er, one for you, one for the risotto, um, a small onion, er, as much garlic as you like,

about 300 mls or half a pint of vegetable stock, um, and that should be warmed, um, and in a saucepan next to the pan that you're going to make the risotto in. Er, a couple of tablespoons of olive oil, and, optional, parmesan to top off with. And then parsley to garnish with.

### Audio 1.9
**Presenter**: Well, OK, well, shall we, er, shall we start, er, going through the method now?
**Ian**: The method. Er, the first thing you do is to chop up the mushrooms, chop up the onions, chop up the garlic, then put the oil in a large frying pan, then let that warm through to, on a medium heat, add in the onions, let them go transparent, for about three or four minutes that'll take. Um, after that, throw in the garlic, let that go for a minute or two, throw the mushrooms in, um, fry them in the oil for about two or three minutes, and if it sounds like it's dry, um, add some more oil in if necessary. Um, give them about five minutes, then put in th-, the rice. Um, then throw in the wine. And once you can hear th-, the wine having boiled down slightly, then put in the chopped, dried mushrooms, then add some stock and then slowly keep adding stock, allowing the rice to absorb the, er, the liquor for about 20 minutes or so.

After 20 minutes, try and fish out one or two grains of the rice and test them. You want them so they've gone and absorbed, but become quite soft. Um, you can go for about 25 minutes, but no more than that because then th-, the rice starts breaking down and it just looks like a dog's dinner. It tastes horrible.
**Presenter**: It's such a fine line!
**Ian**: Well, it's not, it is and it isn't, you can murder a risotto. In fact, I had one on New Year's Eve, um, I was so appalled with it, I, I had to send it back, it was dreadful.
**Presenter**: What, in a restaurant?
**Ian**: Yes, in a restaurant. As I say, once you're happy the rice is cooked through, then turn it, take it off the heat basically and serve. Um, now if you wanted to, you can either scrape some parmesan on top of that and work it through. If you want to enrich it, I would add a knob of butter, at the very end of the cooking, and then put it on the plate and then just go on as you would w-, with fresh parsley, and then serve.

## Lesson 5 Pronunciation for listeners 1

### Audio 1.10
1 going about in a T-shirt
  we were up there for a week
  put them in a bowl
  I'd booked a room
2 eight and a half
  more and more complex
  hiding underneath it and trying to sit on top of it
  it is and it isn't
3 minutes or so
  metres high or something
  one or two grains
  60 grams or two to three ounces
4 older I get as well
  get about as much as you can
  er, as much garlic as you like
  tall as the moon
5 clearest of days
  one of my daughters
  er, a couple of tablespoons of olive oil
  there was sort of 30 of my family

6 spend an average
  to an Italian deli
  you live on an island

## Audio 1.11
1 a cup of tea and a biscuit
2 one or two bags of rice
3 try and eat a bit of fruit
4 a pint of milk and a loaf of bread
5 as cold as a block of ice
6 a piece of cake and an ice cream

## Audio 1.12
1 and, er, it's warm
2 but when the sun's shining, um, excellent mood
3 I thought, um, I'd do a mushroom risotto
4 and, er, we were up there for a week
5 er, indeed, yes, um, right, this is probably enough for two people
6 er, one day, you want to send your, um, your daughter
7 and, er, family's very important
8 the older I get as well, um, it obsesses me more and more

## Audio 1.13
1 and if you wanna go to an Italian deli, you'll find that
2 I guess you see, you know, there's all these, sort of
3 then put in the rice
4 and I, I think it's, er, it's good for me
5 I think, yeah, I, I would like to have the lifestyle
6 and then, so that's how I knew that I absolutely loved it
7 'cause he was taking part in this, er, TV show
8 particularly in terms of the impacts of climate change and
9 so when the opportunity was presented to me
10 which is not that oil's going to run out
11 in our local community to become more resilient
12 I now have to learn to like

## Audio 1.14
1 I think, I think it's looking positive
2 with, er, with a load of Chelsea supporters
3 I think it's eight, eight and a half metres
4 and that should be warmed then in a, in a saucepan
5 to add to the, er, to the risotto
6 and then just garnish it with, er, with fresh parsley and then serve
7 especially maybe if you, if you had children as well
8 for example, um, if you're, if you are famous person
9 so that was, that was incredible
10 it's like, it's like adding spice to food
11 the impact of, of increasing energy costs
12 and again how, how we depend on huge shopping centres
13 and begin to create that kind of, er, that kind of future for ourselves
14 and I think a lot of, lot of the ideas that are coming out of that

# Lesson 6  Fame

## Video 3, Part 1
**Tom**: Yeah, I, I got in from my flight yesterday and, um, I, I'm not sure who it was, but I saw a, a guy just surrounded by people in the airport, I guess he must have been a famous person or something, and I kind of wondered like, wow, I wonder, you know, is that a good thing or a bad thing to, you know, have people, kind of, could be like, almost harassing you, or, I dunno, how would you feel if, if you were famous and someone, you know, a load of people just came up to you, right?

**Thuy**: To be honest, I like it. I, I like the way people look at me and admire me because I'm a famous person, um, and I … I think it's a, it's good for me, er, for example, er, if you are a famous singer, er, you can d- … many many fans give flowers to you, and they are 'bravo' after your performance. [Yeah, yeah.] It's good, your feeling, it's very good, and you proud, you proud your ability. [Yeah.] How about you?

## Video 3, Part 2
**Ezgi**: Yeah, it's good, but I think it limits your private life. You, I, I can't do everything in, on street so … I, I can't walk free and I can't go everywhere. For example, a very famous singer, they can't go to cinema, er, it's, it's really bad I think, that's why I don't want to be [Yeah.] famous people.

**Tom**: Yeah, I guess you see, you know, there's all these sort of magazines where all the photos from the paparazzi of, just invading their private lives, you know, and I think, especially maybe if you, if you had children as well, and you, you didn't want them to be in the limelight, um, but nonetheless, they're, the paparazzi are taking photos of you and, you know, you, yeah, you just don't have any privacy, you can't go and buy a pint of milk without someone [Yeah.] bothering you.

**Ezgi**: And always the press they follow you and … It's bad, [But …] it's bad.

## Video 3, Part 3
**Thuy**: But if, er, you look another side of that pro-, er, that issue. For example, um, if you're, if you are famous person, er, one day, you want to send your, um, your daughter, your children into a famous school, and when they recognise you are famous person they wi-, will give you another try, and many many advantages for your children. It's good. Why not?

**Tom**: Yeah.

**Ezgi**: Yeah, but also, I think it's … affects them also, they, they can't be free. Freedom is so important for me, that's why … being famous, I don't think so, really, I don't think so.

**Tom**: I think, yeah, I … I would like to have the lifestyle that fame affords you maybe, you know, usually if someone's famous, they usually have a fair bit of money and can do most things that they would like to, but yeah, then there's usually a camera lens in your face.

**Ezgi**: Yeah, you have to care your clothes, you have to follow the fashion, but [Yeah.] if you don't wear the fashionable clothes, and tomorrow, you will see yourself on the magazines as bad clothes, it's bad, I don't think so.

# Lesson 7  Talent-show winner

## Audio 1.15
**Mary-Jess**: I took Chinese Mandarin as an extra-curricular GCSE, that's how I knew I absolutely loved it – I mean, it's such a fascinating language.
I've always wanted to be a recording artist.
It just looked like the most exciting opportunity that's ever been presented to me, so I definitely just went for it.

## Audio 1.16
**Mary-Jess**: Well, it all started when I was 12, 'cause I took Chinese Mandarin as an extra-curricular GCSE, and then, so that's how I knew that I absolutely loved it – I mean, it's such a fascinating language that … I've always wanted to

be a recording artist, so when I went to university, I took music, in order to try and help follow my dream, but I knew that it was such a fickle industry, and so hard to get into, so I had Chinese as my backup, and, um, while I was studying for my degree, on the second year, you go out to China, so I went out to Nanjing University and it was there that I entered the show.

Um, I've entered all the competitions that I could here really, um, just to try and get my foot in the door for the music industry, so when the opportunity was presented to me to take part in the show, I thought 'Great, this looks amazing!' so I, I knew it was live and it went out to a lot of people, I didn't quite know how many at that point, um, and it just looked like the most exciting opportunity that's ever been presented to me, so I definitely just went for it.

### Audio 1.17
**Mary-Jess**: It was really strange the way it happened, actually, because I went to the studios with a friend initially, 'cause he was taking part in this, er, TV show, which ended up being absolutely hilarious, and it was a really good day, and while we were there, we got to explore round the huge studio complex that we were at, and it was over the other side that I noticed this singing competition was going on, and it, honestly, it looked amazing, so I ran round the studios trying to find the producer, and he said, 'OK, well, we'll think about getting you on the show. Sing.' So I was, 'Oh, all right, fine, I'll sing,' so I had to sing for him there and then on the spot, and he said, 'OK, we'll get you on the show,' but when they called up two weeks later, I had the worst flu I think I've ever had in my entire life, and I was trying to explain to him in my then quite broken Chinese, 'Look, listen to me, I'm so ill, I can't even talk properly,' and that was, that was horrible for me because I didn't think I'd get another chance to do it, and it's live on Chinese TV, it's like the best opportunity that I've ever had, and I couldn't even speak.

### Audio 1.18
**Mary-Jess**: G-, ah, the process was crazy. It was so surreal. My mum put my story in the local paper on the Monday, and at that time I thought, 'Oh, great, tha-, that's nice, I can keep that for the future, show the grandkids that I was in *The Citizen*, brilliant,' and because it was my life, I just didn't, I couldn't comprehend how people would be interested by it, but as I said, that was on the Monday, and on the Tuesday it was in all the national papers, on the Wednesday, Decca were on the phone, and then Thursday, I met the representative from Decca, and on the Friday, not only was I on BBC *Breakfast*, but I was in Decca's demo studio, recording a demo so that they could see how my voice sounded on record, and that was in the space of a week!

There's an EP that will be out on the 11th of July, and then the album will come out on the 8th of August, and so, it's just so exciting to see what people'll think of it, because, as I said, I've been working on it for over a year, and I've co-written seven of the tracks and I had a big hand in the production 'cause I knew what I wanted it to sound like and then, all the recording process was amazing, we recorded the Royal Philharmonic string section in Studio 1 at Abbey Road.

**Interviewer**: Oh my goodness!

**Mary-Jess**: As soon as Abbey Road was mentioned, I had my fingers crossed saying, 'Please let it be Abbey Road, please!' and, er, so that was, that was incredible, and we also recorded some native Chinese instruments for the album as well, and we went to Beijing to do that, and when they're coupled with the Western strings and the Western instruments, it's like, it's like adding spice to food, it just brings out all the flavours of it, and it's so unique and so different.

## Lesson 8  Life without oil

### Audio 1.19
and again, how, how we depend on huge shopping centres
fix these things for us, er, we can do it ourselves.
it's about … having, giving people the opportunity to, to think creatively

### Audio 1.20
**Paul Goodwin**: And we're talking about Transition Towns this morning with, er, Trevor Sharman. N-now, how were you first inspired about this?

**Trevor Sharman**: Well, I've really been very interested in what's going on in the world and, er, and how the future is panning out, particularly in terms of the impacts of climate change, and I was particularly struck in hearing first about the idea of peak oil, which is, not that oil's going to run out, er, tomorrow, but we're really reaching a point where we've reached the maximum level of extraction of oil possible. And that's going to mean that oil is going to become much more expensive and perhaps more scarce, and what is really quite concerning is how vulnerable we are as a society because of our huge dependence on oil. And so I was very interested when I came across the transition idea, which is really looking at what we can do locally, in our local community, to become more resilient and be more able to withstand some of the challenges that are coming our way, um, which will be coming our way in terms of the impact of, of increasing energy costs. So the transition in the title is the transition, the move, the change from a society and a way of doing things that depends hugely on oil and on petrol, on cars, and on all the things that we get from oil, to one where we're much more local and much more resilient in terms and reliant on each other, reliant on our local community. Er, instead of waiting for somebody else to fix these things for us, er, we can do it ourselves. We can get together, we can think about, first of all be aware of what the issues are. And, I mean, that's what we've started, we, we started by trying to raise people's awareness by showing films and having talks and conversations about, well, OK, these are the problems, now what are we going to do about it? And that's really what it's all about. It's about having, giving people the opportunity to, to think creatively, to get together, to begin to do something that they are really interested in, and really passionate about.

### Audio 1.21
**Paul Goodwin**: 'Cos one of the films you showed, what was called *The End of Suburbia*, isn't it? Tell us a little bit about that.

**Trevor Sharman**: Yes, it's a, an American film, um, probably made about four, five years ago, and it's jus–, it showed really how absolutely dependent – particularly American society, but also applies to us – how dependent the whole society's become on the car, and how we, we seem to feel that we need a car as a third leg to get around on. And what this has done to the design of towns, an–, and again how, how we depend on huge shopping centres for our, er, our food supplies and so on, and how this isn't really sustainable. It's not going to be something that's going to continue for the, in the long term. And so we also need to be thinking about, well, how we can be more resilient in the future. How can we become less dependent, less vulnerable. So it was also coming up with some ideas about how that could begin to be done.

## Audio 1.22

**Paul Goodwin:** How have things kind of moved away from how we want them to be or kind of how they were, you know, in the last few decades, Trevor?

**Trevor Sharman**: Well, I d-, I think the transition thing is not about looking backwards, it's about looking forwards. I think what's important, and what the transition idea invites people to do is to think what kind of society and world we want for the future, have a vision. Er, lots of things we say about our present life is that yes, we, we're very affluent and we've never had so much money, although that might be changing quite rapidly, but people are also concerned that we have to work so much. Er, we work the longest hours in Europe in this country. We seem to be obsessed with working and we spend all our time worrying about how we're going to pay for all of the things that perhaps we don't really need. Um, we've got not enough time for our children, and we're worried about our children. These are things that worry us now. We could start to be thinking, 'Well, how would we like things to be? What difference would we like to have in the way we work and the way we are within our communities and family,' and begin to create that kind of, er, that kind of future for ourselves. And, it's really about building community, building relationships with our neighbours, looking at how we can, as a, as a local community, perhaps look after our children between us, er, share more, instead of, er, having all of our own things, like everybody having a car, perhaps we could share more, er, in terms of our transport. We could share more in terms of food, er, how we actually produce and, and, er, cook it and so on. So, we could be thinking, 'Well, what's actually the way of life we'd like to have?' And I think a lot of, a lot of the ideas that are coming out of that vision for the future make much better sense in terms of being less impactful on the environment, requiring less energy, er, and, and also creating a much more positive life for us all.

## Lesson 9 Living with failing eyesight

## Audio 1.23

**Maggie:** I've tried to not let it affect my work life; in fact, the one area that seems to have held sort of steady is work, in that I can still see the computer and I can alter the print on the screen to suit my needs, I can change the contrast. Doing research is a lot more difficult and slower because print appears very distorted to me, so I can't read standard print, but I can still read my computer screen, and so I, I spend a lot of time on the computer.

## Audio 1.24

not let it affect (x3)
sort of steady (x3)
very distorted (x3)
I spend a lot of time on the computer (x3)

## Audio 1.25

**Maggie:** Some of my employers don't know because I work remotely, and to them it doesn't make a difference. Um, I still conduct a lot of interviews on the phone, and then the employers who, who *do* know have been very supportive, they've basically said, 'Well, whatever you need, let us know if there's anything we can do to help,' and, and so far, um, I haven't had to ask for any specific help, but there, there may come a time, but I, I think, actually, journalism may be one profession where it almost doesn't ma… It depends what you do, obviously, but you can do a lot of things on the phone, you can do a lot of things by computer, people don't mind whether you can see or not, and I think that it's a good profession for somebody who can't see.

My friends and family have been great, and again, a lot of open-ended offers of help. I think what I've struggled with is taking them up on it and, and accepting help – that I find really, really difficult. First of all, I don't even know what kind of help I need. It's, it's so overwhelming, I don't know where to begin, but that's been fine, I do find I have a very good support network in London, and, um, and then when I go home, of course I've got my friends there, who are very accommodating, they'll come and meet me at the bus stop, they'll take me to the shop, they'll go shopping with me, you know, a lot of the things that I used to do on my own, that I can't, that I feel I can't do on my own, and again, it may be an irrational perception, but for now, I don't feel I can do some things on my own.
A lot of people that I grew up with knew that I didn't have great eyesight then, and maybe they thought it was worse than I did. I didn't really realize what I couldn't see until very recently when I started to notice what I couldn't see, you know, I didn't feel like I was missing anything until recently, when I noticed from week to week that I can't see something that I could see last week.

## Audio 1.26

**Maggie:** My life is definitely completely different, and what I'm trying to come to terms with right now is how do I make it better than it was before? Because I think that's, that should be your goal anyway, in life, is to try to, to strive for constant improvement, either professional achievements, personal relationships, culturally, etc., so I'm going to have to learn to enjoy different things than I enjoyed before. I mentioned reading books, it's a really simple pleasure to be able to sit down and read a newspaper or a magazine, something that I took for granted and I th-, and of course, people who are sighted take for granted. I now have to learn to like audio books. If I want to read a book, that's how I'm going to have to read it. Even newspapers, I'm going to have to learn to listen to somebody else reading the newspaper to me, and thankfully, there are so many resources for these kinds of recorded material that didn't exist even ten years ago, and it's now the norm, audio books are for sighted people, they listen to them in their cars, they listen to them while they're ironing, so it's something that is part of natural cultural life that maybe wasn't available ten years ago, and now I'm going to have to learn to like it, and so for me, I guess that the future, the challenge that I set for myself or that's facing me, is, yeah, trying to find, um, a substitute for a lot of the things that I did before that I feel that I can't do now.

## Audio 1.27

I'm going to have to learn
learn to like
going to have to learn to like it
trying to come to terms with
how I'm going to have to read it

## Lesson 10  Pronunciation for listeners 2

### Audio 1.28
It's gonna be a big one.
Have you ever had a complete …
Take a look up at the sky.
You never know what you're gonna get.
Now I think that's very British as well.
There's gotta be something wrong if I can't eat.
It's not gonna be something that's gonna continue.
… music in order to try and help follow my dream …
… looked like the most exciting opportunity that's ever been presented to me …

### Audio 1.29
1  We were up there for a week
2  didn't think anything of it
3  I was staring up at the Red Planet
4  We really need good weather this summer.
5  I implore you to take a look at the sky tonight.
6  could be like almost harrassing you
7  I've always wanted to be a recording artist
8  I've entered all the competitions that I could
9  I didn't think I'd get another chance
10  I knew what I wanted it to sound like
11  Tell us a little bit about that.
12  trying to come to terms with right now

### Audio 1.30
**Mel**: end of March and, er, it's warm
heard, have you heard about this
they've got the world's biggest deckchair
**Steven**: weather disaster
not having a care in the world about the weather
just going about in a T-shirt
**Ian**: per person
er, the first thing you do
put the oil in a large frying pan
fresh parsley and then serve
**Bechara**: to go to Mars
we might learn
how that works here on Earth
more and more complex
that liquid water could flow

### Audio 1.31
**Maggie**: whatever you need, let us know
you can do a lot of things on the phone, you can do a lot of things by computer
before I started using it
better than it was before
**Trevor**: make much better sense
waiting for somebody else to fix these things
what we've started, we started by trying to raise
to think creatively, to get together

### Audio 1.32
1  for a period of about six years in total
2  21st birthday
3  they did a pretty good job of sorting it out
4  a computer program created
5  and it's a sort of search strategy
6  it was the first album ever that they wrote every song on it

## Lesson 11  Going places

### Video 4, Part 1
**Tom**: Well, er, I like, I think I've always liked living near the sea, I like having the beach there, although it's a bit disappointing in Portsmouth because there's no surf, um, so I'd like to go somewhere where there are some waves and … maybe not hotter, necessarily, but, er, just, er, more, um, reliable climate, I just don't really like the rain. Yeah.
**Maria**: It definitely should be a warm place with a warm climate, and with the sea. For example, I like Portsmouth really, because I, here I live not far from the, from Southsea, and I have an opportunity to go to the beach every day after classes, or go jogging, which is also very lovely, so I think that an ideal place for me would be a place with a warm climate and the sea, yeah.
**Alan**: For me personally? Um, I think anywhere near the sea and the countryside really. Um, I'm not a big city person.

### Video 4, Part 2
**Tom**: Well, before anything, I think the, the people you go with, you know, it's, er, it's good to share that sort of experience with friends 'cause you can then talk about it later in life, um, although I did just go on holiday this year on my own, but I, you know, that way you're kind of forced to interact with people there, and you, I sort of met a lot of interesting people through doing that, um, but for me, yeah, I mean if it's, er, sort of summer, yeah, I definitely, I, I like to be near beaches and to be able to swim and just enjoy that, or I also like winter holidays, not that I've been on one for many years now really, but you know, like snowboarding – that's great fun.
**Maria**: I definitely should spend my best holidays with a friend, with the people I love, for example, with my parents or with my friends, and, er, the ideal holiday for me is spending time, um, at the seaside, enjoying the sun, sunbathing, playing beach volleyball probably, but it gets boring in two or three days, so there should be places I can visit and probably know something, learn something about the foreign culture or history, so it should be both educational and relaxing.
**Alan**: Er, a good holiday, um, to be absolutely honest, where I can sit by a swimming pool, er, and drink an orange juice, read a book, go swimming and do nothing. I'm not very adventurous in terms of holidays.

### Video 4, Part 3
**Tom**: Um, well, I think, about a year ago, there's a couple of places I've been recently, actually, I went to, er, Cambodia with a friend of mine, er, which was really interesting just 'cause it's so different to England, you know, the food and culture, and, er, there's also, I mean we went to several sort of places of historical interest, um, er, obviously there's, there was the sort of Communist, er, uprising, and we went to some pretty, some pretty horrible places really, but, er, sort of interesting and eye-opening in a sort of a historical way, um, and there was also some, you know, some beautiful temples and stuff as well, on a, on a brighter note.
**Maria**: I think that it is Mexico. I visited it, er, in, this April, yeah, this April. I was, er, really impressed by the Caribbean Sea, by the sun and beautiful beaches, sandy beaches with white sand, and of course, people, people impressed me very much, they were very open-minded and, er, their level of English also was very good, so I had an opportunity to talk to people, to natives.
**Alan**: Yeah, er, two places in France, I went to Antibes in the south of France last summer, and then later, Normandy,

and, and France is just great, er, Antibes especially, with the weather, old town, um, Picasso museum, just a really good atmosphere, although a bit expensive to be honest, um, eating out is ridiculously expensive.

### Video 4, Part 4
**Tom**: Um, well, I mean, I guess you, most of the time should visit the capital of a country, um, but bear in mind that London is not everything, you know, and there are lots of nice sort of pockets of, er, rural land, and I mean I, I really like Cornwall as a place to go and spend some time, er, you've got some lovely sort of beach front there and, um, and if you like surfing and stuff like that, there's sort of lots of outdoor activities you could do, er, don't be put off by the usual stereotype that British food is not good, I completely disagree with it really, and also, you know these days we have a lot of food from all kinds of different cultures, so if you really don't want to eat it, you could probably find something from your culture anyway.

**Maria**: If you are going to go to Russia in winter, I would, I would like to advise you to take more warm clothes because in winter it can be really cold. For example, in area where I live, it's not far from Moscow, the win-, it can be 20 below zero, but there are, there is a lot of snow and you can enjoy playing snowballs and skiing, skating, and all kind of these activities, and if you go in summer or in autumn, I'd like to advise you to go to St Petersburg because it's one of my favourite cities, and it is very beautiful, has a lot of beautiful palaces, magnificent temples and churches, the Neva River and em-, and embankment also will impress you much.

**Alan**: Yeah, coming to England, um, I think really just get, er, get used to the, the way of doing things over here, really, on the roads, be on the right side, that's key advice, but also, um, queuing – in my class today, we were discussing, um, that you should queue, because English people are fanatical about this, and, um, other countries don't have that culture, so, er, don't queue-jump, would be an important thing, and, er, it's, it's worth knowing in all kinds of situations.

## Lesson 12  Raby Castle

### Audio 1.33
**Katie Wallace**: What a stunning, stunning view.
  This is absolutely an amazing room.
**Katie Blundell**: It really is spectacular.
  You know, it's a real stunning location.
**Claire Owen**: It is the most stunning and sumptuous room.
  It's the, um, really impressive entrance hall.

### Audio 1.34
**Katie Blundell**: up at the castle (x3)
**Claire Owen**: to the castle (x3)
**Katie Blundell**: absolutely stunning (x3)
**Claire Owen**: it is the most stunning (x3)
**Katie Blundell**: open room (x3)
**Claire Owen**: when we're open (x3)
**Katie Blundell**: I've never seen so many paintings in my life (x3)
**Claire Owen**: all the paintings are members (x3)

### Audio 1.35
**Katie Wallace**: Raby Castle is one of England's finest medieval castles and has been home to Lord Barnard's family since 1626. However, I am ashamed to say that even though I'm born and bred only a few miles away, I've never ever been inside, so today I've been invited to come into the spectacular grounds and get a full guided tour of all the different rooms by the Curator. First, though, I'm off to speak to Katie Blundell, the Marketing and Events Manager, who's waiting for me up at the castle … First of all, Katie, what a stunning, stunning view!
**Katie Blundell**: It really is spectacular, the park's absolutely beautiful, especially with all of the deer – we've got nearly 400 deer here in the park – so yeah, it, it's beautiful.
**Katie Wallace**: I mean, just there for example, we've got cannons, we've got deer running across the field right in front of us. This is better than working in an office, isn't it?
**Katie Blundell**: Oh, it certainly is, yeah, absolutely, beats the usual rat race that people have to do, it's, it's, you know, it's a real stunning location to come into work here each day, it's, I feel really lucky.
**Katie Wallace**: How many people on average do you get here per year visitor-wise?
**Katie Blundell**: Last year, we had over 35,000, [Really!] which was a really good year for us, 'cause we just open seasonally, we open for three days over Easter weekend, and we open from May until the end of September, so we had an excellent year for visitors, um, which, which we think was, was due in part to some new events that we had here, so it was an excellent year for us.
**Katie Wallace**: Just looking at the, er, at the castle here, how much of it is actually open to the public?
**Katie Blundell**: We actually have about 11 rooms open to the public, and they're the, the real, real focal points we have of a visit to Raby Castle, we've got the Baron's Hall, the Medieval Kitchen, the Victorian Octagon Drawing Room, so it's, yeah, it's about 11/12 main rooms on the public route.
**Katie Wallace**: Well, hopefully, I'm going to pick your colleague's brains, Claire the Curator, and she will be able to tell us a little bit more about the history of the castle. Well, Katie, thank you so much for today, and good luck with all of the events that you've got coming up this year.
**Katie Blundell**: That's my pleasure, thank you very much.

### Audio 1.36
**Katie Wallace**: Well, I'm with Claire Owen, the Curator here at Raby Castle. My first impression of walking into this room – you can tell me a little bit more about it in a minute – is wow! What *is* this room where you've brought us to, Claire?
**Claire Owen**: Right, this is the Octagon Drawing Room, Katie, and you've got absolutely the right reaction there, because it is totally wow. It is the most stunning and sumptuous room in the whole castle, actually, um, built originally by an, a Scottish architect who did a lot of work here, called William Burn in 1848, um, it was built for the second Duke of Cleveland to really impress his friends when they visited.
**Katie Wallace**: Tell me a little bit about this room, Claire. First of all, I'm sure that people can hear, it's a big, open room.
**Claire Owen**: It's the, um, really impressive entrance hall to the castle, and when people come in here, they are truly impressed, um, looking up, you can see a magnificent example of gothic vaulting, and it was built at the request of the second Earl of Darlington, who lived here at the time and it, his son was away on a grand tour of Europe, and he was coming back to celebrate his 21st birthday, and so the Earl of Darlington at the time asked John Carr of York to make this magnificent entrance hall, raise the roof of the former lower hall that was here, so that he could actually arrive back to Raby and arrive in his carriage, and the carriage could drive in one side and out the other.
**Katie Wallace**: Oh wow.

**Claire Owen**: Truly impressive.
**Katie Wallace**: What is, personally, what is your favourite room?
**Claire Owen**: I think I do love the Baron's Hall, where we're going to see in a minute, um, which is absolutely vast.
**Katie Wallace**: Right, let's go and see that, then! … This is absolutely an amazing room, we've got bookshelves, pai–, I've never seen so many paintings in my life. Talk us through what this is, Claire.
**Claire Owen**: This, Katie, is the Baron's Hall, where it is reputed that the rising of the north, um, was plotted here, and 700 knights actually met here to plot against Elizabeth the First, in support of Mary, Queen of Scots, back in 1569. Looking up in here, we have a super oak ceiling.
**Katie Wallace**: That is pheno–, that ceiling is phenomenal.
**Claire Owen**: Oak roof, I would call it, really. It isn't original, that's about 150 years old. Originally, it was a flat, oak hammer-beam roof.
**Katie Wallace**: OK. Who are all the paintings of on the walls?
**Claire Owen**: All the paintings are members of the Vane family, who've lived here since 1626, so the, um, one that goes back the furthest is Henry Vane the Elder, who originally bought the castle in 1626, and it goes right through up to, the most recent is Lord Barnard's, the current Lord Barnard's, er, grandmother, which is a rather beautiful watercolour.

## Audio 1.37

**Katie Wallace**: Tell me a little bit actually about what your job entails as Curator of Raby Castle.
**Claire Owen**: Right, my job, although it's just part time, um, is, involves the conservation and restoration of the chattels as we call it, all the paintings, the furniture, all the items in the castle, as well as being responsible for sort of, the presentation of the public route to the public. And also I'm responsible for the guides, sort of taking them on, training them, making sure they're all organized, know what they're doing, um, when we're open to the public, and actually we have the guide training session very soon coming up now.
**Katie Wallace**: The scenes are absolutely stunning, the castle itself is absolutely stunning, and, er, the best of luck with your job, 'cause you've got a big job, haven't you there really?
**Claire Owen**: I absolutely love my job. I think I'm very, very lucky to work in such a place as this, and then you arrive to work at Raby Castle, I think you're very fortunate and life is good.
**Katie Wallace**: Definitely. Well, thank you very, very much for your time today. It's been an amazing journey you've taken me on. Thank you!
**Claire Owen**: Thank you.

# Lesson 13 The friendly virus

## Video 5, Part 1

**Lucy**: Is there such thing as a good virus? Now this might seem like a strange thing to ask. When we think of viruses, we tend to think of the big baddies like flu and HIV, that are exceptionally good at spreading disease. Even Hollywood's cottoned on to our fear of viruses, and has brought them to the red carpet as evil, fast-spreading, quite deadly villains. But what if we could use viruses to treat diseases, like cancer?

## Video 5, Part 2

**Lucy**: Now, this idea has been around for about a century, and it's based on a natural phenomenon. Doctors treating children with cancer noticed that some who got a measles virus infection had a spontaneous reduction in their tumours. It turns out that the measles virus prefers to grow in tumour cells, as they're programmed to just grow and grow and grow, and this is exactly what the virus wants to do. So, it can really thrive in them. The beauty of this is that, when the virus has grown enough, it sets off small explosions in the cell, to bust the cell open. This kills the tumour cell, and it allows the virus to escape and spread through the tumour.
Now, we've known about this for a long time, but what's exciting is that we now have the tools and the technology, and the knowledge, to do something about it. We know how the measles virus works, so we can ensure that it will only infect cancer cells and not healthy cells to prevent any bad side effects.

## Video 5, Part 3

**Lucy**: So, for a measles virus to get into a cell in our body, it uses a key on its surface. It's cleverly developed this key to fit a lock on the surface of our cells. Now, when the key fits the lock, it opens a doorway for the virus into the cell. We also know that when a cell becomes cancerous, it changes its locks compared to healthy cells. So, we can modify the virus key so that it has a, it will only open the lock on cancer cells, allowing it to invade like a well-targeted SWAT team. We can also give this SWAT team a secret weapon: the virus can carry in a protein that will convert a harmless drug, that you can give the patient, into a highly lethal substance, to poison the cancer cells from the inside, in a double-whammy cancer-killing effect. It's not just the measles virus that could be good at this. Scientists are staging all kinds of virus-versus-cancer battles with some exciting results. It might take a while to match the right virus with the right cancer, but if this therapy works, these villainous viruses could be the good guys in disguise.

# Lesson 14 Complaining

## Audio 1.38

**Peter**: Complaining has never been so public or so instant. In the last five years, email has replaced the phone as the preferred method of making a complaint. Three-quarters of us fire off an email following a poor customer experience. I'm very pleased to say that on the line we have Corrine Sweet, psychologist, to talk about complaining. Right, well, complaining – are we complaining more, are we complaining less, wh-, what, what's the trends?
**Corrine**: Well, we're complaining much more than we were five years ago, and particularly online. Where you are, about five years ago, you would have written a letter or made a phone call if you were upset about something. Now, 76% of you are emailing and you're going either to the company concerned, or you're going to a social network. And that's a huge shift in your behaviour.

## Audio 1.39

**Peter**: It is, isn't it? D-do you think, I think it's more to do with the fact that it's dead easy to send an email off, or do we have more to complain about?
**Corrine**: Well, I think both those things are true. I think we are more picky, we've got higher standards, we want more, and, I think at the same time, we want to have

immediate gratification. We want not to stick a letter in the post and it goes off and it gets lost and it takes ages and it sits in an in-tray and eventually you might get something back. We want to say, 'I don't like this and I don't like it now,' and then, 'I want to hear "What do other people think?"' So, with things like Twitter and Facebook, you know, straight away, people will be saying, 'Actually, I don't like it either,' and 'It didn't taste good' or 'It didn't look nice' or 'It was a horrible experience'. Um, we're having a kind of people power.

**Peter**: I guess it's hard to generalize, but, er, do you get a feel that, er, people are kind of right to complain?

**Corrine**: I think that's an interesting question, because I think in the British psyche, er, we don't like whiners, we don't like moaners, and we tend to sort of queue up quietly, [Yes] but I do think we get a bit passive–aggressive, which means that we quietly take our ball away and go and play somewhere else and we don't actually say, we don't like the confrontation, we don't like being assertive in an American way. But I think, actually, we've gone from one extreme to the other, so I think, funnily enough, there is a happy medium, which is to learn to complain online in a very constructive and positive way, and to say what you want and be assertive.

### Audio 1.40

**Peter**: Yeah, tha-, that's quite interesting. Th-there's several interesting points there. And, I was thinking, sending off an email prevents the sender having to be confrontational, they're not questioned immediately, are they? They, you don't have to respond, you just kind of put your case forward and right, that's got that off my chest, so which is, er, a nice feeling, it's …

**Corrine**: Well, I think it makes people, people who are shy, um, will feel empowered by being able to complain online, but people who, er, use that anger and their frustration against other people, may feel frustrated by that because what they really want is to fight, um, but that's often very counterproductive. If you are over-aggressive about things, you are somebody that people avoid, so I think, using online complaining effectively, um, making sure other people know what's happened, getting collective response to things, means that you actually begin to get, you know, a collective conscious and unconscious, you know, in the world, that we begin to actually change things for the better.

**Peter**: Yes, I think the, the sites where you buy things from, eBay and Amazon, are good examples of that, where people can respond and mark people, pe-people do, it does make a difference, doesn't it, when you've got a decision to make, do you pay an extra couple of pence to get, um, something off somebody who's giving a good service compared to somebody who's giving a poor service? I would say good organizations would probably encourage people to give positive feedback.

**Corrine**: Yes, I think in, there are certain companies that have spent years building a customer base, and they're often more old-fashioned companies or they're family companies where they really care about the customer and they make the customers feel psychologically stroked and I think there is a lot of other companies who don't care, and they just want you to hand over your money, and I think people are feeling, the word is abused, but really, people are feeling, um, used.

### Audio 1.41

**Peter**: Indeed, yeah. Well, c-can we just finish off by then saying wh-wh, as an individual then, and to the listeners, what's the best way, then, if you don't think you've had a good service, to complain in one form or another?

**Corrine**: Well, I personally would say that if you really want to achieve something, you always have to think about who you're complaining to, and that works both ways. Um, you should be polite, you should be courteous, you should be clear, you should say, um, 'I have this experience. I've got this goods or this, this trip or whatever it was you had, and it didn't work, and here's the date, the time, the place, the colour, the serial number,' – all that stuff – and then say, 'This is what I would like you to do' and be very polite about it. And say something positive. And I think then you actually get further, and you get what you want.

**Peter**: Well, that sounds like sound advice. And, er, I suppose we ought to say, to end with, that, er, I have absolutely no complaints about, er, your interview. It's been wonderful talking to you.

## Lesson 15 Pronunciation for listeners 3

### Audio 1.42
… and it's actually literally true! (x6)

### Audio 1.43
actually
actually
time actually
think actually
we actually have
and actually we have
I actually love it
we do, actually
and he actually texts me
before it'd actually started
we don't actually say
and we were actually on the, the outskirts
how much of it is actually open
means that you actually begin to get
it happened actually because I went
but actually he did really, really well
I was actually watching it on TV
places I've been recently, actually, I went to
tell me a little bit actually about what your
he'd actually arrange for their marriages

### Audio 1.44
1  yeah, definitely computers, you know
2  you know, obviously celebrate something
3  I was particularly struck
4  they've basically said, well
5  I'm particularly pleased because
6  It was definitely the best year of my life.
7  earlier and of course he, one of the things he
8  um, you know, basically the focus of Lohri is
9  panning out, particularly in terms of
10  so wh-, what do we need for this? Obviously mushrooms
11  and of course, people who go to visit
12  er, obviously there's, there was the sort of
13  because obviously after George
14  well, of course, it's terribly important

## Audio 1.45
**Anisa**: and I sort of slept on and off (x3)
**Tom**: it's kind of like radio that you can choose (x3)

## Audio 1.46
1 for sort of the presentation
2 lots of nice sort of pockets of
3 there were sort of 30 of my family
4 but I kind of stumbled into a karaoke place
5 I mean, we went to several sort of places
6 and you just kind of put your case forward and
7 people are sort of crowding round it and
8 er, you've got some lovely sort of beach front
9 people are kind of right to complain
10 know with the big, you know, kind of plastic discs
11 and we tend to sort of queue up
12 maybe a car that sort of runs on water, you know
13 for me kind of sums up the whole of, of the kind of, you know, the start
14 um, until he kind of stood up
15 and I kind of think you're missing out a little bit

## Audio 1.47
1 and also just the lifestyle
2 and then just walking around and
3 um, just to try and get my foot in the door
4 and, um, I'd just wanted to get out of the heat really, so
5 you know, just cars that use alternative fuel
6 it was, it was just wonderful
7 definitely just went for it

# Lesson 16  Risk

### Video 6, Part 1
**Maria**: I would like to try to jump with the parachute.
**Alan**: Really?
**Maria**: Yeah.
**Alan**: Seriously?
**Maria**: I think that it is one of the things that I would like to do before I die, but …
**Ning**: Before you die? OK, come on!
**Maria**: I'm not going to die when I jump, but one day … but all of my friends say that I am crazy, that it is really risky and I shouldn't do that, but …
**Ning**: I think so. I agree with them.
**Alan**: Are you afraid of heights, though? When you look out the plane, would you be really scared?
**Maria**: I think that I'm not afraid of heights, but I think that it is up to the moment I am on the plane and I look down and decide, 'Oh my God, I won't do that!'. So, would, would you, would you do it?
**Alan**: I don't think so, I think at the last minute, I would chicken out.
**Maria**: Oh really?
**Alan**: Because, I don't know, just, heights, er, no, I wo-, wouldn't want to throw myself out the plane. I think I'd like to try, um, scuba diving or something like that, [Yeah!] but it's a bit risky.
**Ning**: Yeah, I like scuba diving, but, but I can't swim, you know, it's just a dream.
**Alan**: It's a big disadvantage.
**Ning**: I always tell myself, 'OK, maybe next week I will to do more exercise and find a tutor to teach me how to swim,' but no, it never worked.
**Alan**: You wouldn't try it? It would be great, though, wouldn't it, to just go under and see all the fish and stuff, but it's risky, there, there's always a risk.
**Ning**: The colourful fishing.
**Alan**: Yeah, it'd be fantastic.
**Ning**: But you need a, a qualification.
**Alan**: Yeah, tha-, that's the problem. So you wouldn't be able to do it.
**Ning**: Yes, that's the problem.

### Video 6, Part 2
**Alan**: Would you go, would you do a risky holiday like mountain climbing, or learning to, um, do, like, hang-gliding, or something like that, would you fancy that?
**Maria**: Yeah, I'd like to try mountain climbing really, and some of my friends did mountain climbing in Russia, we have an impressive mountain, and one of my friends did mountain climbing at the top of Everest.
**Alan**: Did they like it?
**Maria**: Yes, he said it was amazing.
**Alan**: The top of Everest, really?
**Maria**: Not at the top, but he tried to reach, but he didn't, but the thing is that it tooks, it took him about several days to go there, and they stayed in the, uh, in the tent, and they couldn't just, sunset and sunrise and then go for it, I think that it is amazing but it's dangerous because the pressure differs, and people may feel not very well.
**Alan**: Yeah, you have to be very fit to do this, very fit and very strong, I think.
**Ning**: I don't imagine, because I'm afraid of height.
**Alan**: It's the last thing for you to do then, really.
**Ning**: Yes, and I live near the coast, coast, so I don't like mountains, and I, I really don't like the cold weather.

### Video 6, Part 3
**Alan**: No. I'm quite cautious generally, I don't like to take many risks, just I, for example, with money, I don't, sort of, risk, um, on an investment or something like that, either.
**Ning**: What, what would you do if, if you earn a lot of money, I mean if you maybe find you, someone give you some money, a large amount of money, what would you do?
**Alan**: I don't know, 'cause I'd probably be quite cautious wi-, with it, I wouldn't, wouldn't risk losing it all on some crazy scheme or something like that. Um, would, would you ever gamble with money, would you ever go to a casino and take a risk?
**Maria**: No, never, I think no, because I usually have a bad luck in such sorts of entertainment, so for example, if I want to, to bet, or, I don't know, to play, I usually lose, so I'll, I'll never go to casino too.
**Alan**: Yeah, I sometimes use the lottery, maybe [Lottery?] just one pound every month perhaps, never win.
**Maria**: But you pay two pounds for a lottery ticket and you win one pound.
**Alan**: Yeah, I did actually win two pounds once, so I got twice my money back.
**Ning**: It's still good luck.
**Alan**: Some people do though, don't they, in England, people queue up to buy lottery tickets.
**Maria**: Oh really?
**Alan**: Yeah, on a Friday, you want to buy a newspaper, and there's a huge queue of people trying to buy a lottery ticket.
**Ning**: Oh, I remember last month, last month, er, all the things is about the royal baby.
**Alan**: Oh really?
**Ning**: Yeah, they, they pay for the royal baby, they guess the name of the baby.
**Alan**: Yeah, English people are like that, they gamble a lot on stuff.
**Ning**: Yes.
**Alan**: They gamble away at whether it will snow on Christmas Day and they sort of …

**Ning**: Yeah, like the name of the royal baby.
**Alan**: Yeah, so, er, they gamble on all kinds of stuff.

## Lesson 17  Baltic voyager
### Audio 1.48
**Phil Beer**: I've had some very lucky experiences, but it seems like, sort of, you know, like once every five years I get a chance to do something. Um, this one came up, um, er, er, with an accidental conversation, I was actually, um, with, er, a young man called Diggory Rose, um, who is a sailing skipper, and he had just got the job, er, of skippering this boat, the Pegasus, for The Island Trust, which is a sail-training organization down in Salcombe, in Devon. Diggory told me about the new boat he was, er, gonna be running, and he happened to mention, um, er, the possibility of doing Tall Ships in 2009, so I jumped up and down and said, 'I'll do it.'

### Audio 1.49
**Interviewer**: Tell me about the Pegasus.
**Phil Beer**: Pegasus, she's absolutely beautiful, she's 56, 57 feet in the water, seven-, 70 feet overall with the bowsprit right out. Um, and, er, she's very beautiful-looking boat, and she's quite fast, as we discovered a little bit later on, um, so four, we had four standing crew and, um, then we had, er, a bunch of lads from the Liverpool Fire Service, the Merseyside Fire Service, and they were our trainees for the trip.
**Interviewer**: So, how did you fare in the races?
**Phil Beer**: OK, first race leg, we'll never know 'cause we broke the boat. We had a glorious 36 hours, absolutely steaming along and then, unfortunately, um, we had a problem with the mast, um, we detected a bit of movement, you know, and quite a lot of noise, and we realized that it was actually working loose. So we had no option, actually, but to, er, quit racing, so we'll never know what happened there. We got to St Petersberg and then a whole bunch of work was done. Er, Diggory's a shipwright as well, so, er, he was able to direct and do most of the work. We just had to get the, the tools and materials in, so we did, er, they did a pretty good job of sorting it out. And then we were cruising in company, the next part of Tall Ships is you're always cruising in company, so we actually did the whole of the Finnish archipelago for, er, nine days or so, 10,000 islands in nine days, all the, that sort of stuff, which was lovely, it was really good fun. And then, um, we put it to the test again, and the second race-leg was from Turku, in Finland, down to, er, Klaipeda in Lithuania, and we came first in our class, and second overall.

### Audio 1.50
**Interviewer**: What was the weather like, then?
**Phil Beer**: Mostly glorious. So, that's like the upside of it. Most of our cruising in Finland was lovely. Rained a bit in Russia, we certainly had a few, er, heavy-duty storms, very unpleasant journey up into the Elba to get into the Kiel Canal, that was quite unpleasant, um, but then, apparently, it's often quite unpleasant, and then, um, we also had a, a, er, coming back again across the North Sea, um, we were bashing our way through a, a near gale and, of course, when you, when you're just nose on to it, you know, and you're trying to avoid fishing fleets and oil rigs and all the rest of it, it's, er, quite unpleasant, but …
**Interviewer**: Was anybody sea-sick?
**Phil Beer**: Um, surprisingly, um, I always get sea-sick, or hitherto I have, I managed to avoid it this time. I think there's just so much to do, when you're working, that you just forget about it 'cause you get on, that's what you get on with, you know. Er, yeah, I think, I think one or two people were slightly sea-sick, um, odd occasions, but generally, it was all pretty good really, considering the, the heavy-duty weather that we encountered on a couple of occasions. I think everybody came out of it really well, so …
**Interviewer**: Did you sing any sea shanties?
**Phil Beer**: Yes, lots of singing sessions. Er, we visited a lot of ships and did a lot of sing-songs, yeah, it was great.

## Lesson 18  Under the volcano
### Audio 1.51
**Malcolm**: It must have been absolutely terrifying [I think] for people 'cause it, because [good question, yeah, because] it's not, it's not a highly populated area, is it?
**Jenny**: Um, no, it's not very populated, but, er, you can see that volcano from Portland, Oregon, which is a city probably about the size of Bristol.
**Malcolm**: So, the bulge started [Yeah] and then, and then what happened, er, after that? [Well, the bulge started] So, I mean, er, did, did, people like yourself, volcanologists, sort of run …

### Audio 1.52
populated (x6)
started (x6)

### Audio 1.53
**Malcolm**: Er, a little bit, er, later on, we're going to have some science news, but I'm really delighted to welcome, er, my guest today, Jenny Riker. Hi, Jenny.
**Jenny**: Hello. Yep.
**Malcolm**: Er, Jenny's a, er, volcanologist – you study [Yes] volcanos and you've got a specialism, haven't you? Er, er, something which I have actually seen, er, Mount St Helens.
**Jenny**: Yeah, so I'm a PhD student at the University of Bristol, and, er, and my PhD work is centred on Mount St Helens volcano, which is in Washington State. I'm from Oregon State, so Mount St Helens is not very far away.
**Malcolm**: Sorry … we should explain. Sometimes people get confused. [Yeah] Washington State, up on the north, er, west. [Yes] It, it's an entire state on the [Entire state, very big, bigger than the UK]. Very, very big up on the north-west coast, er, not to be confused with Washington, DC, [Not to be confused] capital on the east coast. And, and, um, j-just tell us the story of Mou-, er, Mount St Helens, because it was, er, a pretty big blow-out, wasn't it?
**Jenny**: Yeah, so, yeah. I guess i-, in the recent history of Mount St Helens, a lot of people are familiar with, er, the 1980 eruption of Mount St Helens, um, which actually went on for a period of about six years in total, but what most people remember was, um, in 1980, er, what was generally had been a quiet mountain in Washington State, um, began to develop a little bit of a bulge on its side, um, so I think that, um, seismologists in the area noticed an increasing level of, of earthquakes and things that, that, um, seismic activity in the region, but, er, eventually over time, um, that activity became something that people could actually see, the side of the volcano began to stick out a little bit.
**Malcolm**: It must have been absolutely terrifying [I think] for people 'cause, because [Good question, yeah] because it's not, it's not a highly populated area, is it?
**Jenny**: Um, well, you know, it's, it's not that far from the very

large cities of Seattle and Portland, um, so the volcano itself, no, it's not very populated, but, er, you can see that volcano from Portland, Oregon, which is a city probably about the size of Bristol. So it, it might have been a bit unsettling, I think, for people in the region, yeah.

**Audio 1.54**
**Malcolm**: So, the bulge started [Yeah] and then, and then, what happened after that? [Well, the bulge started] So, I mean, did, er, did people like yourself, volcanologists, sort of run, did they run towards the site, or did they run away from it?
**Jenny**: So, I, I was, er, I was two years old, so couldn't run very fast, um, but, um, people, for example, people that I work with now, were very involved in monitoring that eruption, and I think a lot of people did, scientists who were interested in volcanoes, did start flocking to, to Mount St Helens from all over the US, um, because they were interested in what was going on, and an opportunity to observe an active volcano, um, and, er, yeah, like I said, I think, I think one of the most useful monitoring tools at the time was seismicity, it, er, certainly still is today and, er, I think it became very clear, um, after a period when the bulge was growing and seismic activity was becoming more frequent and larger in magnitude, that something was going to happen, yeah.
**Malcolm**: And then it did [And then it did, yeah, so] So, so, I, as I recall, th-, there didn't, er, first another bulge appeared, didn't it? Somewhere, er, if, if my memory serves me right.
**Jenny**: So, so I guess, er, um, so my understanding is this bulge, um, that manifested itself at the surface of the volcano, was actually, e-, er, a very shallow body of magma, what we would call a cryptodome, being emplaced, er, beneath the surface, but very near the surface. Um, and, um, eventually, the stresses related to the emplacement of that bulge became such that the side of the volcano collapsed. What actually triggered this huge eruption that people are familiar with in 1980, at Mount St Helens, was, er, a landslide effectively, um, and so, a whole side of the volcano, er, sloughed off, and, er, the release of pressure from, so the slumping of the side of the mountain, that release of pressure, er, actually causes, um, gases that are dissolved in magma beneath the surface, to suddenly expand, and that expansion of gas is what drove the very huge, er, eruption cloud that people are familiar with seeing in images from the 19-, May 1980 eruption on St Helens.
**Malcolm**: And, and what's left there now? [Yeah] What remains?
**Jenny**: It's a very different volcano now. So, um, …
**Malcolm**: So, it's still busy, it's [It's, it's still busy.] still active.
**Jenny**: It's a national monument in the US. It's still, of course, it's still active, in fact. Most recently, it was, er, active again and erupting, small eruptions, um, in 2004 through 2006, there was renewed activity, um, much quieter than, of course, than the 1980 eruptions that people are familiar with, but, um, yeah, still active. There's, er, quite a chasm where the side of the volcano used to be. And there's a small, um, small, what we call a dome, a small bit of very, very sticky lava, sort of, um, sitting there in the chasm left by the landslide and the eruption of 1980.
**Malcolm**: Obviously, it must be incredibly dangerous for your colleagues who are in the field and when you've been in the field yourself, er, there's these things bubbling away. I'm reminded, er, I, I, not very long ago, I, I, er, read, er, the, um, Robert Harris story, um, about the, um, the big eruption – and as I say it, I've forgotten the name of the volcano – Vesuvius. [Oh, Vesuvius]. Yeah, that's it, yeah, the big, the big, er, ['79 '80, OK.] Yeah, the big eruption when Pliny, [Yeah] er, the, um, the, um, historian [the first volcanologist], writer and scientist and, er, yeah, the first volcanologist lost his life because he was wandering round saying, 'Oh, this is terribly interesting, I'll go and have a closer look,' and nobody ever heard of him again. Um, so it is, er, very dangerous and, and so on. How do you know when it's too dangerous to keep going?

**Audio 1.55**
**Jenny**: That's, er, that's a very good question. Um, so people that I work with and myself, you know, we work at volcanoes all over the world, lots of different volcanic environments. Er, I think, certainly, certainly, if something is erupting explosively and rocks are falling from the sky, volcanologists are generally not going to stay out of the way! Um, I think, in certain volcanic environments like Hawaii, um, that tend to produce lava flows an-, and only rarely produce explosive eruptions, um, I think, er, it's much easier to work in those environments, to approach lava flows because they, they tend to advance quite slowly. Most people can outrun, er, most lava flows. Um, so, i-, it really just depends on the volcanic environment, yeah, yeah.
**Malcolm**: 'Cause people who go to visit the site where, er, Pompeii was [Yeah], Herculaneum and [Yeah] places like that, there are these weird and eerie preservations, aren't there, [Yeah] where people are just frozen [Yeah] in, in, in the act of whatever it was they were [Yeah], whether eating a meal as, I, I think there's a dog [M-m], isn't there [Yeah], that's sort of encased in [Yeah]. Wh-wh-, er, I mean, what's happened there?
**Jenny**: Well, er, so I, I have to preface this by saying, um, I'm not so familiar with the science of that process, but, er, I imagine what happens is that, um, th-the eruption, of course, the flows approach very quickly. People don't have time to get away, um, and maybe they don't have a lot of warning, so they haven't even stopped what they're doing. Um, and once, th-, you know, the body is mostly carbon and such and organic material and i-, it burns away, but, um, the ash that hardens outside of the, of the organic, you know, being, or living thing, um, can be preserved and so, there, er, these are effectively shells of, of people and dogs and things that were there at the time of the eruption.

## Lesson 19 Mystery on Mount Everest

**Audio 1.56**
**Interviewer**: *Everest Needs You, Mr Irvine*, one of the greatest legends of mountaineering, retold by writer and historian Julie Summers, is going to be at the Darlington Arts Centre on Friday the 14th of October. I'm very pleased to say that Julie is on the phone to talk to us about the performance. First of all, give us an overview of, er, what the whole thing's about.
**Julie**: Well, the whole thing's about, er, Sandy Irvine, who, with George Mallory in 1924, disappeared on the upper reaches of Mount Everest. They were never seen again alive, although Mallory's body was found in 1999. But, when they disappeared, their, their loss was felt very keenly in Britain, and they became part of, the sort of the greatest mountaineering legend of all times. And so what I'm going to do in the performance is to really bring alive,

um, Sandy Irvine, who has always been the historical cipher. He was the youngest member of the Mount Everest expedition. He was only 22, er, when he died, and he was also, interestingly, the only member of the expedition who hadn't fought in the Sec-, in the First World War because he was only 12 at the outbreak of the war. Um, but it's a very beautiful era and it has a lot of, er, drama, a lot of, a lot of humour – he was a very funny young man – and I want to sort of conjure up, um, the Edwardian era that represented the backdrop to the early Everest expeditions.

## Audio 1.57

**Interviewer**: Now, I suppose it's fairly obvious why you would kind of patron the, the lovely story, then, the very interesting story, why you would be interested because, um, you're the great-niece of, er, Sandy, as well, aren't you?

**Julie**: That's right, his, um, his older sister Evelyn was my grandmother, and she married Dick Summers, which is where my, my surname came from. But he was, he was the third of six children and very much the, the sort of liveliest member of that family, and his story just came down to us as, as part of the family legend and really, until I was in my late 30s, I knew very little about him except he was Uncle Sandy who, who died on Everest. We all knew, as children, that, um, his sister and brothers were devastated by his death – o-, of course, they would be – and my grandmother refused ever to speak about him in any detail, even when her own children questioned her. So, he was very much, sort of, you know, a very deeply loved family member. But when I came actually to look at his life and to, er, explore his biography, it was absolutely action-packed. He, he managed in his short 22 years to cram in what most people wouldn't be able to do in twice that period. He went to Spitzbergen in 1923 – he, he crossed the Arctic island of Spitzbergen – he rowed in the Oxford and Cambridge boat race twice, losing once and winning once. He, er, did have a love affair with his best friend's stepmother, er, and he went to Everest. Now that's quite an achievement for a young man in his early twenties.

## Audio 1.58

**Interviewer**: Isn't it just, yes. And have you been in touch with the Mallory family at all about, um, you know, the, the things that they may have had, and that sort of thing?

**Julie**: Yes, um, in fact, ironically, um, one of the members of the Mallory family, Virginia Arnott, er, who is Mallory's granddaughter, lives just down the road from me – I live in Oxford and she lives in Abingdon – and our boys were at school together, so there were Irvine and Mallory boys in the same school for a couple of years, which was, n- neither of us knew that that was the case. Um, but yes, I, I've spoken to the Mallory family, um, because obviously after George Mallory's body was found, there was a huge amount of interest in the story, um, and we all hope, I think, um, that in, in the end, um, nobody finds Sandy Irvine's body, which is, there's a hunt for his body of course, because people want to know the ultimate truth of this tale and, um, I think the Mallorys share with me the hope that no more bodies will be found on Everest linked to 1924.

**Interviewer**: Oh, right, because I understand there's even an expedition this year that's actually hoping, er, to find Sandy.

**Julie**: Yes, there's an American, um, historian who's taking a, er, a group of climbers up Everest, I think in November, and they're hoping to track down, er, Sandy's body, and

th-, the distressing thing for us is that, i-, if the body that they found in 1960, seen by a Chinese climber, is in fact Sandy Irvine's body, then his face will be visible because he's lying apparently on his back [Oh dear] and it will not be a pretty sight and he was an incredibly good-looking young man and I really fear what it'll be like to see photographs of, of that corpse. I hope, I hope against hope they won't publish them because it will be horrible.

**Interviewer**: Indeed, indeed.

## Audio 1.59

**Julie**: And the mystery's so wonderful [Yes]. It was such an extraordinary era, and all this bravery after all the sort of terrible slaughter of the First World War, and I think the romance of the story captures people's imagination. It, it still does, even today.

**Interviewer**: I imagine over the years and, and particularly at the time, as we kind of live in a society of conspiracy theories, er, what sort of stories ha-, have kind of sprung up about it. And do you kind of hold any credence to any of them?

**Julie**: Do I listen to the conspiracy theories? I'm fairly sceptical about them, but the debate that still rages today about whether or not they got to the summit, er, is fascinating, and people have gone into huge studious detail about how many oxygen cylinders they were carrying, and did they cross this particular piece of mountain at that particular time, um, and the climbing community is divided. Some believe they did, and some believe they didn't.

**Interviewer**: And I guess – or it w-, would have been solved by now – but, er, there was no way of telling from anything they may left at the summit so …

**Julie**: Well, the, the, Mallory always said that he was going to leave a photograph of his wife and a British flag – a union jack – on the summit, and the conspiracy theory, when Mallory's body was found, that was raging, was that in his pocket there was neither a photograph of Ruth Mallory nor a flag, and therefore people concluded that they must have got to the summit. But, conversely, when Hillary got to the summit in 1953, he had the courtesy, and I think the sort of gentle humour, to look at the summit and see whether he could find a, any evidence that Mallory'd been there, but it's a snow peak and, you know, 29 years later [Yes], there'd be no vestige of, er, of information. Um, so, I-, I think it's, I think it's, er, quite fun to think that, um, you know, people believe that, er, Mallory did leave that photograph up on top, but there's no evidence of that at all. In fact, finding Mallory's body raised more questions than is answered about how they had died and whether, you know, how far they'd got on the mountain.

**Interviewer**: Right, yeah, absolutely fascinating [Yeah].

# Lesson 20 Pronunciation for listeners 4

## Audio 1.60

1 I was two years old
2 my watch is broken
3 the man, who was a doctor
4 there was only one left
5 it must have been terrible
6 the place has changed a lot
7 the birds are singing
8 they must have gone
9 I thought you were French

## Audio 1.61
1 which is in Washington state
2 because they were interested in what was going on
3 and this is exactly
4 Evelyn was my grandmother
5 I was two years old
6 for your colleagues who are in the field
7 things that were there at the time of the eruption
8 what's exciting is that we now
9 and we realized that it was actually working loose

## Audio 1.62
they were never seen again alive
it must have been absolutely terrifying [I think]
is that when the virus has grown enough
although Mallory's body was found
that they must have got to the summit
oxygen cylinders they were carrying
complaining has never been so public
or it w-, would've been solved by now
he was going to leave
email has replaced the phone
you would have written a letter or made a phone call
it might have been a bit unsettling

## Audio 1.63
| | | |
|---|---|---|
| 1 quite fast | very fast | (x3) |
| 2 snow on Christmas Day | how are you doing today? | (x3) |
| 3 how do you know | to let me know | (x3) |
| 4 people can outrun | first run | (x3) |
| 5 it's small science | and there's a small | (x3) |
| 6 a lot smaller | a lot of open-ended | (x3) |
| 7 there's a dog | people and dogs and things | (x3) |

## Audio 1.64
coming our way
I've gotta say
clearest of days
with a stranger
the change
how are you doing today
when he came back
is there any better way
why today
I am ashamed to say
can't see something
up at the castle
just there for example
in the whole castle
a photograph of his wife
to the castle
for examples
for example
example of gothic
go abroad
actually causes, um
life for us all
that liquid water could flow
having talks
thought it was
the lottery
got the job
my surname came from
from
people and dogs and things
the bus stop, they'll take me to this shop
there's a lot of interviews on the phone
near the coast
the new boat

well, you know
the science of that process
to let me know
turn over
you know
I don't know, I just don't know if
how do you know

## Lesson 21  First impressions

### Video 7, Part 1
**Maria**: So before I, before I arrived, I've heard a lot of stereotypes about England, for example, people told me that English people are very reserved and cold-hearted, and of course I've heard a lot of stereotype about the weather, and people told me that it is always raining and the sky is grey and, er, that I always should carry my umbrella, and, er, when, when I came here, all the stereotypes I've heard were absolutely ruined because people I met here are real-, are really open-minded and I was really impressed by their hospitality, and, um, their desire to talk to me and to know more about my country, and about, um, about the style of life in my country, so it was really pleasant impression, because I lived in a host family, and I was also impressed by the way they talk to each other and they raise they children, and also the weather was surprisingly good, for example, I've been staying here for about three weeks and, er, there were only two or three times when I had carry on my, with my umbrella, so yes … but there were also some very strange things, which surprised me – for example, you have two taps with hot water and cold water and I still don't understand why English people need these taps, and for example, um, when I take shower, the temperature changes, even, even if I don't want, so I don't do anything with the taps, but first it is very hot and then it, it, it's cold and then it is something in the middle and I just have to, I don't know, jump and then co-, come back again, so yeah, it was strange … Also, people told me a lot of different things about British food, some people told that it is awful and a lot of potatoes and that you overcook everything, but really, I like fish and chips and, um, but really, here, here, people eat a lot of potatoes, for example, if I, when I go jogging in the evening in the seafront, I see a lot of people carrying fish and chips and eating potatoes, so it was quite strange for me because in Russia, I usually don't eat potatoes, but yeah, yeah, well, it is OK … and I also like the English style of life, probably, er, my im-, my impression is a bit wrong, but I, I, I think that people here, um, are not so stressful, and, um, like in Russia, and also people told me that London is very unfriendly city, but I went here with my friends and I understood that it is not, for example, I was, we we-, we took, we hired a bicycle and spent all day cycling across London, and I was really impressed by the way people respect each other on the roads, for example, um, cars didn't try to force us to go faster, or – I don't know – double deckers when they had to go to the bus stop, but I wasn't afraid of the double decker – it always waited for me to come further so it was really nice, yes, and surprising, and I think that the general impression of England is very good, I like this country, and probably I would like to stay here. Yeah.

## Video 7, Part 2

**Ezgi**: Yeah, it was good and bad, because when I first arrived, OK, I saw a lot of people who came from different countries, for example, in the Saudi Arabia, I think, yeah, it makes me, it makes me surprised because this means that, er, British people are so open-minded and it's, it's really good, and the other things, I think tap, yeah, taps in your bathroom is so, er, comp-, it's completely different from Turkey, for example, you have two taps, which one is the for cold and the other one is the warm, well, what is the, how can I, how can I adjust the temperature, it's so, it's so hard, for me, but I don't, I think, I ask my host family, but she can't explain, I don't know, because nobody knows. The other thing's, taxi, in Istanbul, you can, er, take a taxi on street, it's, it's normal, but in the UK, you can't, you have to call the taxi station or somewhere, you can't take a taxi on the street, I think, yeah, it's good and bad and raining time, in raining weather, it's bad.

## Video 7, Part 3

**Thuy**: Um, to be honest, I'm very happy, er, when, at the first time I came here, um, my, er, first feeling is, er, I look at the sky and I feel very relaxed, extremely, er, familiar with, er, life in my se-, in my, er, country and stuff, yeah. Um, and one more things, er, because I live in a hostel, and I just, er, live alone, so, mm, a little bit feel, feel lonely, but, er, after that, I feel better, because, er, British people, the way they behave, er, with another people make me feel warm, and they very qu-, friendly, for example, um, whenever, er, I want a d-, a help from them, they very friendly, they say, 'Oh yes, it doesn't matter, I will help you, please take a phone numbers or something, if you have some problems, please talk with me,' and to be honest, one day, I, um, don't know how, I do-, I cook something and, er, my pot is damaged, so I very scare, I don't know how to say with the reception, 'Give me another ones,' and I, er, went to desk reception, and I said my kitchen, er, tool is damaged, but I don't know how to, er, describe this pot, but I don't know, I don't know that word, and he open, he turn on his computer and – Google – and, er, write, type 'kitchen tool', and is appear 'pot', and he show me this image, and he give me another one, and I feel relaxed and … and another things is when I go out, and, um, I don't know how the way to go, and I usually ask the people, er, 'Please show me the way to go there,' and they very friendly, they help me, and always they say, 'OK, don't worry, you live in Portsmouth in UK and you should relax yourself,' and I think when I come back to my country I will tell this story to my friends and my family, and I think, if, um, someone come here, or me come back here again, they will feel very happy about that.

# Lesson 22  Rescuing tradition

## Audio 1.65

**Peter**: This is Peter Dixon for Radio Teesdale and in the studio I have with me at the moment two of the members of Dautenis. Hello, guys!

**Piotr**: Hello.

**Małgorzata**: Hello.

**Peter**: Well, it's great to see you. You've come all the way from the north-east of Poland and, er, you're over here for a week.

**Piotr**: Exactly.

**Peter**: So, the name of the group, then.

**Małgorzata**: We're called Dautenis, we call ourselves Dautenis, and the name comes from the old language that was used in our region many, many years ago, it was long before Polish was established, er, as a language, and it is a name that refer to two lakes in our region, they are nowadays called Dowcien. We chose this name because this is a symbol for us of the old culture, of, um, what we do with the old songs and dances, melodies. We try to bring them back to life and so the name that was used years ago and is now u-, in use again is a symbol of getting the old culture back in, in life.

## Audio 1.66

**Peter**: It's hard for our listeners to tell how old you are, but I can testify for the fact that you're a very young group. It's great to see that you're actually playing those traditional pieces of music from, from your area.

**Małgorzata**: Well, I think it's, mm, it's becoming more and more popular because people start getting interested about the things that used to happen around them before, and the, instead of having what everybody has, we try to find out who we are, and the only thing to find this out is to get deeper into the culture that surrounds you, so we speak to the elders, we try to find out what was going on in the area, er, what was, what were the rules that the people lived according to, er, what was the fun that they used to have, we try to find out what was the source of the things that created our culture, our way of bringing up children, the, the legends, the songs, the dances, everything. So the only way to identify yourself is to get to your roots, and that's what we try to do now. The situation that we are now is also the result of the communist regime, er, because during that time, they tried to, sort of polish the folk culture and the folk customs, they tried to adapt them, er, to the modern way that they tried to make, er, available for everyone, so this culture was sort of, would you say, 'washed and ironed', and then sold to people in a sort of picturesque way. You would colour it up, you would dress the dancers neatly, you would make them sing like a choir in a church in a nice and educated way, and this rural, er, would you say, atmosphere would just be gone, this, there was nothing natural in the way this music was presented, so I think that's probably why the young people would stop feeling so familiar to this, because this was sort of, er, an unnatural way of presenting this music, and we're trying to get back to the roots now.

## Audio 1.67

**Peter**: So how does your music and your performances sit within Polish music? In England, we have, er, a lot of pop music, of course. Do you have that in Poland as well, or is music generally of a more traditional nature?

**Małgorzata**: No, no, it's just like everywhere else, we have pop music, and we have lots of music from England, everybody knows The Beatles and everybody knows Oasis, and, er, we follow, you know, on the charts in Poland, you have all the hits that you can find. Th-, There are also many people who are interested in the music from Ukraine or Bulgaria, because we feel familiar with these countries, and Romanian music as well.

**Peter**: You come from the north-east of Poland – how does the north-east of Poland compare to the north-east of England? A-, is there any similarities, or is it quite different?

**Piotr**: Er, we feel, er, a bit, er, like at home, I think, 'cause we also have, er, many open spaces like, like here, but not so, not so, not so huge mountains and but it's …

**Małgorzata**: No sheep!

**Piotr**: … but it's very familiar for us to, to be here. It's also, er, wild and, er, very, very beautiful landscape.

**Małgorzata**: What happens here is like, the landscape

changes every minute and you have, ha, you have say a postcard here, a postcard there, so we cannot stop taking pictures like Japanese tourists, but, um, we had a chance just to see the Barnard Castle down there on the way up here to the radio, and, but the views were really nice and we liked the colour, maybe we are not, er, really fascinated with the weather, it could have been more stable, I could say, because, um, well, it's really green here, we saw, so I hope we have some more time here in Teesdale to, to find out what nice things you have to offer.

**Peter**: Very good. OK.

## Audio 1.68

**Peter**: Very good. OK. Wh-, wh-, what style of music will people expect to see when they come to Cotherstone on Saturday?

**Małgorzata**: Well, you can sum it up by saying that we used old traditional songs and dances that, er, as Piotr said, we learned from the elders of our land and archive recordings, but, mm, what we do is arrange them in a modern way, or 'modern', um, meaning our own, so we combine tradition and, er, would you say 'modernity'? And we use old instruments, traditional instruments from our region, combined with new ones like guitar, and even our set of drums is the best description of what we do because you have the old drums used for dance music, the frame drums, combined with some new stuff that you would find in a rock band or a jazz band.

**Peter**: Absolutely delightful, and it's great to have you in the studio, and thank you very much for taking time out of your tour, 'cause I know this is one of your rest days today, so very mu-, great thanks for coming in.

**Małgorzata**: Yeah, what can we say? *Zapraszamy*!

# Lesson 23  From thought to action

### Video 8, Part 1

**Hazem**: So we're often asked to think outside of the box, but for a brain scientist, the brain *is* the box. And so sometimes it really helps, when you're trying to study humans, to think like an alien.

Now, I want you all in the audience tonight to think like aliens with me. I'm going to conduct a little experiment, and I promise no alien abductions, I just need everybody in the audience to raise the left arm up. Thank you, excellent job. The experiment is over!

Um, well, if you think that this was dull or boring, it's probably because you were still thinking like a human, but if you were thinking like an alien, you'd be amazed at how the thought that came to your mind changed into action. You'd ask yourself questions like: what is thought to begin with? How does is transform into action? Where does this happen in the brain? And what can possibly go wrong? And they are exactly these questions that make neuroscience search for the answers. And some of the answers we've found out I want to share with you tonight. Some of them you already know, but I hope I'll add a couple of new things.

### Video 8, Part 2

**Hazem**: Well, first, you all know that we have two halves of our brain, er, one is blue and one is red. Just kidding – they're both blue, of course. So, anyway, um, in front, um, of a little crack that you have in your brain, there's what we call the motor area, or the primary motor cortex, and this is basically the part that's responsible for the movement of the opposite side of the brain. But, even before this area, there's what we call the supplementary motor area, which is, basically, sort of an intention centre, because this is where all the planning takes place. So, whenever you only think of an action, or imagine a certain movement, this area is the first part to light up. And when there's good communication between your intention centre and your motion centre, your thought turns into action. So what could possibly happen, if there was a disconnection between your intention and your motion?

### Video 8, Part 3

**Hazem**: So, what could possibly happen, if there was a disconnection between your intention and your motion? Well, in this case, something which is quite amazing happens. A very strange condition arises, in which the person feels as if their hands, their arms, have acquired a mind of their own. And that specifically happens with the left arm, the one that you so easily raised a while ago. And patients with this condition, um, believe that their arms are behaving on their own and, often when they're engaged in really serious stuff like talking to an amazing crowd like you guys, they would discover that their arms are actually moving on their own and they would sometimes never realize what's going on until they see the results of their action, and this could be very embarrassing, especially when they're being judged.

Anyway, this sort of thing is exactly, um, what makes neuroscience so amazing because it tells us so much about our very free will and our consciousness. And there are people like that who have to struggle every day just to make sense of why their bodies are behaving the way they do, that makes us, the healthy people, have to think more of why we go around in our lives feeling completely indifferent to how amazing our brain works.

So, I really think it's a good idea, from time to time, to sit back from your life, enjoy how amazing it is, and think like an alien. Thank you.

# Lesson 24  Read my lips

### Audio 1.69

**Mike**: The same is true for *m*, *m* for *Michael* and *n* for *Nicholas*. They actually sound rather similar, but they look rather different, and so what you find is – this is just sort of gross examples, there are also … it goes more subtly than that – but what you find is if you can see a person – and this is true for people with perfect vision – if you can see a person, you get much more of the content of their speech than if you can't.

### Audio 1.70

**Interviewer**: Just how important is facial expression in communication? Well, joining me now in the studio is Professor Mike Burton, who's a professor of psychology. Hello, welcome to the show, Professor.

**Mike**: Good morning.

**Interviewer**: Now, how important is facial expression when we come to communication?

**Mike**: Well, of course, it's terribly important. Um, faces actually carry all kinds of information, more than you might just think, if you first think about it. So, from somebody's face, you can tell who they are – that's something that's terribly important, of course. You can also tell, roughly, what emotion they're feeling from their expression, um, and it doesn't really matter if you don't know the person or not, you can tell if they're angry or if they're happy, so that's another piece of information. And, er, a third piece is what they're saying, um, most people who have a good view of a face actually use lip-reading a lot more than they realize. So, there's all these different sorts of information that come from faces that we pick up all the time to help us with our communications, and, um, it's only when you sort of lose one of these that you notice – you lose all of them and then you're in a bit of trouble.

## Audio 1.71

**Interviewer**: H-, how much of this is actually, kind of, um, genetic and stamped on us from birth?

**Mike**: Well, what seems to be very clear is that, um, there is a mechanism for noticing faces. Our visual systems are set up to look for them. For example, if you're born and brought up in Japan, you will have a sensitivity to the variations amongst Japanese faces. If you're born and brought up in Scotland, you'll have sensitivity to those variations, and, actually, you'll be worse on the opposite, er, sorts of face. So, I think that what is there from birth, is something rather basic, to look for face, but it doesn't allow you to get the subtleties. The subtleties come later.

**Interviewer**: Because y-, you will find somebody who'll say, er, with a newborn baby, 'Oh, that, that expression, that's just his dad.'

**Mike**: Yes. That's right. A lot of people, er, do say that. I think there's, there's a lot of social and cultural in that, don't you? Where one, one is trying to bring the baby into the family and so forth. Um, the, er, there's some rather unconvincing evidence that you really can tell much about the face from birth, really, about the likeness.

**Interviewer**: So, er, a lot of it is learned behaviour?

**Mike**: Yes. Yes. Now, when it comes to emotions, which is, er, where you started, there, um, there certainly do seem to be some emotions that, er, are just universal. Everybody has them. Er, these I call the big five emotions: happiness, anger and so forth. But the more subtle things certainly are, er, learned and they're more cultural. So, if we go back to the Japanese case, er, Japanese people use certain sorts of smiling for politeness, but it's not the smiling that one would get for, er, spontaneous laughter, for example. So, again, the story seems to be that, what we've got, all of us, all humanity have got, is the basics and then we refine it and make it more subtle, er, according to our cultures and our upbringing.

## Audio 1.72

**Interviewer**: Now, taking it to a, a kind of closer … personally speaking, I have central-vision problems. Now, I've noticed over the years that my hearing's fine, [Yep] but when I'm in a crowded place or quite loud, or in a place with bad light, I seem to not be able to hear what people are saying.

**Mike**: That's, that's such a interesting observation and it is completely borne out by, er, research, um, over many, many years. You know, people with perfect vision use lip-reading all the time, and they don't know that they do it, and, and here's, er, an example of, of where this becomes obvious. I used to live in a village called Fintry, which starts with an *f* for *Freddy*. I never have to spell that out if I'm face to face with somebody, whereas if I'm on the phone, they say is that an *f* or an *s*? And if you think about it, *f* and *s* look really differently, even though they, they sound quite similar. The same is true for *m*, *m* for *Michael* and *n* for *Nicholas*. They actually sound rather similar, but they look rather different, and so what you find is, this is just sort of gross examples, there are also, it goes more subtly than that, but what you find is if you can see a person, and this is true for people with perfect vision, if you can see a person, you get much more of the content of their speech than if you can't, and people have indeed found that in noisy environments, allowing people, for example, er, video-conferencing, er, gives them much better comprehension than telephony. Now i-, in your situation where you are, a, you just cannot, er, resolve the person's lip movements, because you can't see them, you are inevitably going to suffer some loss in, er, in what sounds like hearing, but it actually, it's the full comprehension of the sentence. So, yes, I'm afraid this is a well-documented phenomenon, well known.

**Interviewer**: An-, an-, and as sighted people, we take it for granted, don't we?

**Mike**: Absolutely, don't even notice that you're doing it. So I say this is why one uses the telephone example just to sort of point out a situation where sighted people actually can't see each other routinely, and they say, 'Oh yes, people do ask me to spell it out in that situation.' So, yes, er, studying psychology does give one an appreciation of the things that we all take for granted, actually. You don't even notice they're difficult until you lose the, er, facility with them.

## Audio 1.73

**Interviewer**: So, how, let's take it from a sighted person's, er, point of view. Um, how can you compensate for this, would you think, in a conversation?

**Mike**: Well, one of the, um, things that, er, psychologists have learned is that these, that the different parts of information in a face are processed in rather different ways. So, for example, it's possible to lose the ability to recognize who somebody is, through some brain damage, but still, nevertheless, retain the ability to recognize a, an emotional expression or read lips, and you can us-, lose these things independently. If you actually know what you're aiming at, as it were, if you know what the, er, what the thing, what is being lost by the perceiver, then you can emphasize that. Just take a simple example of emotional expression, I said there were some universal emotional expressions, some are more easy to see than others. So, a smile is a good example, that's by far the easiest thing to see. It makes the biggest effect on the actual physical face, it's a thing that you can see in noisy environments quickest, it's very easy. So, one can imagine accentuating that, as, as the person, er, communicatingwith a partially sighted observer, for example.

**Interviewer**: Professor Mike Burton, it's been a fascinating conversation. Thank you for joining us here on Insight Radio.

**Mike**: Thank you.

## Lesson 25 Pronunciation for listeners 5

### Audio 1.74

1
so there's all these different sorts of information that
there is a mechanism for noticing faces
er, there's some rather unconvincing evidence
there are also, it goes more subtly than that
and I said there are some universal emotional expressions

2
that we pick up all the time
evidence that you really can
some emotions that, er, are just universal
and people have indeed found that in noisy environments
don't even notice that you're doing it

3
you lose all of them and then you're in a bit of trouble
set up to look for them
er, gives them much better
because you can't see them

4
sensitivity to the variations
but the more subtle things certainly are
you get much more of the content of their speech
why one uses the telephone example
retain the ability to recognize

5
it goes more subtly than that
content of their speech than if you can't
some are more easy to see than others

## Audio 1.75
1  I bet you're very proud
2  and I started to cry
3  tell you how I feel about him
4  'cause I knew he was excited
5  and I did, I got very, very emotional
6  but I couldn't bear to watch it
7  I get very nervous for him
8  and I hadn't realized
9  and he had the scars when he came back
10  I'll do it
11  we'll never know 'cause we broke the boat
12  I think one or two people were slightly seasick
13  because, er, you're the great-niece
14  you know what I mean
15  she had very young friends
16  but I can still read my
17  you can do a lot of things on the phone
18  and they'll come and meet me at the bus stop

## Audio 1.76
1  That's, that's such an interesting observation, and it is completely borne out by, er, research, um, over many, many years, you know, people with perfect vision use lip-reading all the time.
2  … in your situation, where you are, er, you just cannot resolve, er, the person's lip movements because you can't see them, you are inevitably going to suffer some loss in, er, in what sounds like hearing, but actually it's the full comprehension of the sentence.

## Audio 1.77
1  it looks absolutely incredible
2  look really differently
3  you've got absolutely the right reaction there
4  it is the most stunning and sumptuous room
5  really impressive entrance hall
6  this is absolutely an amazing room

## Audio 1.78
1  Wow! What is this room where you've brought us to, Claire?
2  A: Three months! That's a long time, isn't it?
   B: That is a long time, actually.
3  A: Now that's bold!
   B: That is bold!

## Audio 1.79
Just how important is facial expression?
There is a mechanism for noticing faces.
A lot of people, er, do say that.
There certainly do seem to be some emotions.
Oh yes, people do ask me to spell it out in that situation.

I think I do love the Baron's Hall.
Studying psychology does give one an appreciation
I think it does obsess us as a nation.
and people have indeed found that in noisy environments
things that, er, psychologists have learned
you will find somebody will say
that you really can tell much about the face

## Lesson 26  University

### Video 9, Part 1
**Alan**: Tell me a bit about universities in your country. What's, um, are you going to university at the moment?
**Ning**: Yeah, I'm still a university student and, er, er, I have graduated from … graduate school [Mm] and I'm planning to, um, go to university in the UK.
**Alan**: Oh great, excellent.
**Ning**: Yeah, I love this place.
**Alan**: It's good, nice to hear, how about you, Maria, are you, um …?
**Maria**: I'm also a student and, and I studied the university in Russia, but probably I will take my Master's degree at the university in the UK, I don't know …
**Alan**: That's nice. Is it expensive to study in your countries?
**Ning**: Actually, I think it depends, because, if you want to, um, enter a private school [Yeah], of course it's really expensive, I mean, and, er, but, if you just, er, at some state university [Yeah], um, it doesn't cost a lot.
**Alan**: Yeah, in England, a lot of students are, are unhappy because it's now maybe £9,000 a year for, [Wow] they have to borrow this from the government, a student loan, and so a lot of students, to be honest, are [It's just a loan] Yeah, and they've got to pay it back. [Yeah, yeah, pay it back.]
**Ning**: So that's the reason why they needed to take a gap year?
**Alan**: Yeah, some people just, er, go away and try and earn some money to, to help, er, do this, um, [Oh!] um, so, so they have a lot of debt at the end of, of their time, so in England at the moment, this is a bit of a, a big issue and, um, student numbers are actually falling a bit, um …

### Video 9, Part 2
**Alan**: How do you pay for it in, in Russia and China, do you have to pay yourself or does the government help?
**Ning**: Actually, if you are doing the Bachelor degree [Yeah] you needed to pay for yourself … but, er, if you, you can enter the postgraduate school to get a, a higher degree like a Master or PhD, um, you don't needed to pay anything. [Oh, that's] you [Really] you can get a, er, get a different amount of money [Yeah] to support your living cost.
**Alan**: That's quite nice, and in Russia, do you, do you get mu-, help from the government?
**Maria**: Er, personally, I don't pay for my studies [Nice!] at university, because, er, in, I think that, er, in almost all the universities in Russia there are several positions [Um] for students with the best results [Um] of the exams who can get scholarship …
**Alan**: Oh, that's great!
**Maria**: … from the government [Yes] and so I don't pay for the university, and every month government gives me a small amount of money to support myself [Ah, excellent, yes] and you also can apply for different grants and, um, yes, er, I don't know, a foreign, different money, for example, if you do some research, [Yeah] you can, um, present your project to judges and they will decide if, whether they give you money or don't.

**Alan**: That's a really good idea. That's really nice. And i-, d-, is it hard work at university, as a student, do you have to get a lot of homework, are you working …

**Ning**: Actually, it's kind of different from the high school [Be honest] be, be honest, yes, um, it's easier than the, than the studies where you … [Is it really?] Yeah. [Easier than high school?] There is, actually, no homework, I mean, only, er, maybe [Yep] little homework, yes, you, you are not forced to do the homework, you can, if, you, even if you got it, the homework, [Yeah, yeah] you can just leave it away, and, er, have some fun …

**Maria**: But it stays until the end of the term, and at the end of the term you have to do everything.

**Ning**: The last two weeks, the last two weeks …

**Alan**: Yeah, so that …

**Ning**: … is hard … [Busy!] Yeah!

### Video 9, Part 3

**Alan**: And what's the accommodation and things like, er, is it easy to find a, a place to live at university, or do they help you with this, or do you have to live in a student house?

**Maria**: If you don't pay for the university, and if you get scholarship, the university provides you with a student's house, [Oh, that's really …] with a room at the student's house, but, er, normally, er, the accommodation's not very good, frankly speaking, in Russia, so, oh, most, some students prefer to, for example, to rent a flat [Um, yeah] or to share a flat with someone, so it is not [Yeah] so expensive, but it's better.

**Alan**: That's nice, yeah.

**Ning**: Actually, in China it's quite different because you, no matter which degree you want to get, um, the university will pro-, pro-, provide you the accommodation.

**Alan**: Do they really? That's quite good.

**Ning**: Yes, and it's cheap, it's quite cheap. So, um, nearly all of the students they choose to stay in the apartment or residentials, yes.

**Alan**: Ah, nice. In England, it tends to be the first year you get a hall of residence, but then the next two years or three years you've got to find your own, your own place.

**Ning**: You need to move out?

**Alan**: Yeah, you have to move out, um, they don't guarantee, er, accommodation now after the first year. Sometimes you …

**Ning**: Because there is no enough?

**Alan**: No, there's not enough and the, they always let the new students go there first [Oh] so experienced ones get, um, well, it's, it's fun, but it's sometimes quite expensive, um, [Yeah] you know, you've got to find accommodation for, for everyone.

**Maria**: But I find that, for example, if you study at the university of Cambridge, you, it is compulsory to stay, er, in the halls of residence and pay for, for it.

**Alan**: Er, yeah, some of these, Oxford and Cambridge, I think, you get more opportunity to stay within the small colleges so they're, they're in a slightly better position.

## Lesson 27  Speed on ice

### Audio 2.1

**Presenter**: Julie has arrived. Hello, Julie. [Hi] Hello, how are you doing today?

**Julie**: Fine, thank you.

**Presenter**: Julie is, of course, er, John, who is currently over in, er, Vancouver at the Olympic Games, John Jackson, in the bobsleigh. This is his mum. I bet you're very proud.

**Julie**: I am – very, very proud of what he's achieved. I can't explain, I can't tell, start to tell you how I feel about him, [Um] just bursting with pride.

### Audio 2.2

**Presenter**: Julie has arrived. Hello, Julie. [Hi] Hello, how are you doing today?

**Julie**: Fine, thank you.

**Presenter**: Julie is, of course, er, John, who is currently over in, er, Vancouver at the Olympic Games, John Jackson in the bobsleigh. This is his mum. I bet you're very proud.

**Julie**: I am – very, very proud of what he's achieved. I can't explain, I can't tell, start to tell you how I feel about him, [I] just bursting with pride.

**Presenter**: I was going to say, what sort of, you've just said it's quite hard, but what sort of emotions were you going through, even when you see him? For example, er, in the opening ceremony, knowing that he's going to be there. What was that feeling like?

**Julie**: Well, he actually, er, we sat up and he actually text me at ten past one in the morning, before it had actually started at quarter to three, quarter to two, and he'd said, 'Oh Mam, I'm lining up now to go out, you know, for the ceremony.' And I started to cry, I got very emotional. It was just 'cause I knew he was excited and so proud of himself to do that, to let me know just how he was feeling. Um, and I did, I got very, very emotional. I'm just so proud of him. Yeah.

**Presenter**: What is it like, from a mother's point of view, watching your son go or get up to 95 de-, er, miles per hour in a little bit of a cart thing on some ice?

**Julie**: Um, well, I try to watch. There was one race he had in Germany, the first run, oh dear me, he rattled down the ski sl-, like the slope and, um, I was, I thought, I was convinced he was going to turn over. And so, he made it through, and he went to the second round, so I sat on the stairs, I wouldn't watch it, but actually, he did really, really well on the second run. I think he just gets nervous first run, but I couldn't bear to watch it, but I watched it, the replay, back and it was fine. It's, I do get nervous, I get very nervous for him.

**Presenter**: Has he, um, has he ever had any accidents doing his sport?

**Julie**: Oh, yes, yeah. Um, he was once, as he was driving, but he was brake man, um, for the GB1, and I was actually watching it on TV and I hadn't realized it was John that was pulled out of the back of the sled, the speed, um, until he kind of stood up and hung over a wall and I thought it was just the actions. I knew it was him. Um, and he had the scars when he came back, ice burns right down his back, on his elbows, shoulders. It was really bad. Um, but you just, he said, you've just got to get back in and do it, otherwise you wouldn't, you wouldn't get back in again.

### Audio 2.3

**Presenter**: Now, I imagine, I imagine a lot of people have mentioned this before, but the film *Cool Runnings*, does, is John totally sick of people sort of making comparisons between, er, him and *Cool Runnings* in any way?

**Julie**: No. But believe it or not, that was the, er, film that they requested to play on the plane over to Vancouver, so they played that, 'cause he said it's quite amusing, yeah, they say they look at that, but you can see the funny side to it, you know, as well, so …

**Presenter**: And has he got a lucky egg? That's the question? Does he kiss his lucky egg?

**Julie**: I don't know, I'll have to ask him about that, if he has, um, if he's got, you know, a set little way of what he does before he sets off. I know he likes to hold his, he puts his, um, hand up to his head. He has certain mannerisms. Just before he sets off. [Same ritual, isn't it?] Same, yeah, every time.

**Presenter**: Is he quite superstitious, then?

**Julie**: I don't know. I just don't know if that's just the way he likes to set off with his hands, it's a salute [What does he do when he's driving the car?] Oh, yes, when he drives the car, oh, he'll tell me off for this, he does a hundred-point check before he sets off. His mirror, wide mirror, this, knobs, everything. Then he'll set away. It takes him ten minutes.

**Presenter**: His normal car? When he just jumps in a car?

**Julie**: Oh yeah, everything has to be right.

### Audio 2.4

**Presenter**: What do you think his chances are of a medal? Has he spoke about this?

**Julie**: Um, he wants to get within te-, top ten, 15, but I know how determined he is, and anything can happen. I've been watching the skiing and, you know, there's people that they say, 'Ah, these are the top three,' fine, but actually the pressure's on them to perform, where with John it's not. And he's really very determined person. He likes to be perfect and they've been practising, so I believe he could win a gold. You want, but you've got to have that belief. You can't go there without having a belief, a-, but he'll give it his best. That's all. He'll give it a hundred and ten per cent. That's all I can say.

## Lesson 28  The science of the small

### Audio 2.5

1 not quite as small as what they do (x3)
2 smaller than the width of a human hair (x3)
3 bigger than an atom (x3)
4 a lot smaller than, for example, a bacterium (x3)

### Audio 2.6

**Interviewer**: And we're in for a treat now on, on the show because, er, we're joined by, um, Annela Seddon, nanotechnologist, and the word 'nanotechnology' is bandied around all, all, all over the place, er, what is it? And, er, what's, what does it mean? So we're going to find out about that because i-, it, it is one of the most exciting areas of science, and certainly one of the most important. OK. Well, we should talk about what nanoscience is.

**Annela**: 'Nano' actually comes from the Greek for 'dwarf', so the whole idea that it's small science, um, I think the particle physicists would argue that it's not quite as small as what they do with their quarks and subatomic particles, but nanoscience itself, um, the 'nano' bit, tells us that we're dealing with objects on a scale that are one billionth of a metre.

**Interviewer**: Yeah.

**Annela**: So, about ten thousand times or so smaller than the width of a human hair. So, bigger than an atom but a lot smaller than, for example, a bacterium or a red blood cell or something like that, so, um, that kind of size range. We talk normally about one to a hundred nanometres is the sort of nanoscience area. We work in that size range, particularly because, at that sort of size scale, the properties of materials get really interesting and they start to change, and it's these kind of properties that we want to harness and be able to actually use to do kind of cool new experiments.

### Audio 2.7

**Interviewer**: How did th-, this idea f-, well, the, the, the subject itself come into being, you know, because, yeah, we've, er, over the years, we've been digging deeper and deeper and deeper and understanding more and more about the atom, but suddenly people were talking, wh-, when I was a kid, people weren't talking about nanoscience, I mean not, it wasn't a, a common thing to hear, but, but now you hear it all the time.

**Annela**: So there was a lecture in 1959, quite a famous lecture, and, and, it's, um, it's written up faithfully in, er, a fantastic book, er, by Richard Feynman, it's called *The Pleasure of Finding Things Out*, and the lecture is called *There's Plenty of Room at the Bottom*, and Feynman set out this idea that the science of the future would involve manipulating materials, manipulating matter on the atomic scale, actually being able to pick up and place atoms exactly where we wanted them to build molecules, to build materials, to build everything from very tiny things all the way up to huge things, but exactly how we wanted them, and he set out a challenge to scientists to work out a way that we could actually do this, to work out a way that we could measure and manipulate things on this scale, 'cause at the time, we didn't really have that kind of technology, we didn't really know how to do this, and it wasn't until about the early eighties that, um, people started to invent different types of, er, methods, um, to actually not only see things on the atomic scale, but to manipulate them.

**Interviewer**: Er, um, you were talking about Richard Feynman, er, earlier, and of course he, one of the things he memorably sai-, I mean he's al-, he's frequently quoted chap, um, an-, an-, and for anyone who doesn't know him, he, he, he was a very famous, er, physicist, er, did some really significant work, but he was also very good at talking about himself and telling stories about himself, which are wonderful and, er, and very entertaining, and he, he was a great popularizer of science, but one of the things that he said, of course, about, about this was, 'If you think you've understood quantum mechanics, you haven't understood quantum mechanics,' because it is such a weird and mysterious world, isn't it, where really odd things happen?

### Audio 2.8

**Annela**: When you think about some materials that we think we know very well in our metre-scale world, and we think about what happens to them when we make them smaller, even on that scale things get really, really strange. So if I give you a piece of aluminium foil, for example, that you could wrap round a chicken and put it in the oven and cook it, if I took that piece of aluminium foil and I cut it up and I cut it up, and I made it smaller and smaller and smaller until it got down to the nano-scale, it would become explosive, and it's to do with how the surface of that particle changes, the surface of that material changes as it gets smaller, so more of the material is on the surface as the particle gets smaller, and that means that all of the properties, all of the things we know that happen on the metre scale stop behaving how we expect, which is really quite interesting, so a material that's totally inert in the normal world, as soon as it's shrunk down to the nano-world suddenly takes on a whole set of properties that we didn't expect – it might change colour, it might change electrical conductivity, it might become magnetic, it might do anything, and the great thing, I think, about working on this scale is sometimes, we have no idea about what the material is going to do when we make it smaller, and this is where we can start to harness these interesting properties, and we can actually start to do interesting science with them, and so that, that for me, I think, is one of the greatest things about doing this type of sciences, this whole raft of unpredictable properties that, you know, you would never expect something that you can make an aeroplane out of, that's hopefully fairly inert, suddenly becomes explosive when it comes down to that, that tiny size scale.

**Interviewer**: That's really freaky and very, very interesting indeed.

# Lesson 29  Studying abroad

## Audio 2.9

**A**:  Now, with tuition fees set to rocket up to £9,000 a year for university students starting their courses next September, many young people are looking at alternatives like studying abroad. The Netherlands is becoming more popular with British students, who can take their degree courses in English, and in many cases, it costs less than studying a similar course in the UK.

**B**: I imagine, you know, when, when, the, when the fee prices go up for us next, I imagine it, I'd expect the amount of people applying to go up, but Dutch isn't a popular language in Britain, so do you reckon, do you reckon it would be easy for students to study at the university, or would it take a bit of work?

## Audio 2.10

**Interviewer**: This is The Basement on Pure. Now, with tuition fees set to rocket up to £9,000 a year for university students starting their courses next September, many young people are looking at alternatives like studying abroad. The Netherlands is becoming more popular with British students, who can take their degree courses in English, and in many cases, it costs less than studying a similar course in the UK. Sandra von Beit, from the University of Applied Sciences Utrecht, is our guest. Welcome to The Basement, Sandra.

**Sandra**: Thank you.

**Interviewer**: Um, so, have you seen an increase in applications from British students already, or does it still seem to be a bit under the radar?

**Sandra**: Er, not as many as we expected, er, we've got 36, er, students from the UK here at the moment, and, er, we're expecting more applications from the UK, but we haven't seen that many yet.

**Interviewer**: I imagine, you know, when, when, the, when the fee prices go up for us next, I imagine it, I'd expect the amount of people applying to go up, but Dutch isn't a popular language in Britain, so do you reckon, do you reckon it would be easy for students to study at the university, or would it take a bit of work?

**Sandra**: No, er, there are students from all over the world that go to Holland, um, I think there are 1,500 English, er, degree programmes in Holland at the moment, so yes, it's, it's quite famous for its, er, er, English programmes. I know, for example, Germany, you would really have to learn German to go there, or France, the same, but in Holland, you know, people speak English on the street, and, er, or they'll speak Dutch, but everybody pretty much speaks English on the side as a second language, and, er, yeah, and, er, the degrees, or the programmes are in English.

**Interviewer**: So Sandra, tell me a little bit more about your university.

**Sandra**: OK, the University of Applied Sciences Utrecht has about 40,000 students, so it's quite a large university, er, also quite international – the students come from, er, all over the world, er, we've got five English-taught Bachelor courses, which are mainly, er, business-related or communications, um, it's a university of applied science, which, which means it's very practical – you'll be doing, er, two internships, for example, you'll be working in projects and in companies at the same time.

**Interviewer**: Um, so, Sandra, some students might fancy the idea of studying abroad, um, but be worried that future employers might not value the final qualification. Do you think this is the case?

**Sandra**: No, I don't think they have to worry about that – er, a Bachelor in Holland has the same value as a Bachelor in the UK, and all our courses are internationally accredited, so they shouldn't have to worry, and, er, I know in a lot of cases they can do a double degree, where they will get a, a degree from a UK university as well, we've got quite a few partners, er, in the UK.

**Interviewer**: Fantastic.

## Audio 2.11

**Interviewer**: And now I'm, I'm going to bring in Paul Holloway now, he presents our punk show on Thursday nights, um, the reason being he's actually studied in Utrecht. So, er, Paul, you know, what was it like? Would, would you recommend the lifestyle?

**Paul**: Oh, definitely. Um, I mean it was 15 years ago that I was, er, a student in Utrecht, um, but it wasn't, I wasn't there for the full time of my, er, course, I was only there for, er, my year out, and I spent six months, er, at the university in Utrecht, which has fantastic facilities, at the Applied Science university, which is out of town on a great campus, and then I spent six months working in the south of Holland in Eindhoven for Phillips. You learn so much about yourself as well as the country where you are, um, 'cause when you go backpacking, you, you kind of get a feeling for a place, but you never really get under the skin of a country until you've lived there for a couple of months and really integrated into the way that people do things. You learn so much about yourself. You learn so much about the place where you're staying, but you also learn things about Britain, some things which, very subtle differences in business and in the way that we socialize. The Dutch do things differently. Sometimes you might think they've got it right, sometimes we've got it right. Um, but it opens your mind, and, er, it's, it's a fantastic experience for young people and I'd recommend it. I met my wife when I was out in Utrecht, although she is English, I've got Dutch friends, I've been invited to weddings in France and Italy, it was definitely the best year of my life.

**Interviewer**: Fantastic.
**Paul**: I had a fantastic time.
**Interviewer**: But I suppose, um, one thing that a lot of people want to know is what is it like as a student city …

## Audio 2.12

**Paul**: Oh, Utrecht is absolutely, what do you think, Sandra? It's, it's a brilliant student town, isn't it, there's a big student population.

**Sandra**: It is, yeah. It's very popular with Dutch students as well, I mean, um, it's very close to Amsterdam, but it's, you know, it's the biggest student city, I think, er, one out of every five residents is a student, so no, it's, it's, it's a lot of fun.

## Audio 2.13

**Paul**: And there's really great café culture, the c-, old canal that winds through the middle of the city is really pretty, er, there's s-, I mean, if you're worried about missing out on popular culture, you don't have to worry about that, because there's a, a train that goes right into Amsterdam, right through the night, so you can go and see all the, I mean, you see some great bands, all the biggest bands like Oasis and Radiohead, that are playing stadiums, we could see them in small venues in Utrecht or in Amsterdam, so there's plenty going on out there, and I think also, a lot of students nowadays in, specially in Stockport, there's this feeling that when you're choosing a university, because Manchester's such a great city, [Mm] and it's on our doorstep, it's only seven miles away, and there's three or four really good universities to choose from, a lot of people take that decision to stay at home, and I understand that because it's so expensive, so much more expensive than when I was a student, but I kind of think you're missing out a little bit on the student experience, because you only get to do this once, [Yeah] and I know how much debt students have to get into nowadays and I know it's hard, but getting away from the town where you grew up, and getting away and meeting new people who are doing the same thing as you, you find out so much about yourself, and that is so much part of the student experience, and to do it in a foreign country is even more of a step, isn't it? But Utrecht, it's so close, [Yeah] it's so cheap, um, to get over there on a cheap flight or even on a coach if you book it in advance, and if you need to get, if something terrible happens at home and you need to get back in a hurry, you can be back in a couple of hours, it rea-, you know, it's not like you're going to the other end of the world.
**Interviewer**: Yeah, um, so, I suppose best get down to the figures side of it now. Um, Sandra, what's the typical cost of a course at the university?
**Sandra**: Er, it's 1,672 euros per year, which works to 1,400 and something pounds, I think.
**Interviewer**: That's i-, that's just, it is a no-brainer, that's more than *half* the current fees, never mind when they, when they go up, how do they manage to keep it so cheap?
**Sandra**: Well, the government subsidises for all European students, so that's why it's quite low, um, and what students can do is they work on the side sometimes, you know, if they work for 32 hours for example in a bar, or in a, in a restaurant or in a supermarket, they can get an additional, er, grant, but if you work it out, then I think in the end it's, it's cheaper to study in Holland than stay in the UK with, er, with those fees.
**Interviewer**: You're not kidding, I mean, that is, that is mind-blowing figures, that's, you know, really is making me think twice anyway about where I'm going, um, but so, where can people find out more?
**Sandra**: www.international.hu.nl, um, there's a lot of information on specific programmes, what the costs are, they can chat to international students and get, you know, read blogs from other international students.
**Interviewer**: Thanks a lot for chatting to us today, Sandra, it's been, it's really helpful for me anyway, being a student myself, um, yeah, all the best in the future.
**Sandra**: Great, thank you so much for this.
**Radio ID**: Stockport's Pure 107.8 FM.

# Lesson 30 Pronunciation for listeners 6

## Audio 2.14

| | | |
|---|---|---|
| 1 | bigger **than an atom** | the na natom (x4) |
| 2 | **it's written up** faithfully in, er, a fantastic book | it srit nup (x4) |
| 3 | **and we think about** what happens | an we thin kabout (x4) |
| 4 | **even on** that scale | eva non (x4) |
| 5 | **cut it up** | ka ti tup (x4) |
| 6 | **suddenly takes on a** | suddenly take so na (x4) |
| 7 | **the great thing I think about** | the great thing a thin kabout (x4) |
| 8 | I know how **determined he is** | determin di yiz (x4) |
| 9 | **stopped at the scene** | stop tat the scene (x4) |
| 10 | covering his **mouth and nose** | mau than nose (x4) |

## Audio 2.15

| | | |
|---|---|---|
| 1 | smaller and smaller and smaller | small a run small a run smaller (x4) |
| 2 | they're able to, like, vote for a nest | they're reible to like vote fa ra nest (x4) |
| 3 | lay more eggs rather than laying their own | lay more reggs rather than laying their rown (x4) |
| 4 | to be able to actually use | to be yable to wakshaly use |
| 5 | funny side to it | funny side to wit (x4) |
| 6 | lucky egg | lucky yegg (x4) |
| 7 | at around two a.m. | at around two way yem |

## Audio 2.16

1 tell us a little bit about, about their intelligence
2 tell me a bit about universities in your country
3 develop a little bit of a
4 tell me a little bit more about
5 could you tell me a little bit about that
6 to tell us a little bit more
7 stick out a little bit
8 in England at the moment, this is a bit of a, a big issue
9 can you tell us a little bit about that?
10 you can tell me a little bit more about it in a minute
11 tell me a little bit about
12 in a little bit of a cart thing

## Audio 2.17

1 they have something called *nomihodai* (x3)
2 but, er, sort of, interesting, and (x3)
3 something occurs to me (x3)
4 but exactly how we wanted them (x3)
5 what is it like from a mother's point of view (x3)
6 the way he likes to set off with (x3)
7 ten per cent drop in premature birth rates (x3)
8 quiet mountain (x3)
9 what it involves, etcetera (x3)
10 I don't know nothing about it (x3)

## Audio 2.18

1 he turn on his computer
2 when I go out
3 and I usually ask, er, the people
4 you live in, er, Portsmouth in UK
5 I will, er, tell this story to my friends and my family
6 because I live in a hostel

# Lesson 31  Technology

## Video 10, Part 1
**Ezgi**: Er, I, maybe 20 times, I always check my email, it's so important for me, I, I always look at Facebook, what else, yeah, just email and Facebook.

**Tom**: Um, well, I do use Facebook quite a lot to stay in touch with people, um, I also use a program called Grooveshark, which is sort of free music streaming, you don't get to keep the music, so it's not theft, which I disagree with, so it's kind of like radio that you can choose almost, yeah. And YouTube.

**Thuy**: I think I am not use, er, much technology than the other one, um, I just use this in my job, and after that, after I come back home, I, um, never, never touch this, and I think it's good because I don't want to relies on technology too much, it will interfere my privacy, and I think we have to enjoy our life in many ways, not, er, not only depends on technology.

\*\*\*

**Tom**: Um, well, I guess my phone is something that I … I guess I could live without it, but it would make my life very, sort of difficult, compared to what I'm used to now, um, certainly, I, sort of, can't really imagine, you know, having to remember all my friends' phone numbers, and phone the landline to their house now, so, yeah, my mobile phone, er, also for the internet access, you know, if ever something occurs to me, 'Oh, I wonder what, you know, this is or that is', you know, I can quickly Google it and find out about it, so it's, yeah, it's really useful, I wouldn't like to part with that.

**Thuy**: In my case, er, I myself can't live without a washing machine, because I think, um, I think I'm lazy person, so, and my, er, job, very busy, er, so I, usually put on my clothes, er, into a washing machine almost, er, two times, er, per week, so I think I can't be, I can't live without it, and it's useful.

**Ezgi**: iPhone! You know, nowadays, people, er, love, people love iPhone because, er, you can download a lot of apps, it's easily important, especially the social media, er, apps, for example, Facebook, Twitter, er, Skype – Skype is really important for me because I live in, I am living in the UK so I want to contact with my family, er, that's why I just use Skype to contact them, it's really important. Facebook, you know, it's very, it's, er, so pop-, Facebook is so popular.

## Video 10, Part 2
**Thuy**: My favourite, er, website is, er, BBC, er, BBC, er, world news, I usually, um, surf internet about that website because it's useful to my, to my job now, I'm editors and every day I have to make world news, so I have to locate it, locate the news and some information a-, around the world so I usually use it.

**Ezgi**: Yeah, my favourite website is, yeah, Science Daily, Science Daily that's called, it's really, how can I say, benefit for me because I'm engineer, so I have to follow, er, developments in my area, in my special area, for example, I'm chemical engineer, so I have to foll-, I'm, er, spec-, specialized in energy, so I have to, er, follow which developments to-, today, er, which developments, er, happens, for example, about biomass or … bioreactor or the other things, new energy, renewable energy.

\*\*\*

**Tom**: Er, yeah, definitely computers, you know, um, I mean, I remember being six years old and there was a BBC computer with a big, you know, kind of plastic disks with like two colours on the screen or something. Now, I mean in the, in the palm of my hand on my phone, it's just, it's as vivid as real life, pretty much now, it's amazing, you know.

**Ezgi**: Telephone, I think, cellphone – cellphone is really important. When I was young, there's no cellphone, so yeah, I was, after I was, er, ten years old, yeah, my brother, er, had first cellphone, so I am, I can't believe this, you can, er, contact to him whenever you want, it's really important, I think and, yeah, actually, no, definitely cellphones.

\*\*\*

**Thuy**: I think, er, in the near future, um, maybe mobile phone, smartphone, will be more and more developed, and people will have more idea about, er, invent, inventing new kinds of smartphone, er, because especially young people, they like to use it, because it's useful, and, er, it have our life more and more convenient, and more and more comfortable, and I think in the near future, the, this will be a famous trend in, er, smartphone.

**Tom**: Um, well, I guess, I mean there, there seems to be some progress being made on, um, sort of, electric cars, or you know, just cars that use alternative fuel, and, maybe a car that sort of runs on water, you know, if we can separate the molecules and sort of use the hydrogen or something.

# Lesson 32  Breaking news

## Audio 2.19
1  A man was found dead (x3)
2  The man, who has not yet been named (x3)
3  Police were called (x3)
4  where he was pronounced dead (x3)

## Audio 2.20
**Announcer 1**: 91.8 Hayes FM
**Announcer 2**: Local news summary
**Presenter**: A man was found dead in the early hours of Tuesday morning at Hanwell Flight. The man, who has not yet been named, was discovered at around 2 a.m. by a stretch of the Grand Union Canal. Police were called to the Grand Union Canal following the discovery of the body. The 41-year-old man was taken to hospital, where he was pronounced dead. Enquiries are underway to establish the circumstances of the incident.

## Audio 2.21
**Presenter**: A tube passenger who was killed after falling onto tracks has been named as 23-year-old Michaela Hayden from Uxbridge. Miss Hayden was pronounced dead at the scene of the incident on the Jubilee Line platform at Finchley Road station on April the 16th. The police have said they do not consider the death to be suspicious.

A teenage boy is in a serious but stable condition after a crash in Heston. The 15-year-old was involved in a collision with a car in New Heston Road on Tuesday the 24th of April at around 1 p.m. He was taken by helicopter to the Royal London Hospital in Whitechapel with a head injury. The boy, believed to have been a Hounslow Manor School pupil, had just got off the 111 bus heading towards Hounslow when the incident happened. The driver of the car involved in the collision stopped at the scene. No one has been arrested. Anyone with any information is asked to contact the police on 101.

## Audio 2.22
**Presenter**: Police are appealing for witnesses after two extremely valuable watches were stolen in broad daylight during a violent mugging. The 23-year-old victim was on

his way to sell the watches, worth between 20 to 30 thousand pounds, when he was confronted by two men at around 2.30 p.m. on Wednesday the 15th of February. He began walking in the direction of the Broadway, when the suspects then punched him and threw him to the floor. They grabbed his bag containing the watches and ran off in the direction of West Avenue. He needed hospital treatment, but was later discharged. The first man is described as white, around six feet tall, and aged around 26 to 27. He was wearing a grey scarf around his face covering his mouth and nose. The second male was black, around six feet tall, and also aged around 26 to 27. He was wearing a dark-coloured hooded jumper with the hood up, and a black-and-white scarf around his face covering his mouth and nose. Anyone with any information is asked to contact the incident room on 0208 721 7253.

Police and ordinance experts have removed an unexploded Second World War bomb from the former national air-traffic control site in West Drayton. The device was taken to the Stockley Park area and safely detonated shortly after 3 p.m. The Portisway site is now a housing development, incorporating a garden village with nearly 800 homes. Police say the suspect device was found in the Park West area of the site and all the relevant safety precautions were taken.

Two film students from the University of West London have won a prestigious festival award for their documentary. John Gordon and Nico Alijoki, from the University's Ealing School of Art, Design and Media, were awarded the British Film Institute's Future Film Festival documentary award for under-25s.

## Audio 2.23
**Presenter**: And finally, since Scotland was the first to introduce a ban on smoking in public places, there has been a ten-per-cent drop in premature birth rates, a drop in heart disease and childhood asthma, to name but three. Though not conclusive yet, the body of evidence seems to suggest a link. So, is it time to shift the emphasis on the home and confined spaces like the car when children are present?

## Audio 2.24
**A**: When the people want to smoke, they will smoke anyway. Yes, you can do some kind of campaign, even more to raise the awareness of the, that influence of the smoking when children are around, but I think, like a instinct is telling you once you are pregnant, you don't want to smoke if you are seriously thinking about your child. If you don't, no matter who will say and no matter how much they will know about this, they will still, still smoke, otherwise there will be like a police country when everything will be from the government say you can do this or you cannot do that, but on the other hand, how are you going to punish people at home? What are you going to have cameras in the house? Then you cannot press the charges against, so that is against their human rights.

**B**: No, I think the parents should show responsibility if, if they are smokers in the home or in the car, to know that smoking's bad for the children, so leave it to the parents, that's up to individuals themselves. People are well aware of the dangers of cigarette smoking, so they should show responsibility to their children.

**C**: I don't personally smoke, but obviously, parents should know not to smoke round their kids obviously 'cause of the asthma, so it's a good idea in some ways, but then parents sh-, should know not to smoke around their kids? But no, I don't think it would work, 'cause it's people in their own cars, isn't it? So …

**D**: No, I still think people should have the choice to be able to smoke in their cars or in their homes, even if there are children around.

**Presenter**: That's all for now. My names is Anu Baines. If you have a local news story, email our office at hayesfm.org or call 0208 573 7992 with your details. Up next is a summary of the weather and travel, and that'll be followed by what's on and things to do in your area.

**Announcer**: That's your local news, working together with local papers, *The Gazette*, *The Times*, *The Leader* and *The Chronicle*.

## Lesson 33  The future of paper
### Video 11, Part 1
**Monika**: Time is passing by all the time. And although everything that surrounds us seems to be stable and durable, it is in fact constantly drawn by a mechanism that slowly but consequently leads to its total discomposition. And if we wanted to preserve an idea for hundreds of years, what do we save it on? On stone? Well, the storage capacity is not very big. On parchment? It's too costly and not very humane. On magnetic tape? It will start to demagnetize in about 30 to 50 years. On CD-ROM? We begin to lose information after two to five years. On USB? Well, my last one burnt after a year. In the clouds? So shredded bytes of information stored all over the world.

### Video 11, Part 2
**Monika**: Well, yes, as a civilization, we really had a lot of ideas what to store our data on, like these big floppy disks, or tape memory banks that, er, data from probes – Viking – to Mars were stored in. Well, 20 per cent of that precious data is already irreversibly gone. The rest can be read by a digital archaeologist – and yes, a job like that exists already. So, let's think of good old paper for a moment. Paper, therefore cellulose, therefore long chains of repeating fragments. Each fragment is a ring, um, composed of atoms of carbon, hydrogen and oxygen. Each ring is bent in a very energetically stable chair conformation in which the molecule can take a long rest – therefore paper is stable, it's long-lasting.

### Video 11, Part 3
**Monika**: Of course, unless we don't improve on the paper-making process, and the, it becomes less durable, and we did just that in the middle of 19th century when we used a very acidic component, er, in the paper. And I'm sure you, you know what I'm talking about: it's the books that smell in a specific way, have yellowed pages, and we've, when we try to read them, they decompose in our hands. Well, why's that? It's because in the paper, the acidic environment left an intruder in the form of cat-, er, hydrogen cation. This cation accelerates breaking of the chains in a process called hydrolysis. Now, shorter chains means weaker paper. Fortunately, today we can de-acify the book, and thus get rid of the annoying intruder.

So books printed nowadays on a good-quality paper can last 300, 400 years, and what's best is we can read them with tools most available to human beings, which is the eye, the brain and the hand.

Time is passing by all the time, but we as a civilization are not yet ready for the book to pass away. Thank you.

# Lesson 34  A life in the music business

## Audio 2.25
yeah, no, you know, it's just one of those things like anything else
so that, you know, that was quite a while ago
and so you don't really stop, you know
but it wasn't until like, you know, The Beatles
but I, you know, so it, I just got involved and
artists didn't do that back then, you know, you did covers
a guitar and, you know, 40 years of songs

## Audio 2.26
**Katie**: Dennis, the voice of Dr Hook, welcome to Radio Teesdale today.
**Dennis**: How are you?
**Katie**: I'm really good. How are you?
**Dennis**: Good. It's been a long time since I've been the voice of Dr Hook, though!
**Katie**: Does, does it really seem that long ago?
**Dennis**: Er, well, yeah, no, you know, it's one of those things, like anything else, it, sometimes it seems like it was yesterday, but if I really take a deep breath and think about it, the farewell tour was in 1985, so that, you know … that was quite a while ago!

## Audio 2.27
**Katie**: I mean, the, if you actually, I think sometimes you actually probably have to pinch yourself because the, the statistics of this are amazing. You were the recipient of over 60 gold and platinum albums, gaining number one in the charts in 42 different countries. It's just craziness, isn't it? Do you ever have to sort of stop and pinch yourself sometimes?
**Dennis**: No, you know, you know why I don't, because that all happened, that all happened, like, in sequence and it just kind of happens, you know what I mean, it's not until it's all over and you look back on it, and you think, wow! You know wh-, when I really realize that? When somebody like yourself introduces me.
**Katie**: So you, when you were in your height of fame, in Dr Hook, did you never, did none of you guys ever think, 'Do you know what, we're massive?'? Was it just sort of, like, the eye of the storm, as it were? You were just in there and everything else [Yeah] was going on.
**Dennis**: Yeah, you know what it is? Every time you had a hit record, you'd think, now we have to have another one, you know what I mean? Everything you do makes you think about the next thing you need to do, and so you don't really stop, you know.

## Audio 2.28
**Katie**: Now, your voice is instantly recognizable. When did you first discover you had this talent to sing?
**Dennis**: Um, I always liked music when I was a kid, and my mom was very young. My mom was 19 years old when I was born. So, in some ways, she was a still kid herself, and she had very young friends, and she listened to a lot of music and she loved singers. She loved all the great voices back then, er, Nat King Cole and Johnny Mathis and Arthur Price and Dinah Washington, Sam Cooke and so I grew up listening to a lot of really good voices. But, um, so I was always a fan, but it wasn't until, like, you know, The Beatles, and all the groups started coming to America, that I thought, ooh, maybe I should do this. So it was probably because I saw a bunch of girls screaming and I was 14 and I thought, 'Ooh that looks like a good job. Probably, if I was a plumber, they wouldn't do that!' you know. But I, you know, so, it, I just got involved and, and then it, it just carries on, I suppose.
**Katie**: Now, you're a massive fan of The Beatles, is that right? [Yeah, yeah] You're a huge fan.
**Dennis**: Yeah, yeah, yeah, yeah, huge fan. I mean, a-, a lot, the music was wonderful, the band was wonderful, the personalities. It just changed the face of show business and the music business, but, again, for me, like I just told you, it was the thing that opened my eyes, you know. It was really the thing that opened my eyes, and thought 'Ooh, maybe, maybe this is something that I should be involved in.' So, yeah, I, if you came to where I live right now, and look around, you would think I was in The Beatles!
**Katie**: Nothing wrong with Dr Hook mania, that's something to dream for! Um, what was your favourite album by the way, an era of The Beatles, are we going for early stuff, later stuff?
**Dennis**: I like *Rubber Soul* and the reason I like *Rubber Soul*, I think, was because it was the first album ever that they wrote every song on it, and artists didn't do that back then, you know. You did covers, you did whatever songs. But that was, that was the first album that r-, every song on there was written by John and Paul or George, and it was like, wow, that's really wonderful, but yeah, *Rubber Soul*. *Rubber Soul*'s probably my favourite out of all of them.

## Audio 2.29
**Katie**: Now, the song-writing in Dr Hook, how did that work? Tell me about the dynamics of that.
**Dennis**: Um, my, my song-writing works the same way it worked then, the same way it works now – if I get an idea, I write something. Um, I get an idea when I get an idea, and sometimes when I get an idea, I get this thing and it hits me and I write the song in 30 minutes. You know, and then sometimes I deliberate over it, but, er, so yes, that's always how song-writing, I mean, on my, on my last album, my album that just came out, *Post Cool*, all the songs on there I could tell you why I wrote every single song, you know. Er, so in some ways I guess it's autobiographical, um, as I tend to write things that mean something to me. I don't tend to make a story up as much as, I might embellish it, or change it a little, but the root of it usually comes from something solid like that, you know, it's …
**Katie**: I've always wondered this, do you write the lyrics first or do you write the music?
**Dennis**: Um, you know, it's better when it comes at the same time, because if I write a lyric, I struggle over a melody because I want that, the lyric and how it scans is really important to me. It's usually the rhythm of the whole song, and so I always want the melody to fit exactly, I don't like to start changing the words, to bend it for another melody. So, it's better when it happens at the same time. But if only had to get one, I think I would rather just get the words, 'cause you know what you've got when you, when you have words, you know. These days, I, I tour a lot, sometimes I have a band – I did last year – but this year I'm touring by myself, it's just me and a guitar, and when you do it that way, you wanna have songs that say something. As a matter of fact, you want to have songs, that, if you didn't sing them, if you just said the words to somebody, they would register, you know.

## Audio 2.30
**Katie**: Right, let us move on to your tour. Whey! [OK]. So, it's you, a guitar.
**Dennis**: Yeah, well, a couple of guitars, yeah, but just, yes,

it's me, me, a, a guitar and, you know, 40 years of songs, you know, that I can draw from. And some are hits, and some are album tracks, and some are from my solo things and, you know, I, I've been playing a lot of my solo stuff for a while now, so that people know that as well. I mean, people are disappointed when I don't play things from my solo album and that's, that's what you want, you want everything to be included, you know. You just do.

**Katie**: Now I've just heard your third, it's your solo album, isn't it, which is called, er, *Post Cool*? [*Post Cool*] Do you know, I absolutely love it, I do [Thank you] honestly. You'll have heard this a hundred thousand times but, you know what I'm going to say, my mam was a massive huge fan, [OK!] you know.

**Dennis**: My mom was a fan, my mom was a big fan. When Dr Hook broke up she went 'What?!', I was like I'd taken *her* career away!

**Katie**: Dennis, the best of luck with your tour [Thank you]. I cannot wait to see you at Darlington Civic Theatre.

**Dennis**: Thanks very much.

**Katie**: Thank you, Dennis. You take care now, [Bye bye] bye.

## Lesson 35  Pronunciation for listeners 7

### Audio 2.31
It's written up faithfully in a, a fantastic book, er, by Richard Feynman, it's called *The Pleasure of Finding Things Out*, and the lecture is called *There's Plenty of Room at the Bottom*. (x3)

### Audio 2.32
1. now I've just heard your third, it's your solo album, isn't it, which is called, er, *Post Cool* [*Post Cool*]
2. er, they knew this very wealthy American lady called Emily Grigsby
3. computers use something called an 'ant algorithm'
4. they looked at the, what's called the *mitochondrial DNA*
5. I was actually, um, with, er, a young man called Diggory Rose
6. well, we work with one species of ant primarily called *temnothorax albipennis*
7. built originally by an, a Scottish archi-, architect called William Byrne
8. which is the beginning of spring, which is called *morgh*
9. and it was the home of a chap called Frank Potter
10. we're called Dautenis, we call ourselves Dautenis

### Audio 2.33
1. according to a report from a, a *Scientific American* story
2. in front, um, of a little crack that you have in your brain there's what we call the *motor area*
3. according to Eleanor Jones of Uppsala University
4. and this house is called Beechwood
5. we're joined by, um, Annela Seddon
6. and a company called Penguin Books
7. and the word *nanotechnology* is
8. *nano* actually comes from the Greek for 'dwarf'
9. from my supervisor, Nigel Franks
10. but the most significant person in the Punjab was, er, a gentleman called Dhulla Bhati
11. the word *Guyana* means 'land of many waters'
12. a computer program created by Professor David Cope of Santa Cruz University
13. there's what we call the *supplementary motor area*
14. it was owned by, um, a family pre-, previously to the Second World War called Mollinson
15. and there's another famous book called *The Ants*
16. it was, er, built about 1709 by a chap called George Cowdry
17. it is a name that refer to two lakes in our region, they are nowadays called Dowcien
18. one of the members of the Mallory family, Virginia Arnott
19. um, there's a really good one about bees, um, by Thomas Seeley called the *Honeybee Democracy*
20. they have something called *nomihodai*

### Audio 2.34
er, also for the internet access, you know, if ever something occurs to me, you know, 'Oh, I wonder what', you know, 'this is or that is', you know, I can quickly Google it and find out about it.

### Audio 2.35
1. well, yeah, no, you know, it's one of those things like anything else
2. it just kind of happens, you know what I mean, it's not until it's all over
3. now we have to have another one, you know what I mean
4. and so you don't really stop, you know
5. they wouldn't do that, you know
6. but I, you know, so, it, I just got involved
7. it was the thing that opened my eyes, you know. It was really
8. and artists didn't do that back then, you know. You did covers
9. I write the song in 30 minutes. You know, and then sometimes I deliberate over it
10. I could tell you why I wrote every single song, you know
11. something solid like that, you know
12. um, you know, it's better when it comes at the same time
13. me, a, a guitar and, you know, 40 years of songs, you know, that I can draw from
14. you want everything to be included, you know. You just do.
15. can't really imagine, you know, having to remember all my friends
16. well, I guess, I mean, there seems to be some progress being made on, um, sort of, electric cars or, you know, just cars that use alternative fuel
17. definitely computers, you know, um

### Audio 2.36
1. it was like the best opportunity that I've ever had
2. but it seems like, sort of, you know, like once every five years
3. that all happened, like, in sequence
4. was it just sort of, like, the eye of the storm
5. but it wasn't until, like, you know, The Beatles
6. it was like, 'Wow, that's really wonderful'
7. um, really, like, good robust decision-making
8. a seemingly, you know, like, simple creature
9. um, their nest choice behaviours are, like, very democratic
10. so collectively, they're able to, like, er, vote for a nest
11. the sun represents, like, on the one hand the rays of light
12. and it's like, it's a pagan, pagan ritual
13. and they've got, you know, like, say lorries and buses
14. like, if I see a cyclist now, I'm like, 'Oh no'

# Lesson 36  Advertising

## Video 12, Part 1
**Tom**: Do you ever find that you, you get sort of adverts in your emails that you just really don't want, I don't know, does that ever happen to you? Do you ever …
**Ezgi**: Yeah, junk mail [Yeah], I hate that, [Yeah] really, [Yeah] a lot of it, every day, um, some companies sent me a lot of junk mail and I don't like that.
**Tom**: Yeah, I find, yeah, it's usually something I really don't want or need, you know.
**Thuy**: But I think it depends on the kind of email, so some, some emails is good, for example, I myself I want to apply, er, to, er, universities, and many universities send me an email to explain about, er, their policy, er, their systems or something like that, about, um, and I think it's useful. [Yeah] Sometimes it's useful.
**Tom**: I suppose it depends on what the advert is, you know, yeah, yeah.
**Thuy**: Or, um, you want to buy a watch, and you don't know which one is suit to you, and, um, maybe one day you receive an email and advertise about, this is good, this is good, why not, and I think it's, it's good.
**Ezgi**: It depends on the kinds of products.
**Tom**: Yeah.
**Thuy**: Yeah, I think this depends on the, the number or the, the way they, er, com-, approach you, er, it make you, um, comfortable or not, and for example, when we, er, turn on our programme, and, er, we were watching a, a film, a famous film, and after that, it ad-, advertisement, advertising and it too long and it make us disturbed.
**Ezgi**: Especially when you watch a film or …
**Tom**: Yeah, you get that a lot, definitely, yeah.
**Ezgi**: So every 15 minutes, you have to watch advertising, advertising …
**Tom**: Yeah, yeah, it drives you crazy really.

## Video 12, Part 2
**Hue**: Have you got any ideas about, er, advertising in this moment, maybe it's bothered you or maybe it's make you favour a bit?
**Massimo**: Oh, well, actually I probably got, er, something said about this, 'cause I don't know, you guys, but I receive, constantly receive these, er, spam emails, I don't know, it's something which, you know, they, you know, maybe because, you know, you, well, these days, you know, you try to, or shopping online or you're doing, um, just for, you know, curiosity and you visit some webpage and they, don't know, somehow, you know, manage to track your, you know, er, track your, er, interests, and then you start receiving, you know, this, this spam, you know, this, this, this newsletter, which, well, actually sometimes is probably your awareness, you know, 'cause you're ticking those boxes, I think.
**Anisa**: Yeah, it's your fault really sometimes, yeah.
**Massimo**: But I think there's no way out, you know, you can't really get away from this, you know.
**Anisa**: Well, I don't know about you, but what I tend to do is I have two different email accounts, so I have a personal, private email account that I use for work or for my friends, and then I have the other email account, so when I'm shopping online, I use that one, so I know that when I check that, I'm gonna have about 400 spam emails in a week, and then my other email account, I'll have about two messages, 'cause nobody wants to talk to me, it, it's very sad.
**Hue**: Yes, I totally agree with you in that way, and I think some engineer, computer engineer advised all the customers, try to change your passwords maybe after a month or two months, so you can protect your password as well, so, yeah, and the spam, it means, er, rubbish email, cannot enter your address as well, and the other thing's, er, thing's, sometimes when we buys goods onlines, we'll, is, sometimes it bother me when t-, the quality of goods is not as good as I expect, so – yeah – so I try to find a way to change my goods as well, and it, it also take me long time to change and we also have to search some more information from the onlines, it's problem as well.

## Video 12, Part 3
**Anisa**: I don't know. I think, I think sometimes it is nice when you get some pop-up ads, I, I don't agree with the fact that nowadays with technology, they can track everything you're doing on the internet, so they know what you're interested in, but occasionally, I mean, recently I was looking to buy a new camera, and, er, I was just on the internet, and 'pop!', and I had a little pop-up ad that came, and it was advertising a camera, and, 'Actually, that's exactly what I've been looking for', so OK, you know, one for the advertising, it did work on me, er, but I think I'm really susceptible to advertising, um, …
**Massimo**: So you might end up like, er, buying at the end of the day.
**Anisa**: Oh, you know when you have like the late-night ads on TV and they always, they're advertising something like the, the latest kitchen gadget, um, I'll sit there and go 'Oh my God, I, I, I need one of these! How have I lived my life without one?' and of course, you know, you buy it, you use it once, it doesn't work, you put it in a cupboard, and it, it sits there, you know, for years, so … Would you say that advertising really works on you?
**Hue**: Er, yes, I agree with that, and I have another example, that, er, sometimes I watch a very favourite movies on TVs, that's a film on TV or maybe a football match, where I, we say, that's a very wonderful football match on the TV, so, sometimes adverti-, advertisements break, yeah, break the match or break the new-, the film as well, so I have to pause, to wait, and I feel very tired in that way, so I don't like …
**Anisa**: So you just want to focus on your programme, you don't want to be interrupted by the ads.

# Lesson 37  The language of persuasion

## Audio 2.37
BCFM 93.2 is a charity run entirely by volunteers. That means we are not for profit, so we can put you, the people of Bristol, first. BCFM 93.2 – the station you can count on.

## Audio 2.38
The Social Bar and Café in Stokes Croft, Bristol, is the perfect place to relax and enjoy good food and drinks all day long. The Social serves Fair Trade coffee and provides a daytime play area for the kids, with baby-changing facilities too. With a heated garden, local beers and great food, where else is there to go but the Social Bar and Café, 130 Cheltenham Road, Stokes Croft, near the Tesco Express.
***
**Announcer 1**: For a delicious and different dining experience, Falafel King is the place to go.
**Announcer 2**: With its unique Middle Eastern feel, fresh food and warm welcome, Falafel King is truly a fantastic experience.
**Announcer 3**: So why is Falafel King so special?

**A**: I like the falafel and pitta, and when I go, I always sit downstairs anyway in the calm 'cause it's really comfy, and it's just a nice chill-out, just to myself really.
**B**: Falafel King's good because it's, er, basically you can just come along, grab a snack, you can get a good selection of fresh food, which is nice, falafel's good.
**C**: I like downstairs, it's a very cool place to just chill out. Um, yes, generally a very nice place, so that's why I go.
**Announcer 4**: You can find us at number 6 Cotham Hill, just across the road from the Clifton Down Shopping Centre.
**Announcer 2**: Come to Falafel King because we are the king of falafel!

### Audio 2.39

If you'd like to own a piece of Jamaica, the Jamaica National Building Society can help. Come to the mortgage seminar on Wednesday 14th of November at 6.30 p.m. at Rose Green Centre, Gordon Road, Bristol. As the largest building society in Jamaica and the Caribbean, we are sure we have a mortgage product that is just for you. Come and discuss how your home-ownership dreams in Jamaica can become a reality. We will help you find a way to purchase or build your own home. There'll be information on properties and land for sale in Jamaica, and you'll learn more about home-loan products from the home-enhancement loan plan, to the commercial mortgage and home-equity loans. If you'd like to attend this event, please call 0207 708 2442 or email us at ukrep office@janouk.com. Jamaica National Home Loans – making home ownership a reality.

***

Hi, my name is Mick Siddle. With the recent bad news regarding the increase to energy bills, I want to personally help you to save money. What would you say if I told you I could significantly reduce your gas, electric and telecom bills, plus save you a further 25% off your monthly food and petrol bills? Now you may be thinking, 'I've heard it all before – how can anyone cut my bills?'. Most people I speak to say this. But, by not spending a fortune on advertising, sponsorship, or paying to go on comparison websites, it is totally possible to save, on average, £800 a year. If you want to know more, just call me free of charge for a no-obligation chat. By asking a few simple questions, I will be able to tell you if I can help. I may not be able to help everyone, but there is a great chance I could. Just call me on 0800 954 52 55, and let's start saving money!

### Audio 2.40

**A**: What are *you* looking so happy about?
**B**: I've finished all my Christmas shopping.
**A**: You're kidding! How did you manage that? You've got loads of women to buy for, and we know how difficult *they* can be to please.
**B**: It was easy, actually. The wife's been raving about this shop called Amulet on Cotham Hill for ages. She's hinted enough times that she loves everything in there, so I took a trip down there, and it was brilliant. The staff are really helpful – I mean, the internet's convenient, but you don't get that one-on-one like you get in Amulet. They helped me pick out some great gifts. I bought my wife a Murilo wool scarf, silver earrings for Catherine, a jacket for my sister, a bag for my mum and a few bits for the nieces. I mean, I couldn't believe how easy it was. Hey, where are you going?
**A**: What was that address again?
**Announcer**: Amulet – 39a Cotham Hill, just off White Ladies Road. The nice lady said she'd give you 10% off if you mention their radio advert!

***

**A**: There's fish, then there's fresh fish.
**B**: The Fish Shop on Gloucester Road has some of the best fresh fish and seafood in Bristol.
**A**: Fresh fish delivered daily from Devon and Cornwall. I love that it's fresh and that they always know exactly where a fish comes from, it's never a worry, you know, and even tell you how to cook it. It's fantastic.
**C**: Find out for yourself why people come from all over to buy our fresh fish.
**B**: Mention this BCFM advert to get one pound off a packet of smoked salmon trimmings, perfect for your Christmas starter.
**A**: The Fish Shop, 143 Gloucester Road, Bristol.

***

**A**: Excuse me, mate! Do you know where I can get a table made from recycled wood?
**B**: Yeah. Down at the Bristol Wood Recycling Project. They make all sorts of bespoke furniture. It's excellent quality and at affordable prices.
**A**: Sounds great. Oh, while I'm here, I need to get my missis a present for Christmas.
**B**: They have lots of great Christmas gifts, all hand-made from recycled wood, like chopping boards, wooden clocks, tea-light holders, even Christmas-tree stands.
**A**: You don't have any bird boxes or picture frames by any chance?
**B**: They've got the whole lot. Find out more at bwrp.org.uk – the Bristol Wood Recycling Project. Environmental, ethical, excellent.

## Lesson 38  The intelligence of ants

### Audio 2.41

**Malcolm**: I'm joined now by Antonia Forster, who works in the Brist-, er, the Bristol Ant Lab. I had absolutely no idea we had such a … exciting sounding, um, place in Bristol. Tell us about the ant lab. What does it do?
**Antonia**: Um, well, we work with one species of ant primarily, called, er, *temnothorax albipennis*. It's a really small ant, er, so in the lab, we keep it in between glass slides, and mostly we study its behaviour, er, we give it nest choice experiments, um, one person in our lab, Jamie, studies their fighting strategy, um, so there's all sorts of various things we look at, mostly their collective behaviours.

### Audio 2.42

1 er, individually, ants aren't really capable of, of complicated thoughts or processes
2 so I really wanted to study how, collectively, they can be more than the sum of their parts, which is why I work with ants specifically
3 th-, what we like to say is ants have a 'colony-level cognition'
4 individually, ants *can* do some things
5 they organize the brood within their nest, and they can do that even if there's only one ant
6 um, their nest choice behaviours are, like, very democratic

### Audio 2.43

**Malcolm**: And, er, wha-, I mean, I *have* to ask you, why did you get into this in the first place? I mean, it's a, it seems like, you know, you, you go to a party and people say, 'So what do you do?' and you say, 'Well, I spend my time working with ants' – it's kind of strange and odd, um, I, I think it's fantastic as well, but wh-, I mean *why* did you get into it?

**Antonia**: Um, well, I actually had, er, lectures from my supervisor, Nigel Franks, and, um, his lectures were really great, and I s-, I got really interested in how, er, individually, ants aren't really capable of, of complicated thoughts or processes, but then as a colony, they have these emergent behaviours that are really interesting, and, um, really like, good, robust decision-making, so I really wanted to study how collectively they can be more than the sum of their parts, which is why I work with ants specifically.

**Malcolm**: Now, ants, of course, are really amazing creatures, aren't they? We, we, we sort of protect ourselves from them, I think, we have a, a deep fear of ants, and also we can learn a huge amount from them. Wh-, What, Why do you think – and we're going to get onto some of the specific things – but wha-, wha-, why do you think they have fascinated us, er, over so many years?

**Antonia**: Um, well, firstly, there are a lot of different species of ants; an ant is a family – *formicidae* – and it's not, there are, there are tons of different species of ants and they vary from, you know, enormous ants that are several centimetres long to really, really tiny ones, um, and also there are so many of them, ants actually outnumber humans a million to one, um, and in some places like the rainforest, their biomass outweighs the biomass of all the other creatures put together four to one, um, so the fact that they're so abundant makes them really interesting in a way, but also the fact that, um, their behaviours are just so complicated. It's not what you would expect from a seemingly, you know, like, simple creature.

### Audio 2.44

**Malcolm**: Um, ants are incredibly intelligent creatures, aren't they, so how do they ... te-, tell us a little bit about, about their intell-, do ... now, here's an important question: Do ants have an individual intelligence, or is it entirely a group thing?

**Antonia**: Well, it's, it's an interesting question, um, the, wh-, what we like to say is ants have a 'colony-level cognition', so cognition is the ability to sort of take in information from different sources and adapt it, er, to novel information and apply that to a situation, so it's like problem-solving. Um, individually, ants *can* do some things, like they organize the brood within their nest, and they can do that even if there's only one ant, but, er, their nest choice behaviours are like, very democratic, so collectively they're able to like, er, vote for a nest and choose between a variety of nest qualities and things like that, so in a, in a wa-, I would argue that no, individually, they don't really have cognition, but as a colony, they do.

**Malcolm**: OK, and, and do, do you th-, I mean, this may be out of your, er, area altogether, but do, do you think that they offer us, um, a way to do problem-solving ourselves, do you, do you think that ants can point the way to different ways of problem-solving?

**Antonia**: I think they really do, there's actually, they have been used in that way already, the ... computers use something called an 'ant algorithm', and it's a sort of search strategy to find information among a plethora of other information, so we have used their behaviour in sort of ways you wouldn't expect already, um, I think they offer an insight into the human brain, because in the same way that neurons in the human brain can't individually make decisions but together, collectively, they form a brain. Ants are sort of like that, the colony is kind of like a giant brain.

**Malcolm**: Yes, you add them up and they do something that, um ...

**Antonia**: Is more than the sum of its parts.

**Malcolm**: More than the sum of its parts, yeah.

### Audio 2.45

**Malcolm**: Um, ants have a very particular way, don't they, rather like bees and so on, a fascinating way of organizing themselves. Can you tell us a little bit about that?

**Antonia**: OK, so I think what you're referring to is eusociality, and what that means is there's only one breeder in the whole colony – that's the queen – and the queen lays all the eggs, and all of, all of the other bees or ants in the colony are her daughters, and they help her lay more eggs rather than laying their own, and that's, um, sort of hard to explain briefly, but it's a fact, er, based on the way they divide – when they lay females, they're fertilized eggs; when they lay males, they're unfertilized. What that means is that the females are more closely related to each other than they would be to their own children. So rather than have children, it benefits them to have sisters, so they help their mother lay more eggs instead, so, so that's true of sort of bees, ants and some wasp species as well ... and termites.

### Audio 2.46

**Malcolm**: Um, if there are people listening to this and, and they actually are thinking I'd qu-, I'd quite like, I'm quite interested in bugs and I'd like to know more, and I'd like to help out, are, are there ways that you know, or ideas that you have that, that, er, people could take up?

**Antonia**: Um, there's, there are a lot of different books about this, so there's one called, um, *The Superorganism*, which is a bit of a technical book, but it's really interesting about, er, how ants function as a colony. There's another famous book called *The Ants*, and, um, there's a really good one about bees, um, by Thomas Seeley called the *Honeybee Democracy*, so if you're interested in ant or bee behaviour, those are really good books I'd recommend. Um, you can also find out a lot online by reading papers, um ...

**Malcolm**: And the site of your, um, group is called 'The, the Ant-, The Bristol Ant Lab', yeah?

**Antonia**: Yeah.

**Malcolm**: You can look at it on the web. Um, Antonia, we're delighted that you came in, thank you, thanks very much, and wish you all the best with your research.

**Antonia**: Thank you.

## Lesson 39  A celebration of the sun

### Audio 2.47

**Dea**: And this is Dea, and I'm here today with Taranjit Chana, solicitor by day, and she's kindly come in today to talk to us about Lohri and the celebration and what it involves, etc. Um, Taranjit, what is Lohri?

**Taranjit**: Lohri, um, before I start, Dea, thank you very much to Desi Radio for inviting me and letting me speak about, er, Lohri. Now, Lohri's a fantastic, colourful Punjabi celebration. Um, you know, basically the focus of Lohri is, er, a big bonfire in the evening, and, er, it's a singing, dancing, buying of gifts, *saag*, and *makki di roti*, eating *rewri* and *gur* and throwing peanuts, roasted peanuts, onto the fire.

### Audio 2.48

what it involves, etcetera (x3)
I don't know nothing about it (x3)
Could you tell me a little bit about that? (x3)

### Audio 2.49

**Taranjit**: Beginning of the end of winter, when you mark the beginning of the sun's journey towards the north. Um, it's the last day of *Poh*, which is a winter month, and, er, it's when the sun changes its course, which is th-, the beginning of spring, which is called *Magh*, and it's a welcoming of spring, so it's the new beginning basically. Er, it's associated, er, with the worship of the sun and fire, and it's celebrated by many communities. Um, and again, like I said, it marks the beginning and the coming of spring, the newborn, new crops, and it's a festival of renewal.

## Audio 2.50
**Dea**: Basically, tell me a little bit more about Lohri's origins 'cause I'm gonna pretend like I don't know nothing about it.

**Taranjit**: Er, Lohri dates back a thousand of years and we're talking about the Indus, the Indus Valley civilization. Now, not a lot of pe-, I don't know if a lot of people know this, this, er, civilization is the oldest Punjabi civilization, and it predates any religion, and it's often considered a pagan festival because it's a festival that's dedicated to fire, the sun, the nature, earth a-, and people. And fire is associated with the concepts of health and life, such as water, because it's symbolic of the transformation and regeneration. The sun represents like, on the one hand, the rays of light, and the other with gold. Now gold obviously is the golden fields, all the crops in, and where the farmers have worked really hard, um, i-, it's, this is capable of stimulating of the growth of the fields that have been cult-, cultivated and the over-, overall well-being of humans and animals.

**Dea**: What's actually involved the celebrations of Lohri? C'mon, tell me a little bit about that, c'mon.

**Taranjit**: Well, it's, er, basically, Lohri's celebrated, the main focus obviously being the b-, big bonfire, that's the main focus, but in order to prepare for that bonfire, the whole day takes up, people go to people's houses during the day, collecting food, things like *gur* which is very important, b-, *butria* or *luckria*, er, er, which are needed to fuel the fire. Um, you know, and also involves, um, you know, having *mungfli* available and sesame seeds, because a lot of this food is thrown onto the fire, er, because i-, it symbolizes an offering to the sun god, who's the giver of all life. Er, *saag*, obviously, is cooked with *makki di roti*, you can't have, er, *saag* without *makki di roti*, um, and bonfires are lit. Um, and like I said, you know, people go from door to door collecting all this. Um, the first, er, again, in, th-, the fire is integral to the, er, Lohri celebration and it's the meeting point of social gatherings. There's no real religion, er, religious significance for Lohri, um, if anything it's a greater social significance bus-, because it's the meeting of all communities, it transcends caste, backgrounds and so forth.

I mean, it's all about, um, the new, you know, th-, the first Lohri celebrated by the newborn, the newly married, um, and it's a big occasion where there's a feast and there's exchange of gifts, it's a happy occasion, especially for couples, who are celebrating their first Lohri after their marriage, or it's for a newborn, be it a girl or a boy. And also I'd like to say also when, when the gathering takes place, it's not just a gathering of the community, but it is also the meeting of boys and girls together across the fire.

**Dea**: Cool.

## Audio 2.51
**Taranjit**: And also I'd like to say also when, when the gathering takes place, it's not just a gathering of the community, but it is also the meeting of boys and girls together across the fire.

**Dea**: Cool. And, you know Lohri, i-, it dates back many, many years, which you kind of outlined, and it's like, it's a pagan, pagan ritual which, you know, is almost more than 5,000 years old if, if I, if I remember correctly.

**Taranjit**: Yes, yes, that's right, yes.

**Dea**: And I understand that there were significant characters involved in Lohri and, and, and that up, up, you know, the b-, bringing it to the limelight, the focus, etc., um … Could you tell me about some of the people involved in Lohri in, in the early days?

**Taranjit**: Well, there's lots of, there's lots of legends about Lohri, you know, how the name came about, how it came about and so forth, but the significant person in the Punjab was a gentleman called Dulla Bhatti. He was a freedom fighter in Punjab. He was like a, um, Robin Hood type of character in the Punjab, where he would rob from the rich and, um, help the poor. Um, for instance, you know, he would rescue girls from poor backgrounds who were being forcibly sold in slave markets and you know, he'd actually arrange for their marriages and provide their dowry so they won't be forced to be sold on the slave market, um, and you know, he, that's what he fought for, he fought for, um, the poor, um, and robbed from the rich.

**Dea**: So, new beginnings for the poor to start a new life and for the daughters who didn't actually have a hope, because of the poverty that existed then.

**Taranjit**: That's right, that's right.

# Lesson 40 Pronunciation for listeners 8

## Audio 2.52
first of all, give us an overview
first of all, I'm sure
first of all, you need
first of all, be aware
(x3)

## Audio 2.53
1 and this is exactly
2 infect cancer cells
3 any bad side effects
4 up on the north-west coast
5 perfect vision
6 the easiest thing to see
7 exchange of gifts
8 rainforest
9 the statistics of this
10 the thing is, it's not about looking backwards, it's about looking forwards

## Audio 2.54
1 because (x3); because at the time
2 about (x3); about ten thousand times
3 perhaps (x3); perhaps more expensive and perhaps more scarce and
4 perhaps (x3); perhaps we could share more
5 particularly (x3); I was particularly struck
6 particularly (x3); particularly American society, but it also applies to us
7 probably (x3); er, probably made about four, five years ago
8 responsible (x3); and also, I'm responsible for the guides
9 exceptionally (x3); that are exceptionally good at spreading disease
10 absolutely (x3); I had absolutely no idea
11 collecting (x3); you know, people go from door to door collecting all this
12 traditionally (x3); traditionally in the Punjab
13 hundred (x3); of seven hundred and forty-one feet
14 do you reckon (x3); do you reckon it would be easy for students

## Audio 2.55
1. the good guys
2. and it could be like almost harassing you or
3. the virus can carry in a protein
4. could be good at this
5. we want more
6. you should be polite
7. cruising in company
8. I couldn't bear to watch it
9. can be more than the sum of their parts

## Audio 2.56
**M**: So how do they … te-, tell us a little bit abou-, about their intelligen-, do … now, here's an important question: Do ants have an individual intelligence, or is it entirely a, a group thing?

**A**: In a, in a wa-, I would argue that no, individually, they don't really have cognition, but as a colony, they do.

## Audio 2.57
1. I think it, I think it's looking positive
2. all, all, all over the place
3. um, if I was doing, if I was doing, um, jazz

## Audio 2.58
1. so that it hasn't, it will only
2. hadn't fought in the Se-, in the First World War
3. in your situation where you are, er, you just cannot, er, resolve the person's lip movements
4. to 95 deg-, er, miles per hour
5. again, like I said, it's, it marks the beginning
6. leading a sen-, sedentary lifestyle

## Audio 2.59
1. journalism may be one profession where it almost doesn't ma-, it depends what you do, obviously, but
2. suddenly people were talking, er, when, when I was a kid, people weren't talking about nanoscience
3. wha-, what, why do you think – and we're going to get on to some of the specific things – but wha-, wha-, why do you think they have fascinated us
4. yeah, no, you know, it's one of those things, like anything else, it sometimes, it seems like it was yesterday
5. I mean, the, if you actually, it's, I think sometimes you probably have to pinch yourself
6. with vinyl and stuff, they get, it gets, as it, it gets better, as, as it gets warmer, doesn't it?

# Lesson 41 Arriving in a capital city

## Video 13, Part 1
**Alan**: Tokyo, amazing place, er, it was one of those places which you, you, you can't really anticipate before you go there. Er, the first thing was the trains, er, just completely full of people, but everyone just so relaxed and not a, not a sound, um, and it's actually literally true, when you go to the big stations there, you've got guys in these nice white gloves pushing people on the train, and, and you get pushed further and further into the train, but nobody complains, there's, there's not a sound, and everyone, in complete silence, gets out at their stop and there's, there's no hassle or anything like that, so, so that was great, um, and also just the lifestyle, the, the food, er, the first time I went to one of these *kaiten sushis*, which is, er, like a conveyor belt, er, and the sushi's coming round all the time, everyone, er, you know, just … they're picking out their favourite things, and weird and wonderful stuff comes by, that, that was really good, um, but I think the most surprising thing, and the thing I loved the most in Tokyo was, um, the karaoke, the, the Japanese are crazy about this, and on, on the first day I, I was there, and it was really hot, it was incredibly humid in, in September in Tokyo, and, um, I just wanted to get out of the heat really, so, I had no Japanese, I, I can, I couldn't speak anything, all the signs are impossible to read, so I kind of stumbled into a karaoke place and said in, in very broken Japanese, er, *En-, English*, you know, *igirisu gin dess*, and they gave me a book and they sent me to the room, and it was fantastic, there's a tiny little room, er, air-conditioned, and there's a, a TV and this book with all these English songs, and so you just put a number in, and you just, they come out, you start singing, and they, they bring you a glass of, um, fruit juice, and, er, you can spend hours there, and it was so relaxing, I see why they like it, I mean, it doesn't matter if you can sing or not, it was just, just a great thing, and then I got used to that lifestyle, and, and they go every night, and, um, they have something called *nomihodai*, which is all-you-can-drink karaoke, and so you just get like, er, you can spend about three or four hours and they just bring you beer or, or whatever and you, and you sing, so, um, yeah, Tokyo, amazing place, er, just, er, totally unexpected, and, but peaceful, surprisingly peaceful, so it was good.

## Video 13, Part 2
**Anisa**: It, it was really funny, because I'd been living in another smaller town in Mexico, and then I decided to, to leave and, and go to the big city, so I took a bus in the middle of the night, and it was about a ten-hour bus journey on a very small, very cramped bus, and I was sitting next to this large older Mexican woman with, with all her bundles of food and things, and I sort of slept on and off, er, for the journey, and I remember when I was coming into Mexico City, we were winding our way round the side of the mountain, or it could have been the volcano, and I just remember my, my first glimpse of the city was this huge sprawling area, and we were actually on the, the outskirts, so it was sort of a shanty town, and, and it was a rather ghetto-looking area, but I immediately loved it, it was love at first sight, I got so excited I, I turned to this poor woman and I said, 'God, look, look, look, it, it's Mexico City, look!', and she looked at me as if I was absolutely insane, and, um, I don't know why, I don't know what it was about the city, but it was, sometimes you just get a feeling that you're going to love it and it's amazing, and that's how I felt, and of course, I got to the bus station, and I had all my worldly possessions in one bag, I had absolutely no idea where I was going, I didn't know a soul in the whole city, but I found that everybody was so friendly, and they really went out of their way, you kn-, to help other people and one man could see that I was completely lost and overwhelmed by the size of the city and the, the number of people and couldn't decide where to go and, and he sort of explained the, the metro system to me, and he explained how to get tickets, and he explained, you know, er, 'Don't go to this area, 'cause it could be a little bit dangerous', and he seemed really concerned for my safety, and before I'd arrived in the city, everyone had told me that it's one of the most dangerous places in the world, but I have to say that, after having lived there for, oh, not even a couple of weeks, I, I didn't feel that at all, um, and one of the best things about it was all the food, so you had the people with amazing hospitality, and then you have the food that all these people were cooking, and I met so many nice people that just invited me in for fresh, wholesome, really traditional

Mexican cooking, so it was the combination of really nice people, amazing food, and then just walking around and, I, I couldn't get over the fact that you'd be walking down a street, and you'd have a two-thousand-year-old ruined palace right next to a very modern glass-metal skyscraper, and I thought that contrast of, not even historic but ancient civilization with what people were doing now, and that very modern look, it was, it was just wonderful.

## Lesson 42  Topical chat

### Audio 2.60
1  Well, that's it with iTunes and things like that, though, isn't it? But you get things like vinyl and stuff (x2)
2  some of the original, like, Pink Floyd albums do sound better on record than sort of the digitally remastered, which is a bit bland (x2)
3  Yeah, I know they are, sort of getting better, aren't they? But with vinyls and stuff, they get, it gets, as it, it gets better as it, as it gets warmer, doesn't it? (x2)
4  I think it's really good, isn't it? But like you say, you've got to have the space, haven't you? for them to go [Yeah] (x2)

### Audio 2.61
**Andy**: CD sales have seen a significant year-on-year drop in the first three months of 2012, according to figures from BPI and the official charts company.
**Katie**: Sales fell 25% from 20.5 million in the first three months of last year to 15.3 million this year. Digital sales continue to rise, with almost a third of all albums now being bought digitally.
**Carl**: So guys, are, are, are, um, are, um, CDs out of date?
**Andy**: Definitely. Definitely out of date. That's why they're now cheap, and I can afford lots and lots of music instead of just …
**Carl**: Well, that's it with iTunes and things like that, though, isn't it? But you get things like vinyl and stuff that, I know it's out of date, but …
**Katie**: It's more expensive now.
**Carl**: It *is*, and plus it seems to be coming back and it's a lot more, smoother sound, and I know you get crackling and hisses and stuff, but …
**Andy**: Well, it depends if it's been made for vinyl – if it's been made as a record, then I think it does sound better, like some of the original, like Pink Floyd albums do sound better on record than sort of the digitally remastered, which is a bit bland, but then again, if you've been, you know, if you've got something with a lot of bass like we listen to, like more modern music has a lot of bass, then you tend to, um, need the, um, quality of like online files, like WAVs and CD quality.
**Carl**: Yeah, for it to work correctly.
**Andy**: Yeah. But downloads are so good now.
**Carl**: Yeah, yeah, I know they are, sort of getting better, aren't they? But with vinyl and stuff, they get, it gets, as it, it gets better as it, as it gets warmer, doesn't it? As the record warms up and everything as well …
**Andy**: Well, you'd know that, with all your tapes …
**Carl**: Yeah, yeah, I've got a, really, really old video recorders at home, and they, as you've seen, as th-, as the machine gets warmer, and everything starts to work and everything, more … i-, better, then the actual picture quality does improve, I think, as well, definitely. Katie's just looking 'What on earth?' …
**Katie**: Wow, I'm stunned with this, I'm learning new things here, but yeah, if, if a download costs the same as a CD, then I'd rather get the CD because then you get the sleeve with it, but I mean I'm struggling for space in my room because I've got too many CDs. That's the great thing about downloads is it saves so much space.
**Carl**: That's what my dad likes about the old records though, because like we were talking about, me and Andy went walking with my dad, didn't we?, on the Good Friday, and we was talking about different albums, didn't we?
**Andy**: We just flipped through the records, yeah.
**Carl**: And you … But it, it gives the whole thing of the band, isn't it, what the band did, how the-, how they first came together and this and that and …
**Katie**: Yeah, the sleeve notes.
**Carl**: And I think it's really good, isn't it? But like you say, you've got to have the space, haven't you? for them to go …
**Katie**: Yeah.
**Carl**: … whereas something like on an iPad – iPad or iPod – it's just, it's just there on one unit, isn't it?
**Andy**: I saw an argument recently, though, which said that, sort of like records, without records, and it's just downloads, some artists think it's better because it's just substance over style.
**Carl**: Right.
**Andy**: So people like the music for what it is, they don't like the band because they've got a cool record sleeve.
**Carl**: Right.
**Andy**: It's quite, another way of, an interesting of way of doing it.
**Katie**: It is.
**Carl**: But the thing with CDs is that they will go out of date, but they'll probably come back in again like records have, so …
**Katie**: I don't think cassettes will, though.

### Audio 2.62
**Katie**: Now, the number of cyclists killed or seriously injured rose by 36% this year, but while the number of cycling deaths and injuries rises, other casualties on British roads is on the decrease.
**Carl**: Are bikes just too dangerous to ride on the road? Most people are not properly trained to ride on roads, they knock o-, they *can* knock over pedestrians, cause accidents, as cars are often certain of where they're going, or even, because the wi-, road's not wide enough to accommodate them. But what can be done to improve bike safety?
**Andy**: Well, I don't even drive, um, go on the roads when I'm cycling 'cause I'm just too scared.
**Carl**: I just don't have a bike – that's the safest possible way to be near bikes, just don't have one. But it's just, 'cause there's no, there's not the infrastructure on the roads or pavements or anything to have them, sometimes it's just so dangerous.
**Andy**: Specially when you're going through a town, there's like, just nowhere for you to go now.
**Carl**: No, my flatmate rides his bike everywhere and it's just fr-, he comes in, he's like, 'Oh, I nearly got hit by a lorry,' it's just like … and he's not, he's a bit shaken sometimes when he comes in, there's no way you'd get me on the road.
**Katie**: Yeah, I mean, I think it's obviously really dangerous, um, for cyclists, and they've got, you know, like say lorries and buses pulling out, and cars going to overtake and everything, but I think, as well, cyclists, a lot of them aren't properly trained, like they'll just get a bike, and it'll either not be a road bike, so they're not even cycling properly for the situations, or, like the amount of people that don't

wear helmets and go out all in black in the middle of the night kind of thing, or even in the evening.
**Carl**: Yeah, when you're driving it's …
**Katie**: Yeah, if you're driving, then you're going to be scared of, like, if I see a cyclist now, I'm like, 'Oh no,' specially if you can't see them until you're about five metres away, and you've got then to sort of slow down.
**Andy**: You're right, you know, like, some people, they just don't don't care, do they?
**Katie**: No.
**Andy**: And it's more worrying, they just need like a reflective sash or something, but yeah, it's just a nightmare, so …
**Katie**: I do feel bad for them, though, as well, 'cause like, well cycle lanes, I mean, they have them, but then they just stop really randomly.
**Carl**: They need more cycling proficiency tests and the police to actually pull cyclists over and tell them to get reflective gear on them and fine th-, fine them or something.
**Katie**: Yeah.
**Andy**: Like a licence registration, you should have like a little form that says you've done your cycling proficiency and pull that out.
**Katie**: Yeah.
**Carl**: Yeah, or something like that anyway. But anyway, up now we've got *Just Dance* with Lady Gaga.

## Lesson 43  The silent killer

### Video 14, Part 1
**Aneesha**: Now, most of us would know that at least someone in our family or friends has suffered from heart disease, and heart disease we know today is a number-one killer, especially in the developing world. It affects more than 3.5 million people worldwide, and these numbers are increasing in the Asian continent, because Asians have been proven to be genetically susceptible. Now, if I ask you what are the risk factors that you know of, you would be able to tell me something like smoking, being overweight, or consuming a diet, leading a sen-, sedentary lifestyle, or even something like obesity. But something that not many of us are aware that infections also constitute a very important risk factor for getting heart disease.

### Video 14, Part 2
**Aneesha**: You'll be surprised to know that one of the most common infections is gum infection or gum disease, with almost one in every three adults having some form of gum disease. Now gum disease is something that is often neglected, because it's a silent disease, doesn't cause a lot of pain, or does not cause much problem to the patient. Now, if I come to how these two conditions are linked, I would like to explain a little about how gum disease develops, it's because of bacteria that form on a thin film on teeth areas which are not cleaned. These bacteria then penetrate inside, through the gum tissue into our bloodstream, and once they enter the bloodstream, these bacteria can deposit on the walls of our arteries, they secrete toxins which induce a response within the body, and all this contributes to increase a risk for heart disease.

### Video 14, Part 3
**Aneesha**: Research proves that people with gum infections are twice as likely to develop any sort of heart disease, and this is, gum problem is very, very controllable. With simple treatment measures and maintaining good oral hygiene, the gum problem can be resolved, and not only our oral health but even our general health can be improved. So that's my message for this talk. Thank you very much for your patience.

## Lesson 44  The music of the rainforest

### Audio 2.63
**Interviewer**: And the meaning of *Macusi*, what is that?
**Keith**: Yeah, Macusi is the largest Amerindian tribe in Guyana, and their main instrument is the flute, and I, this year for the first time, nine weeks ago, I was trekking in the Guyanese rainforest, and it was just amazing what happened, how I was able to meet the Macusi tribe. I bought a bamboo flute from there, and you know, so it was really very spiritual.

### Audio 2.64
Macusi is the largest (x3)
and their main instrument (x3)
for the first time (x3)
nine weeks ago I was trekking (x3)
how I was able to meet (x3)

### Audio 2.65
**Interviewer**: And the meaning of *Macusi*, what is that?
**Keith**: Yeah, Macusi is the largest Amerindian tribe in Guyana, and their main instrument is the flute, and I, this year for the first time, nine weeks ago, I was trekking in the Guyanese rainforest, and it was just amazing what happened, how I was able to meet the Macusi tribe. I bought a bamboo flute from there, and you know, so it was really very spiritual
**Interviewer**: 'Cause you grew up with experiences of the rainforest, didn't you?
**Keith**: Yeah, oh yeah, very much so, 'cause, you know, *Guyana*, the word *Guyana* means 'land of many waters', so if you're flying over Guyana, you see all these shades of green, and then little ri-, little waterfalls, mini-waterfalls, and then carrying on, you see more shades of green, and then huge rivers, and then the river O-, Oronoque River, and it leads to the Kaieteur Falls*, which is the world's tallest single drop, of 741 feet, the Kaieteur Falls.

* The Kaieteur Falls are actually on the Potaro River.

### Audio 2.66
**Interviewer**: You've obviously got a lot of affection for Guyana, you must miss it at times.
**Keith**: I do miss it, yeah. Even though I live in England, I've been living in England for a very long time, I go to Guyana every year and experience and immerse myself in the culture, 'cause in fact I have this freedom living in, in the UK, I'm able to take back a lot of the ideas and love to do journeys back to Guyana.
**Interviewer**: And you've always got the palm trees in your back garden, haven't you?
**Keith**: Yeah, well, years ago when my wife thought I was becoming homesick, she went to Ham and bought winter palms, which, they were phenomenal. When I, when I look through my garden during the winter months, I can see huge palm trees in my back yard, covered in snow, and then, down in the garden, there was a pond with about 50 goldfish.

## Audio 2.67

**Interviewer**: The Guyanese rainforest – you describe it as 'magic and mystery'.

**Keith**: Yeah, well, because Guyana, unlike Brazil, is the most pristine rainforest in the world – in fact, it's one of the three pristine rainforests in, is in Guyana, and when you go, a lot of the trees are still there in place. If a tree is, is, fall over or is cut down by, for deliberate purpose, it's rebuilt, so we have a lot of conservation work going on there in Guyana, so it's very magical, and when you're going to, like th-, like, we we-, we had to go and see, loo-, look for something called 'cock-of-the-rock', there's a massive great bird with a big beak, it took us an hour, just waiting around, 'cause he disappears and he checks all the, the area to make sure it's all safe to come back, while you see his nest there. I've been very blessed and lucky in the sense that I, I grew up in a country where a lot of the older musicians and artists were very active and if I was doing, if I was doing, um, jazz, I was helped with the improvisation by amazing saxophonists or a trum-, trumpet players, and then there was also writers who were writing about our rainforests, you know, you should go and see it, you should go and experience all these amazing birds, like, like this last trip I saw an amazing harpy eagle with a, a snake in its mouth going about to feed its, its young one, it's a huge nest, miles up into this tree, you had to use your binoculars to see it, or I saw, you heard howler monkeys, so a lot of people are writing about that, or caimans, writing about the beauty and the sound of the dawn chorus, every morning in. in the rainforest, the birds come together, and they're singing from five thirty till seven, every morning, and I call it, it's, um, phenomenal, the kind of experience of that.

**Interviewer**: How much is the sound of the rainforest synonymous with, er, flutes, for example?

**Keith**: Yeah, well, I think, I think it is, er, I think it, it's also, like my ocarina, you know, this clay one, which you might not want to call a flute because of the shape, but it's also like a lot of flutes, you get – this one plays bird songs.

## Lesson 45 Pronunciation for listeners 9

### Audio 2.68
And ap**par**ently,
er, **mice**,
**Vik**ing mice,
sailed as far as **Green**land.

### Audio 2.69
And ap**par**ently,
er, **mice**,
**Vik**ing mice,
sailed as far as **Green**land.

And ap**par**ently,
er, **mice**,
er, according to a re**port**,
**Vik**ing mice,
sailed as far as **Green**land.

And ap**par**ently,
er, **mice**,
er, according to a re**port**,
er, let me just get this **ab**solutely right,
er, **mice**,
**Vik**ing mice,
sailed as far as **Green**land.

And ap**par**ently,
er, **mice**,
er, according to a re**port**,
er, let me just get this **ab**solutely right,
it's from a, a *Scientific **American*** story,
er, **mice**,
**Vik**ing mice,
sailed as far as **Green**land.

### Audio 2.70
1. DNA (x3)
2. on Iceland and Greenland (x3)
3. in Sweden (x3)
4. dating right back to the Viking heyday (x3)
5. according to Eleanor Jones (x3)
6. mice skeletons (x3)

### Audio 2.71
According to Eleanor Jones of Uppsala University in Sweden and her colleagues, they looked at the, er, what's called the mitochondrial DNA from mice skeletons, or mouse skeletons, on Iceland and Greenland, dating right back to the Viking heyday …

### Audio 2.72
And apparently, er, mice, er, according to a report, er, let me just get this absolutely right, it's from a, a *Scientific American* story, er, mice, Viking mice, sailed as far as Greenland. According to Eleanor Jones of Uppsala University in Sweden and her colleagues, they looked at the, er, what's called the mitochondrial DNA from mice skeletons, or mouse skeletons, on Iceland and Greenland, dating right back to the Viking heyday, which was about a thousand to, um, twelve hundred years ago, and, um, they compared that DNA with that of known Viking mice from the UK and Norway, and what they realized was that, er, these Viking mice travelled all over the world – everywhere Vikings went, mice went with them.

### Audio 2.73
1. it is, isn't it?
2. it is a great way to talk to people though, isn't it?
3. it's going to be a big one, isn't it?
4. this is better than working in an office, isn't it?
5. it's such a weird and mysterious world, isn't it?
6. it's your solo album, isn't it?

### Audio 2.74
1. and you've got a specialism, haven't you? (x3)
2. you've got some fairly extreme weather up there, haven't you? (x3)
3. um, ants are incredibly intelligent creatures, aren't they? (x3)
4. they're not questioned immediately, are they? (x3)
5. it's not a highly populated area, is it? (x3)
6. first, another bulge appeared, didn't it? (x3)
7. ants have a very particular way, don't they? (x3)
8. it's an iconic symbol, isn't it, the deckchair? (x3)
9. 'cause you've got a big job, haven't you, there really? (x3)

### Audio 2.75
1. Well, that's it, with iTunes and things like that, though, isn't it, but you get things like vinyl and stuff (x2)
2. yeah, I know they are sort of getting better, aren't they? But with vinyl and stuff, they get, it gets, as it, it gets better as it, as it gets warmer, doesn't it? (x2)
3. I think it's really good, isn't it, but like you say, you've got to have the space, haven't you, for them to go (x2)

# Answer key

## Lesson 1 Feeling good

**2**

|   | Alan | Anisa | Ning |
|---|---|---|---|
| 1 | ✓ | ✓ | ✓ |
| 2 | ✓ | ✓ |   |
| 3 |   | ✓ | ✓ |
| 4 |   | ✓ | ✓ |
| 5 | ✓ | ✓ | ✓ |

**3**

|   | Alan | Anisa | Ning |
|---|---|---|---|
| 1 Happiness is … | being yourself, relaxing | being surrounded by friends and family, enjoying a relaxed time, no stress | spiritual things |
| 2 What's your idea of fun? | having a chance to do a hobby you like, anything when you get a lot out of yourself, sharing things with people you want to be with | doing something exciting, e.g. travelling somewhere, going somewhere and doing something, e.g. theme park |   |

**4** 1 Anisa  2 Ning  3 Ning  4 Alan  5 Anisa  6 Anisa
**5** 1 A+N  2 A+N  3 A+N  4 N  5 A  6 N
**6** 1 at a restaurant, at someone's house
   2 when the sun's shining
   3 a family party
   4 desserts, food from different countries
**7** a 2  b 3  c 1  d 4
**8** 1 last Sunday
   2 to a family party
   3 because she brought gifts from China
   4 Tuesday
   5 her password
   6 £2.70

**9**

|   | Alan | Anisa | Ning |
|---|---|---|---|
| place | Isle of Wight | Dubai | Shanghai |
| main activities | festivals, outdoor life | keeping cool (swimming), spending time with friends and family | going to the park |

**10** 1 F (It just seems like there's a festival – not just music festivals – every weekend.)
   2 T
   3 F (She says 'When I lived in Dubai …')
   4 T
   5 T
   6 T

## Lesson 2 Obsessed by the weather

**2** 1 to moan  2 basking  3 Diamond Jubilee
   4 (iconic) symbol
**3** 1 raining very heavily
   2 not normal weather (usually weather that causes problems of some kind)
   3 a column of very powerful wind
   4 when your body overheats from excessive exposure to the sun
   You would moan about them because they are all very unpleasant or potentially dangerous.
**5** 1 b  2 b
**6** a 5  b 2  c 3  d 4  e 1
**7** 1 B  2 M  3 S  4 B  5 B  6 M
**8** 1 March  2 in a taxi, in a shop  3 her mum  4 a T-shirt
   5 a week
**9** A a young girl taking her first holy communion
   B supporters watching a football match in a pub
**10** b, e, f, g
**11** b

## Lesson 3 Life on Mars

**4** • The large words are content words. These include verbs, nouns and adjectives. They're normally pronounced strongly.
   • The small words are function words. These include pronouns, auxiliary verbs and articles. They're normally pronounced weakly and may be difficult to hear.
**5** a 1  b 3  c 2  d 4
**6** 1 c  2 a  3 d  4 b
**8** 1 F (Only on clear days)
   2 T
   3 T
   4 F (We already know a little bit about this.)
   5 T

**9**

| chemistry | oxygen, carbon dioxide, heat, liquid water, hydrogen, hydrocarbons |
|---|---|
| astronomy | planet, Mars, moon, Earth, asteroids |
| climatology/geography | polar caps, island, ocean, horizon, wave, climate, greenhouse effect, pressure, temperature |

**10** Without any breathing apparatus

## Lesson 4 Making a meal of it

**2** mushroom risotto
**3** mushrooms (2), dry white wine (8), vegetable stock (4), olive oil (3), rice (1), parmesan (9)
**4** two people; you, the risotto; about ten to 15 minutes; about three or four minutes; a minute; about two or three minutes; about 20 minutes or so; another minute or two; about 25 minutes
**5** 1 carnaroli         50–60; 2–3
   2                    300; 6
   3 dry               glasses
   4 small
   5                    much

Photocopiable © Delta Publishing 2014 from *Authentic Listening Resource Pack*

6  6 vegetable    pint
   7 olive    a couple of
6  1 where to get them (rice, mushrooms); different varieties (rice); what they add (mushrooms)
   2 Warm it in a pan next to where you're cooking the risotto.
   3 parmesan
   4 parsley
7  b
8  first (x1)  now (x2)  then (x13)  after (x2)  once (x2)
   He uses *then* the most.
9  1 dried mixed mushrooms
   2 the oil
   3 the onions
   4 the rice
10 1 onions, garlic, mushrooms
   2 after the garlic
   3 20–25 minutes
   4 (a knob of) butter
11 1 It looks bad.
   2 You can ruin it.

## Lesson 5  Pronunciation for listeners 1

1  2 and   3 or   4 as   5 of   6 an
2  1 a cup of tea and a biscuit
   2 one or two bags of rice
   3 try and eat a bit of fruit
   4 a pint of milk and a loaf of bread
   5 as cold as a block of ice
   6 a piece of cake and an ice cream
3  2 *One or two bags of rice* sounds like *one a two bags are ice* because:
   – the *r* is cut from the word *or* so it's pronounced like *a*
   – the *f* is cut from the word *of* and the *r* of the word *rice* links to the preceding vowel sound.
   3 *Try and eat a bit of fruit* sounds like *try a neat a bitter fruit* because:
   – the *d* is cut from the word *and* so *and eat* is pronounced like *a neat*
   – the *f* is cut from the word *of* so *bit of fruit* is pronounced like *bitter fruit*.
   4 *A pint of milk and a loaf of bread* sounds like *a pine to milk an a loafer bread* because:
   – the *f* is cut from the word *of* so *pint of* is pronounced like *pine to*
   – the *d* is cut from the word *and* so it's pronounced like *an*
   – the *f* is cut from the word *of* so *loaf of* is pronounced like *loafer*.
   5 *As cold as a block of ice* sounds like *as coal does a block a vice* because:
   – the *d* of *cold* links to the following vowel in *as* so it sounds like *cold does*
   – the *f* of *of* (which is pronounced /v/) links to the following vowel in *ice* so it sounds like *a vice*.
   6 *A piece of cake and an ice cream* sounds like *a piece a cake an a nice cream* because:
   – the *f* is cut from the word *of* so it's pronounced like *a*
   – the *d* is cut from the word *and* so it's pronounced like *an*
   – the *n* of *an* links to the following vowel in *ice* so it sounds like *a nice*.
4  2 … but when the sun's shining, ▲ excellent mood.
   3 I thought ▲ I'd do a mushroom risotto.
   4 … and ▲ we were up there for a week …

5 … ▲ indeed yes, ▲ right, this is probably enough for two people.
6 … ▲ one day, you want to send your, ▲ your daughter
7 … and ▲ family's very important.
8 … the older I get as well, ▲ it obsesses me more and more.

5  2 I guess you see, you know, there's all these, sort of
   3 then put in the rice
   4 and I, I think it's, er, it's good for me
   5 I think, yeah, I, I would like to have the lifestyle
   6 and then, so that's how I knew that I absolutely loved it
   7 'cause he was taking part in this, er, TV show
   8 particularly in terms of the impacts of climate change and
   9 so when the opportunity was presented to me
   10 which is not that oil's going to run out
   11 in our local community to become more resilient
   12 I now have to learn to like
6  2 (with), er, a load of Chelsea supporters
   3 I think it's (eight) and a half metres
   4 and that should be warmed then (in a) saucepan
   5 to add (to the) risotto
   6 and then just garnish it (with), er, fresh parsley and then serve
   7 especially maybe (if you) had children as well
   8 for example, um, (if you're) famous person
   9 so (that was) incredible
   10 (it's like) adding spice to food
   11 the impact (of) increasing energy costs
   12 and again (how) we depend on huge shopping centres
   13 and begin to create (that kind of), er, future for ourselves
   14 and I think a (lot of) the ideas that are coming out of that

## Lesson 6  Fame

2 Thuy
3  1 T   2 F (He's not sure if it would be good or not.)
   3 F (She says 'I like the way people look at me and admire me …')   4 T
4  1 He probably wouldn't like to be famous, as he talks about being bothered by people in a public place.
   2 Because they are given to people after a good stage performance.
5  1 E   2 T   3 T   4 E
6  1 You can't walk in the streets freely or go where you want (e.g. the cinema).
   2 Yes, because it might affect your children or your ability to do simple things like go and buy a pint of milk.
7  a 2  b 5  c 1  d 3  e 4
8  **school**: Famous people can send their children to a famous school and they might be given a second chance.
   **fashion**: Famous people have to follow the latest fashion.
   **freedom**: Freedom is important.
   **money**: People usually have a lot of money if they're famous.
9  1 She thinks they would get into prestigious schools more easily.
   2 That they can't be free.
   3 You usually have enough money to do what you want, but you always have photographers following you around, intruding.
   4 Because she says famous people have to be fashionable and care about what they wear, otherwise they will end up being criticized in a magazine for their fashion sense.

## Lesson 7 Talent-show winner

**3** 1 *The X Factor*  2 GCSE  3 Gloucestershire
**4** c
**6** 1 12  2 music  3 second  4 live
**7** 1 d  2 f  3 a  4 e  5 b  6 c
**8** 1 a friend
  2 the other side of the studio complex
  3 sing
  4 She had flu / couldn't speak.
**9** a 1  b 5  c 3  d 2  e 4
**10** No – the order in which she mentions them is: a, d, b, c, e
**11** Name of the local paper: *The Citizen*
  Name of the recording company: Decca
  Name of the orchestra recorded at Abbey Road: the Royal Philharmonic
  She was on TV (BBC *Breakfast*).
  Date of release of the EP: 11th July
  Date of release of the album: 11th August
  She has helped produce the album.
  She has co-written seven of the songs.

## Lesson 8 Life without oil

**1** *Peak oil* is the idea that we have reached the maximum possible level of oil extraction, and that it will reduce from now on.
**3** 1 withstand  2 dependent on  3 extraction  4 sustainable  5 scarce  6 resilient  7 transition
**5** a 1  b 2  c 1, 4  d 3
**6** *Suggested answers*
  **peak oil**: won't run out tomorrow; reached the maximum level of extraction possible; will be more expensive; become scarce; worried about being vulnerable.
  **Transition Towns**: interesting; change so less dependent on society and more on each other; raise awareness with films and talks.
**7** 1 American  2 the car  3 towns
**8** 1 b, d  2 a, e  3 c, f
**9** 1 the transition
  2 (the fact that) we've never had so much money
  3 not having enough time for our children and worrying about our children
  4 food
**10** 1 the British
  2 things we don't need
  3 transport and food (and possibly childcare)
  4 less impact on the environment, requiring less energy, creating a more positive life for everybody

## Lesson 9 Living with failing eyesight

**1** *Suggested answers*: eyesight chart, braille chart, blurred text/vision, glasses, special phone, guide dog, cane, see, problem
**3** b
**5** 1 Yes, those that know I have problems have been very supportive. They have asked me to let them know what I need to do my job.
  2 Yes, they meet me at the bus stop and go shopping with me.
  3 I only started to notice I couldn't see very well quite recently.
**7** 1 F (She says 'I haven't had to ask for any specific help.')
  2 T
  3 F (They have helped by meeting her at the bus stop and going shopping with her.)
  4 T
  5 T
**8** *Suggested answers*
  1 have been very supportive; let us know if there's anything we can do to help
  2 been great; offers of help; meet me at the bus stop; take me to the shop; go shopping
  3 very recently; noticed from week to week; can't see something that I could see last week
**9** 1 try to  2 expect to  3 have to listen  4 easier  5 to like

## Lesson 10 Pronunciation for listeners 2

**3** See script 1.29.
**5** 1 weak  2 strong
**7** 1 American  2 English  3 English  4 American  5 English  6 American

## Lesson 11 Going places

**3**

|  | Tom | Maria | Alan |
|---|---|---|---|
| 1 My ideal place | by the sea, no rain | warm, by the sea | near the sea and countryside, not a city |
| 2 My idea of a good holiday | with friends, be able to swim, winter holidays like snowboarding | with friends / loved ones, at seaside, playing beach volleyball, sunbathing, educational and relaxing | sitting by the pool reading a book |

**4** a 8 (A)  b 2 (T)  c 4 (M)  d 5 (A)  e 6 (T)  f 1 (T)  g 7 (M)  h 3 (M)
**5** 1 T, M  2 M  3 M  4 T  5 T  6 T, M, A
  They all mention the beach / swimming.
**6** 1 Because he likes sharing the experience.
  2 You meet interesting people because you're forced to interact with others.
  3 Being at the seaside, sunbathing, playing beach volleyball
  4 By visiting places and learning about the culture/ history
  5 Not very adventurous
**7** 1 Alan, c  2 Tom, a  3 Maria, b
**8** 1 Because it was so different to England (e.g. food and culture).
  2 Good: interesting and eye-opening historically, beautiful temples
  Bad: horrible places linked to Communist uprising
  3 They were beautiful and sandy with white sand.
  4 They were open-minded with a good level of English. It was important because that made it easier for her to talk to them.
  5 The weather, the old town, the Piccasso museum and the atmosphere
  6 That it was very expensive to eat out.
**9** 1 Alan  2 Tom  3 Maria
**10** 1 F (He says 'London isn't everything.')  2 T  3 F (It's not far from Moscow.)  4 T  5 T  6 T

## Lesson 12  Raby Castle

**2** magnificent, stunning, impressive
**3** c
**5** 1 1626   2 Events   3 400   4 35,000   5 three
   6 11 or 12
**6** 1 no   2 Claire, the Curator   3 at the castle
   4 She feels really lucky.   5 the history of the castle

**7, 8**

|  | Octagon Drawing Room | Entrance Hall | Baron's Hall |
|---|---|---|---|
| people | 2, 4 | 6, 3 | 5, 1 |
| extra information | most stunning, sumptuous room in castle, built in 1848 to impress Duke of Cleveland's friends | gothic vaulting, built by second Earl of Darlington for his son when he returned from Europe, roof of former lower hall was raised so that a carriage could be driven in one side and out the other | has bookshelves and paintings of members of the Vane family from 1626 up to current Lord Barnard's grandmother; 700 knights were supposed to have met there to plot against Elizabeth I in support of Mary, Queen of Scots; has an oak ceiling that was orginally an oak hammer-beam roof |

**9** Responsible for: conservation and restoration of the paintings, furniture and other items in the castle; the presentation of the public route; the guides (hiring, training, organizing)
**10** 1 F (She works part time.)   2 T
   3 F (She says 'You've got a big job'.)   4 T

## Lesson 13  The friendly virus

**3** *Suggested answers*
Is there such thing | as a good virus? | Now, | this might seem like a strange thing to ask. | When we think of viruses, | we tend to think of the big baddies | like flu and HIV | that are exceptionally good at spreading disease. | Even Hollywood's cottoned on to our fear of viruses, | and has brought them to the red carpet | as evil, | fast-spreading, | quite deadly villains. | But what if we could use viruses | to treat diseases, | like cancer?
**5** c
**6** a 1   b 4   c 2   d 3
**7** 1 b   2 c   3 d   4 a
   a this = that the virus kills the tumour cell
   b it = this idea
   c their = children
   d it = the virus
**8** 1 T   2 T   3 F   4 T   5 F
**9** 3 The virus carries a protein.
   5 Many viruses can poison cells.
**10** 1 About a century
   2 In tumour cells
   3 Tools, technology, knowledge
   4 A harmless drug
   5 Exciting results

## Lesson 14  Complaining

**3** We complain more, use email, or go to a social-networking site. We don't write letters or make phone calls.
**5** 1 B   2 B   3 C   4 P   5 C
**6** 1 want to choose exactly what we like
   2 put
   3 takes a long time
   4 feelings, beliefs and ways of thinking
   5 people who complain continuously (*negative*)
**7** 1 The letter might get lost or it might take a long time to get a reply.
   2 British people didn't like to make complaints before, but now they do, although they do it by taking their custom elsewhere or by posting on social-networking sites, without making a direct complaint.
   3 She thinks there is a middle position whereby a complaint can be made in a constructive and positive way without being confrontational.
**8** b
**9** 1 d   2 c   3 a   4 e   5 b
**10** a 2   b 1   c 4   d 3
**12** 1 send off quickly, perhaps in anger
   2 very big change
   3 it's very easy
   4 spoke about something that had been bothering me for a while
   5 feel as though someone cares about their wants and needs
   6 sensible, good advice

## Lesson 15  Pronunciation for listeners 3

**1** And it's actually literally true!
**2** 1 time actually (fragment 3)
   2 and actually we have (fragment 6)
   3 I actually love it (fragment 7)
   4 we don't actually say (fragment 11)
   5 I was actually watching it on TV (fragment 17)
**3** 1 definitely   2 obviously   3 particularly   4 basically
   5 particularly   6 definitely   7 of course   8 basically
   9 particularly   10 Obviously   11 of course
   12 obviously   13 obviously   14 of course
**4** sudduv = sort of, scanna = kind of
**5** 2 lots of nice ▲s pockets of
   3 there were ▲s 30 of my family
   4 but I ▲k stumbled into a karaoke place
   5 I mean, we went to several ▲s places
   6 and you just ▲k put your case forward and
   7 people are ▲s crowding round it and
   8 er, you've got some lovely ▲s beach front
   9 people are ▲k right to complain
   10 know with the big, you know, ▲k plastic discs
   11 and we tend to ▲s queue up
   12 maybe a car that ▲s runs on water, you know
   13 for me ▲k sums up the whole of, of the ▲k, you know, the start
   14 um, until he ▲k stood up
   15 and I ▲k think you're missing out a little bit
**6** 1 and also just   2 and then just   3 just to   4 I'd just
   5 know, just   6 just   7 definitely just
   The fragments all include the word *just*.

# Lesson 16  Risk

**3**  1 Maria    2 Alan
**4**  1 T    2 F (She's not afraid of heights.)    3 T
   4 F (He thinks it's risky.)    5 T
**5**  1 She thinks Ning had misunderstood her.
   2 She won't go scuba diving because she can't swim.
**6**  1 A    2 M    3 M    4 A    5 N
**7**  1 holiday    2 climbing Everest    3 mountain climbing
   4 physical condition    5 mountain
**8**  1 He tried to climb Mount Everest.
   2 Because the air pressure is different, causing people to feel unwell.
   3 She is afraid of heights (she doesn't like mountains) and she doesn't like cold weather.
**9**  a 2   b 4   c 1   d 3   e 5
**10**  1 Because he's cautious and doesn't like taking risks.
   2 Because she says she's unlucky and would probably lose, and she doesn't know how to play the games.
   3 £2
   4 Because they all buy their lottery tickets on a Friday and cause huge queues when he wants to buy a newspaper.
   5 She thinks that English people will gamble on all sorts of things.
**11**  1 Ning (She thought that Maria meant that she would die doing the parachute jump.)
   2 Alan (He would back out at the last minute and not do the jump because he was scared.)
   3 Alan (The fish and other things under the sea that you might see when diving)
   4 Alan (Would you like to try doing that?)
   5 Alan (A plan to make money that involved a lot of risk)
   6 Alan (They gamble on different kinds of unusual things.)

# Lesson 17  Baltic voyager

**1**  2 The Island Trust    3 Tall Ships race
   4 Finnish archipelago    5 St Petersburg    6 Diggory Rose
   7 Elba    8 Devon
**3**  Diggory Rose, the Pegasus, The Island Trust, Devon, Tall Ships
**4**  c
**5**  1 56–57    2 four    3 Liverpool/Merseyside
   4 St Petersburg    5 nine    6 10,000    7 Turku    8 first
   9 second
**6**  1 lovely    2 bad (a near gale)    3 one or two people
   4 sing (sea shanties)
**7**  1 f    2 d    3 e    4 c    5 b    6 a
**8**  *heavy-duty* = strong; *fleets* = a large number of ships; *gale* = very strong winds; *odd* = not many; *rigs* = large structures for removing oil from the bottom of the sea; *shanties* = traditional sea songs
**9**  *bashing our way through* = continuing, with difficulty; *nose on to it* = facing into it

# Lesson 18  Under the volcano

**1**  Mount St Helens, Washington State; 1980
**2**  1 eruption    2 massive, huge    3 earthquake, landslide
   4 bulge    5 magma
**4**  a I think; good question, yeah because; yeah; Well, the bulge started
   b it's not; and then; did
**6**  b
**7**  1, 2, 4, 5
**8**  a 3   b 1   c 4   d 2

**9**  1 c    2 d    3 a    4 b
**10**  1 F (She says 'Volcanologists are generally not going to stay out of the way!'.)    2 T    3 F (She's not familiar with the process.)    4 F (People didn't have time to get away.)
**11**  1 world    2 slowly    3 stop    4 ash

# Lesson 19  Mystery on Mount Everest

**1**  1 on the border of Tibet and Nepal
   2 approximately 29,000 feet / 8,850 metres
   3 Sir Edmund Hillary and Tenzing Norgay
   4 June 1953
**2**  George Mallory and Sandy Irvine
**3**  1 N    2 D    3 D
**4**  Yes, she partly answers question 2 when she says that Mallory's body was found in 1999.
**6**  a 2   b 6   c 1   d 4   e 7   f 5   g 3
**7**  1 Julie's    2 (Uncle) Sandy    3 Julie's grandmother
   4 Sandy Irvine's
**8**  a 5   b 3   c 1   d 4   e 2
**9**  *Suggested answers*
   a He was a good-looking young man, but the body would not be a pretty sight, it would be horrible.
   b There's a hunt for Sandy Irvine's body, but they don't want any more bodies connected to the expedition of 1924 to be found.
   c Julie lives in Oxford and Virginia Arnott (Mallory's granddaughter) lives in Abingdon. Their boys were at school together for a couple of years, although neither family realized it at the time.
   d The body was seen lying on its back.
   e After the body was found, there was a lot of interest in the story.
**10**  1 romantic    2 Some people believe
   3 at the top of Everest    4 1953
**11**  1 Because it's romantic.
   2 She thinks it's fascinating.
   3 Because Mallory didn't have a photograph or a flag in his pocket when his body was found.
   4 He looked for evidence that Mallory had been there.
   5 How they died and if they had got to the top of Everest

# Lesson 20  Pronunciation for listeners 4

**1**  See script 1.60.
**2**  1 is    2 were; was    3 is    4 was    5 was    6 are
   7 were    8 is    9 was
**3**  1 were never seen    2 must have been    3 has grown
   4 was found    5 must have got    6 were carrying
   7 has never been    8 would've been solved
   9 was going to leave    10 has replaced
   11 would have written    12 might have been
**4**  1 fast    2 day    3 know    4 run    5 small    6 a lot    7 dog

# Lesson 21  First impressions

**1**  They talk about people (Maria, Ezgi, Thuy), weather (Maria, Ezgi), food (Maria), transport (Maria, Ezgi).
**2**  People, weather, food, transport
**3**  1 She expected people to be reserved and cold-hearted, and for it to be always raining.
   2 People are open-minded and hospitable, and the weather was surprisingly good.

3 That there are two taps, one for hot water and one for cold.
4 She was told that British food was awful and overcooked, but she likes it – although people do eat a lot of potatoes!
5 She was impressed by the respect that was shown to cyclists by other drivers.
4 In general, she likes the English way of life and would like to stay.
5 a 3  b 1  c 2
6 1 She thought it was an open-minded country because she saw people from different countries, e.g. Saudi Arabia.
2 She says that in Turkey, you don't have two different taps for hot and cold water, and you can hail a taxi on the street without having to phone for one.
7 She talks about the people.
8

| situation | notes |
| --- | --- |
| Where she lives | in a hostel in Portsmouth |
| Problem 1: the broken cooking pot | She didn't know how to explain to reception that her pot was damaged, but the man helped her by looking things up on his computer and gave her another one. |
| Problem 2: going places | People help her when she's lost, give her directions. |
| General impressions | People are very friendly, make her feel warm. |

## Lesson 22  Rescuing tradition

1 *Suggested answers*: a vocalist, electric instruments
2 1 talented  2 melodies  3 combination  4 spectacle  5 traditional
3 bring back to life the old songs and melodies
5 1 f  2 b  3 a  4 c  5 e  6 d  7 a
6 See script 1.66.
7 1 very young  2 want to  3 older people  4 the government  5 are trying
8 a 2  b 3  c 1
9 1 The Beatles, Oasis
  2 Two from: Ukraine, Bulgaria, Romania
  3 many open spaces / wild, beautiful landscape
  4 no mountains/sheep in Poland
  5 views/colour
  6 the weather
10 *Suggested answers*

| old music | new music |
| --- | --- |
| traditional songs old, traditional instruments frame drums | drums rock/jazz music |

11 You're welcome!

## Lesson 23  From thought to action

4 The bold text shows the stressed syllables, and the upwards/downwards positioning of the letters reflects the rising/falling intonation.
5 1 suggest a way of seeing things differently
  2 introduce the main idea
6 a 1  b 4  c 3  d 2
7 a 2  b 1  c 3  d 4
8 1 d  2 b  3 a  4 c
9 1 F  2 T  3 F  4 T

10 1 People's arms and hands move on their own.
   3 Neuroscience tells us lots about our free will and consciousness.
11 1 alien  2 action  3 motion  4 left  5 neuro  6 brains

## Lesson 24  Read my lips

1 *Suggested answers*
  1 1 a  2 e  3 g  4 h  5 b  6 d  7 c  8 f
  2 by using the tone of voice
  3 by using facial expressions
3 *Suggested answers*
  • The speaker branches away from the theme for a moment and then returns to it.
  • The speaker starts to say something, then changes his mind and starts again.
  • The speaker repeats a phrase from earlier in order to return to the main theme.
4 three
5 1 T  2 T  3 F (It doesn't matter if you don't know them.)  4 F (Lip-reading helps.)  5 T
6 c
7 a 4  b 5  c 3  d 1  e 6  f 2
9/10 1 T  2 T  3 F (It's easier if you can see a person's face.)  4 F (Sighted people don't notice until they can't see a person's face.)
12 1 If they are brain-damaged in some way.
   2 No, this is an independent skill.
   3 A smile
   4 Accentuate expressions

## Lesson 25  Pronunciation for listeners 5

1 1 there  2 that  3 them  4 the  5 than
2 See script 1.75.
3 1 What do they eat?
  2 What's her name?
  3 Where did she lose her handbag?
  4 When did he lose his money?
  5 What's your name?
  6 What day's he arriving?
  7 Where are my shoes?
4 *Suggested answers*
  … in your situation, where you are, er, you just <u>cannot</u> resolve, er, the person's lip movements because you can't <u>see</u> them, you are <u>inevitably</u> going to suffer some <u>loss</u> in, er, in what <u>sounds</u> like hearing, but <u>actually</u> it's the full comprehension of the sentence.
5 1 absolutely  2 really  3 absolutely  4 stunning  5 really  6 amazing
7 1 (x2)  2 (x4)  3 (x2)  4 (x2)  5 (x1)  6 (x1)

## Lesson 26  University

2 cost of university education, subsistence payments, accommodation
3 1 aren't  2 have to
4 1 T  2 F (Private universities are expensive, but state universities are not.)  3 T  4 F (They are falling a bit.)
5 1 really expensive
  2 doesn't cost a lot
  3 maybe £9,000 a year / borrowed from the government
6 a 5  b 3  c 1  d 4  e 2  f 6
7 1 You don't pay for a higher degree, such as a Master's or PhD.

2 Because she got a scholarship.
3 They decide if you get a grant for studying / doing research.
4 That if you have fun instead of doing your homework, you have to do it all in the last two weeks of term.
8 1 (x5)   2 (x3)   3 (x2)   4 (x3)
9 1 Not free, but cheap   2 Student house / rent a flat
3 (hall of) residence   4 Hall of residence (first year only)
10 1 Because the university accommodation is not very good.
2 It's expensive.
3 Because it's cheap.
4 Because there's not enough student accommodation for everyone.
11 *Suggested answer*: He has a positive impression, as he makes a lot of interjections such as *Yeah* and *Nice*.

## Lesson 27 Speed on ice

1 1 runners   2 slope   3 speed   4 driver   5 team
6 lucky   7 burns
2 1 Because it's a dangerous sport.
2 Driver, pushers, brakeman
3 Because there is no ice in Jamaica to practise on.
4 By falling out of the sleigh and sliding down the slope
3 *Suggested answers*
In natural conversation, speakers often …
• start a sentence again so they can use a different word.
• leave out words.
• interrupt what they are saying to change the order of the information.
• use incomplete sentences.
• speak at the same time.
4 a 1   b 5   c 3   d 2   e 4   f 6
5 *Suggested answers*
a He's at the Olympic Games.
b He did really well on the second run.
c She got very emotional because she knew he was excited and proud of himself.
d He texted at 1.10 a.m. when he was lining up for the ceremony; it was due to start at 1.45 a.m./2.45 a.m.
e He rattled down the slope and she was convinced he was going to turn over.
f He was the brakeman for GB1 and he was pulled out of the back of the bobsleigh. He had ice burns on his back, shoulders and elbows.
6 1 T   2 F (He puts his hand on his head.)   3 T
7 1 b   2 b   3 b   4 a
8 c
9 1 15   2 three   3 perfect   4 110

## Lesson 28 The science of the small

1 b, d, a/e, c
2 very small
3 1 harness   2 manipulate   3 properties   4 wide/width
4 See script 2.5.
5 1 I   2 I   3 B   4 A   5 A   6 A
6 1 T   2 F (It's a write-up of a lecture.)
3 F (He's a famous physicist.)   4 T
7 *Suggested answers*
**The man**: frequently quoted; famous physicist; significant work; good at talking about himself / telling wonderful/entertaining stories; populizer of science; said 'If you think you've understood quantum mechanics, you haven't understood quantum mechanics'

**The book/lecture**: 1959; book called 'The Pleasure of Finding Things Out', lecture called 'Plenty of Room at the Bottom'; science of the future; manipulating matter on atomic scale; building molecules; challenged scientists to do this, methods not available until 1980s
8 *Suggested answers*
1 talked about   2 type of very small particle
3 researching   4 reproduced repeating what was said exactly   5 person
9 b
10 1 explosive   2 changes   3 expect   4 material(s)
5 properties   6 interesting

## Lesson 29 Studying abroad

1 1 a   2 a
2 1 A   2 B   3 B   4 A
4 a 4   b 2   c 1   d 3
5 a the cost of annual tuition fees (in pounds) in England
b the number of students from the UK studying at Utrecht University
c the number of degree programmes in English in the Netherlands
d the number of students at Utrecht University
e the numbers of partners Utrecht University has in the UK
8 1 15 years ago
2 himself; the country he was staying in; the country he's from (Britain)
3 his wife
4 France, Italy
9 Yes, she does (*It's very popular with Dutch sudents, it's the biggest student city, one out of every five residents is a student*).
10 *Suggested answers*

| UTRECHT | |
|---|---|
| characteristics | café culture, old canal, pretty, near to Ámsterdam, music |
| transport | cheap to get there, easy to get back, plane, coach |
| cost of course | €1,672 (about £1,400) |
| website | www.international.hu.nl |
| MANCHESTER | |
| advantages | near to Stockport (7 miles) three or four great universities meet new people |
| disadvantages | expensive difficult to move away |

## Lesson 30 Pronunciation for listeners 6

1 2 Please wait in the corridor.
3 Do you want an ice cream?
4 It's no good, I can't do it!
5 Most students take the school bus.
6 The Atlantic's an ocean.
7 We walked over the bridge.
8 I phoned him on his mobile.
9 You can see cats' eyes in the dark.
10 I went to work early.
2 2 it's written up
3 think about
4 even on
5 cut it up
6 suddenly takes on a

7 thing I think about
   8 determined he is
   9 stopped at the scene
   10 mouth and nose
3  2 I studied law at university.
   3 I saw him coming out of his house.
   4 Under-age drinking's against the law.
   5 If your ears are cold, put your hat on.
   6 Margaret's got blue eyes.
   7 It's a quarter to eight.
   8 My poor back's starting to ache.
   9 He looks pale – is he all right?
   10 I can't hear – I've got my fingers in my ears!
4  2 they're able to, like, vote for a nest
   3 lay more eggs rather than layout their own
   4 be able to actually use
   5 funny side to it
   6 lucky egg
   7 at around two a.m.
6  2 but, sort of, interesting, and
   3 something occurs to me
   4 but exactly how we wanted them
   5 what is it like from a mother's point of view
   6 the way he likes to set off with
   7 ten per cent drop in premature birth rates
   8 quiet mountain
   9 what it involves, etcetera
   10 I don't know nothing about it
7  2 when / I / go / out
   3 and / I / usually / ask, er, the people
   4 you live / in, / er, Portsmouth / in the / UK
   5 I will, / er, tell this story to my friends / and my family
   6 because / I live / in / a hostel

## Lesson 31  Technology

3  *Suggested answer*: Ezgi probably enjoys technology the most, as she seems to use it both for work and for leisure, and is more in touch with the most up-to-date technologies.
4  1 email   2 Facebook   3 phone   4 washing machine
6  1 Ezgi (it = her email)   2 Tom (it = the Grooveshark program)   3 Tom (it = his phone)   4 Tom (that = his phone)   5 Thuy (it = a washing machine)
   6 Ezgi (it = contacting her family using Skype)
7  1 Th, E   2 To, E   3 Th, E
8  1 F (She checks every day.)   2 T   3 F (He remembers what they were like when he was six.)   4 F (She was ten years old.)   5 T   6 T
9  1 Thuy described the BBC news website and smartphones as being useful.
   2 Ezgi described the Science Daily website as a benefit.
   3 Ezgi talked about the Science Daily website as being important because she's a chemical engineer, specialized in energy.
   4 Tom talked about being able to fit a computer into the palm of his hand.
   5 Thuy talked about smartphones being convenient and comfortable.
   6 Tom talked about alternative fuel for cars.

## Lesson 32  Breaking news

1  *Suggested answers*
   **incidents**
      **accidents**: car crash, pedestrian/road incidents, train crash, bicycle accidents, etc.
      **crimes**: mugging, robbery, house-breaking, petty theft, vandalism, etc.
      **other events**: marriage, entertainment (music, cinema), politics, famous people, festivals, etc.
2  accidents/crimes
3  See script 2.19.
5  **Radio bulletin**      **Article**
   Tuesday               Thursday
   2 a.m.                3 a.m.
   41-year-old           31-year-old
6  **train-station incident**: killed, tracks, pronounced dead, platform, suspicious
   **road incident**: stable condition, collision, head injury, arrested, information
7  1 23
   2 A woman (Michaela Hayden) was killed after falling onto tracks at a Tube station.
   3 April 16th
   4 That the death was not suspicious.
   5 15
   6 The boy was run over by a car after getting off a bus.
   7 Tuesday 24th April, around 1 p.m.
   8 Contact them on 101 if they have any information.
8  West Drayton: 2   Broadway: 1   3 p.m.: 2
   John Gordon: 3   West Avenue: 1   Stockley Park: 2
   University of West London: 3   Nico Alijoki: 3
   800 homes: 2   under-25s: 3   23-year-old: 1
   0208 721 7253: 1
10 b
11 a 3   b 1   c 4   d 2

## Lesson 33  The future of paper

3  Full stops should go after *all the time* and *decomposition*.
5  1 c   2 e   3 a   4 d   5 f   6 b
6  c
7  1 As an example of something that we have used to store data on.
   2 20%
   3 It lasts a long time (300–400 years) and can be read using readily available 'tools' (the eye, brain and hand).
8  a 3   b 4   c 1   d 2
9  1 She uses a chair as an analogy of the stable conformation of the paper molecule.
   2 She uses a chain to help describe the composition of cellulose.
   3 She says that old books smell a specific way, have yellow pages and fall apart in our hands when we try to read them; this is all a result of an acid formerly used in paper-making.

## Lesson 34  A life in the music business

2  1 covers   2 album   3 fan   4 tour   5 charts   6 track
   7 hit
3  b
4  Because it's been a long time since he's been the voice of Dr Hook.
5  b
6  1 c   2 a   3 a   4 b

**7** a 3   b 1   c 5   d 2   e 4

**8** *Suggested answers*
  a Anyone visiting his home would think he was one of The Beatles.
  b She was young when he was born and listened to a lot of music/singers (e.g. Nat King Cole, Johnny Mathis, Arthur Price, Dinah Washington, Sam Cooke).
  c Most artists did cover versions of other people's songs.
  d He saw all the screaming girls and thought that he'd like to be involved.
  e *Rubber Soul* was the first Beatles' album on which they wrote all the tracks themselves (John, Paul or George).

**9** 1 F (He still writes his songs in the same way.)   2 T   3 T   4 F (Sometimes he has to struggle.)   5 T

**11** *Suggested answers*
  a His mum was a big fan of Dr Hook too.
  b His new tour involves just him and a couple of guitars.
  c Some of the songs he performs on his tour are album tracks.
  d When Dr Hook split up, Dennis's mum reacted as though her career had been taken away.
  e Some of the songs on his tour are old hits.
  f Some of the songs on his tour are from his solo stuff [his solo album].

# Lesson 35  Pronunciation for listeners 7

**1** 1 a fantastic book by   2 called   3 called

**2** 1 Post Cool (c)   2 Emily Grigsby (a)   3 ant algorithm (d)   4 mitochondrial DNA (d)   5 Diggory Rose (a)   6 temnothorax albipennis (d/e)   7 William Byrne (a)   8 morgh (e)   9 Frank Potter (a)   10 Dautenis (b)

**3** 1 a report from a   2 what we call   3 according to   4 this house is called   5 joined by   6 company called   7 the word   8 the Greek for   9 supervisor   10 a gentleman called   11 means   12 created by   13 what we call   14 owned by a family   15 famous book called   16 chap called   17 nowadays called   18 of the members   19 really good one   20 something called

**5** 1 well, yeah, no, ▲ it's one of those things like anything else
  2 it just kind of happens, ▲ what I mean, it's not until it's all over
  3 now we have to have another one, ▲ what I mean
  4 and so you don't really stop ▲
  5 they wouldn't do that ▲
  6 but I, ▲ so, it, I just got involved
  7 it was the thing that opened my eyes ▲ It was really
  8 and artists didn't do that back then ▲ You did covers
  9 I write the song in 30 minutes ▲ And then sometimes I deliberate over it
  10 I could tell you why I wrote every single song ▲
  11 something solid like that ▲
  12 um, ▲ it's better when it comes at the same time
  13 me, a, a guitar and ▲ 40 years of songs ▲ that I can draw from
  14 you want everything to be included ▲ You just do
  15 can't really imagine ▲ having to remember all my friends
  16 well, I guess, I mean, there seems to be some progress being made on, um, sort of, electric cars or ▲ just cars that use alternative fuel
  17 definitely computers, ▲ um

**6** 1 it was ▲ the best opportunity that I've ever had
  2 but it seems ▲, sort of, you know, ▲ once every five years
  3 that all happened ▲ in sequence
  4 was it just sort of ▲ the eye of the storm
  5 but it wasn't until, ▲ you know, The Beatles
  6 it was ▲, 'Wow, that's really wonderful'
  7 um, really ▲ good robust decision-making
  8 a seemingly, you know, ▲ simple creature
  9 um, their nest choice behaviours are ▲ very democratic
  10 so collectively, they're able to ▲, er, vote for a nest
  11 the sun represents ▲ on the one hand the rays of light
  12 and it's ▲, it's a pagan, pagan ritual
  13 and they've got, you know, ▲ say lorries and buses
  14 ▲ if I see a cyclist now, I'm ▲, 'Oh no'

# Lesson 36  Advertising

**2** a

**3** 1 E, To, Th   2 Th   3 Th   4 Th, E

**4** *Suggested answers*
  1 They don't like junk mail, as it's usually for something they don't want or need, but sometimes it can be useful (e.g. looking for a university or a watch when you want one).
  2 Thuy wants to apply to university, so she finds it helpful to have an email explaining university policy or systems.
  3 Thuy thinks it's useful to see an advert for a watch if you want to buy one but don't know which one is good.
  4 All three think that adverts during a film are very annoying.

**5** 1 H   2 M   3 A

**6** 1 Because they've been shopping online or have visited a webpage and have been tracked.
  2 No, he doesn't.
  3 Because she uses it for all her personal email, not for shopping online, to reduce the amount of spam she gets.
  4 He doesn't like it when the quality of goods that he ordered isn't very good and it takes him a long time to find out how to return them.

**7** a 2   b 4   c 1   d 3   e 5

**8** 1 F (She doesn't like the fact that people's interests can be tracked.)   2 T   3 F (He says he agrees that he's easily influenced.)   4 T

**9** 1 This is the number of spam emails per week generated by shopping online.
  2 She gets hardly any spam emails in her personal email account.
  3 That the advert works on her, making her feel that she really needs the gadget.
  4 When she's bought it, she finds she hardly uses it at all.

# Lesson 37  The language of persuasion

**1** 1 a a café
    b 26 Station Road, Baker's Green
    c Kate's Kitchen
  2 food and drink
  3 good place to relax; open all day; home-made cakes; fresh, affordable food

**2** *Suggested answers*
  1 space, fast connections, table service
  2 delivery, wrapping, free gift card, unusual choice of gifts

3 free extra courses, small groups, distance learning, experienced teachers
4 cheap, wide coverage; latest models of phone
5 high interest for investment; easy credit; easy access to advisors and account details; lots of cash machines

**3** 1 a a radio station   b Bristol   c BCFM
2 entertainment, news (not explicit)
3 reliability (not run for profit)

**4** repetition of key information (name of the station and its frequency), professionally recorded

**5** **Advert 1**
a bar and café
130 Cheltenham Road, Stokes Croft, Bristol
The Social Bar and Café
**Advert 2**
a Middle Eastern restaurant
6 Cotham Hill (across the road from Clifton Down Shopping Centre)
Falafel King

**6** **Advert 1**
2 all-day food and drink
3 Fair Trade coffee, daytime play area for children, baby-changing facilities, heated garden, local beers, great food
**Advert 2**
2 Middle Eastern food
3 unique, fresh food, friendly, comfy downstairs chill-out room

**7** a 8   b 1   c 4   d 7   e 6   f 3   g 5   h 9   i 2

**8** 1 a mortgage seminar
2 people who want to buy a home or land in Jamaica, or build their own home
3 about properties/land for sale and about home-loan products
4 advice on how to save money on household bills (energy, telecom, food, petrol)
5 'I've heard it all before – how can anyone cut my bills?'
6 Phone him on 0800 954 5255.

**9** Advert 1: gifts
Advert 2: fresh fish and seafood
Advert 3: hand-made furniture and gifts made from recycled wood

**10** 1 Because they're considered to be difficult to please; the advert suggests they can be satisfied by the wide range of goods on offer at Amulet.
2 A Murilo wool scarf, silver earrings, a jacket, a bag and a few other bits and pieces; the staff
3 There's a lot to choose from, and the staff are helpful.
4 Seagulls; that the shop is near the sea and the fish is fresh.
5 Devon and Cornwall; because it means the fish has been caught locally so will be fresh.
6 In the street; that everyone has heard about it and talks about it, so it must be good.
7 They are unusual items and so demonstrate the variety of goods on offer; that there's nothing made of wood that they don't sell.

**11** Advert 1: Christmas song (*Jingle Bells*) and footsteps; set the scene for present-buying and running to the shop.
Advert 2: waves breaking and seagulls screeching; suggest the sea and very fresh fish.
Advert 3: background music, wood sawing, people in a bar; suggest a friendly informal and flexible place which makes things on request.

## Lesson 38  The intelligence of ants

**1** One species of Australian ant has eight legs.
**3** 1 F   2 F   3 F   4 C   5 C   6 F
**4** 1 T   2 F (People have been interested in ants for many years.)   3 F (Some are enormous and some are tiny.)
4 T
**5** a 3   b 4   c 2   d 1
**6** b
**7** 1 intelligence as a group
2 a search strategy
3 Because each ant is like one neuron in a brain.
**8** a 1   b 4   c 3   d 5   e 2
**9** 1, 3, 5
**10** 1 a bit technical, information about how ants function as a colony
2 a famous book
3 about bees, written by Thomas Seeley

## Lesson 39  A celebration of the sun

**3** The words are in italics because they are the names of foods in the Punjabi language, not English.
**5** beginning (x4), sun (x3), spring (x3)
**6** 1 T   2 T   3 F (It's dedicated to the sun.)   4 T
5 F (A lot of food is thrown onto the fire.)   6 T
7 F (Newly married people celebrate at the festival.)   8 T
**8** 1 b   2 b   3 c
**9** 1 c   2 a   3 b   4 d
**10** Dulla Bhatti helped girls from poor families start a new life; Lohri celebrates new beginnings.

## Lesson 40  Pronunciation for listeners 8

**1** first of all
**2** 1 exactly   2 infect   3 effects   4 west   5 perfect
6 easiest   7 gifts   8 rainforest   9 statistics   10 it's (x2)
**3** 2 Would you like a **cold** drink?
3 Who **built** the pyramids?
4 I **felt** very tired last night.
5 I **want** to **hold** your hand.
6 I **went** to the doctor's yesterday.
**4** 2 about   3 perhaps   4 perhaps   5 particularly
6 particularly   7 probably   8 responsible
9 exceptionally   10 absolutely   11 collecting
12 traditionally   13 hundred   14 do you reckon
**5** 1 good   2 could   3 can   4 could   5 want   6 should
7 in   8 couldn't   9 can
**6** There are a lot of false starts and repeated words.
**7** 1 I think it   2 all   3 if I was doing
**8** 1 G   2 W   3 G   4 W   5 G/W   6 W
**9** *Suggested answers*
1 journalism may be one profession where it almost doesn't ma-, / it depends what you do, obviously, but
2 suddenly people were talking, er, / when I was a kid, people weren't talking about nanoscience
3 wha-, / what, / why do you think – / and we're going to get on to some of the specific things – / but wha-, / wha-, / why do you think they have fascinated us
4 yeah, / no, / you know, it's one of those things, / like anything else, / it sometimes, / it seems like it was yesterday
5 I mean, / the, / if you actually, / it's, / I think sometimes you probably have to pinch yourself
6 with vinyl and stuff, they get, / it gets, / as it, / it gets better, / as, / as it gets warmer, doesn't it?

# Lesson 41 Arriving in a capital city

**2** public transport, food/drink, entertainment

**3** 1 He was surprised that even though the trains were really full, everyone was relaxed and silent; there were men with white gloves who pushed people onto the trains.
2 He thought it was really good.
3 He wanted to get out of the heat. He was given a book and shown to a tiny air-conditioned room with a TV. You put numbers in and sing songs in English. They bring you fruit juice. You can spend hours there.
4 'All-you-can-drink' karaoke

**4**

| phrase | topic | general meaning |
|---|---|---|
| no hassle or anything like that | the train | no problems |
| like a conveyor belt | the sushi bar | like a machine carrying plates of food |
| weird and wonderful stuff | the sushi bar | strange but good dishes |
| I kind of stumbled into | the karaoke bar | I went in almost by accident |
| in very broken Japanese | the karaoke bar | in very bad, non-grammatical Japanese |

**5** geographical features, people, danger, food/drink, historical monuments

**6** 1 It was very long (ten hours), the bus was small and very cramped, she slept for some of the journey, she was sitting next to a Mexican woman with a lot of luggage.
2 No, she hadn't planned anything. She doesn't say why.
3 No, she seemed more excited than frightened.
4 She loved it.
5 Yes, because she is so enthusiastic about the food and the people, and she says she fell in love with the city the first time she saw it.

**7 the woman**: large, older than Anisa, with bundles of food, looked at Anisa as though she was mad when Anisa spoke to her
**the man**: friendly, explained the metro system to her (how to get tickets), told her which areas were dangerous, was concerned for her safety

**8**

| phrase | topic | general meaning |
|---|---|---|
| very cramped | the bus | extremely full |
| bundles of food | the woman on the bus | large packages filled with food |
| this huge sprawling area | Mexico City | a very large area that goes in all directions |
| it was love at first sight | Mexico City | she loved it immediately, the first time she saw it |
| all my worldly possessions | belongings | everything she owned |
| they really went out of their way | the people | they did more to help her than they had to |
| I couldn't get over the fact that | the architecture | she couldn't believe that; she was continually surprised by |

# Lesson 42 Topical chat

**2** 1 c  2 a, b, c, d  3 a  4 d  5 d  6 b  7 a  8 b
**3** The vague one – people don't need to be so precise in a casual conversation.
**7** 1 sound  2 record  3 space  4 sleeve  5 cassettes
**9** a 3  b 1  c 2  d 4
**10** 1 d  2 c  3 a  4 b
**11** 1 year-on-year  2 fell  3 continue  4 rose
5 decrease

# Lesson 43 The silent killer

**3** 1 of us would  2 at  3 in our  4 or  5 has  6 from
7 and  8 we  9 is a  10 in the
**5** a 2  b 4  c 1  d 3
**6** a 4 (These bacteria then penetrate inside, through the gum tissue into our bloodstream, and once they enter the bloodstream, these bacteria can deposit on the walls of our arteries …)
b 1 (… one of the most common infections is gum infection or gum disease …)
c 5 (… increase a risk for heart disease.)
d 3 (… how gum disease develops, it's because of bacteria that form on a thin film on teeth …)
e 2 (… gum disease is something that is often neglected, because it's a silent disease …)
**8** 1 F  2 T  3 F
**9** 1 They are twice as likely to develop heart disease.
3 General health is improved if oral health is improved.

# Lesson 44 The music of the rainforest

**2** a
**5** 1 from the Macusi tribe
2 'land of many waters'
3 shades of green, waterfalls, rivers
4 741 feet
**6** b
**7** 1 a very long time  2 ideas  3 (winter) palm trees
4 his wife  5 They get covered in snow.
6 a pond with about 50 goldfish
**8** a 1  b 3  c 6  d 2  e 4  f 5
**9** See script 2.67.
**10** c

# Lesson 45 Pronunciation for listeners 9

**2** a 2  b 3  c 4  d 1
**3** 4
**4** a 5  b 3  c 1  d 6  e 2  f 4
**8** 1 haven't you  2 haven't you  3 aren't they  4 are they
5 is it  6 didn't it  7 don't they  8 isn't it  9 haven't you
**9** 6

# Techniques to improve your listening

| Listening stages | What you can do | |
|---|---|---|
| Before listening | Think about … | the topic |
| | | the speaker |
| | | the text |
| | Decide what you want to listen for | general and main ideas |
| | | detail |
| | | specific information |
| At the beginning | Tune into … | the speaker(s) voice(s): style, accent, intonation, etc. |
| | | the text type |
| While listening | Listen out for … | repeated words, phrases, synonyms, proper nouns |
| | | grammatical words (e.g. pronouns, conjunctions) |
| | Use strategies | Look at body language (for video). |
| | | Listen for key words and phrases. |
| | | Guess the meaning of new words and phrases. |
| | | Remember and summarize as you listen. |
| | | Be aware of how speakers use repetition, hesitation and fillers to give them time to think. |
| After listening | Reflect | Remember what you did and if it worked well. |
| | | Think about what you could do next time. |